Object Oriented Program Design

With Examples in C++

MARK MULLIN

Addison-Wesley Publishing Company, Inc.
Reading, Massachusetts   Menlo Park, California   New York
Don Mills, Ontario   Wokingham, England   Amsterdam   Bonn
Sydney   Singapore   Tokyo   Madrid   San Juan

Library of Congress Cataloging-in-Publication Data

Mullin, Mark M.
    Object oriented program design : with examples in C++ / Mark M. Mullin.
        p.   cm.
    Includes index.
    ISBN 0-201-51722-1
    1. C++ (Computer program language)   2. Object-oriented programming (Computer science)   I. Title.
    QA76.73.C15M855   1989
    005.13'3--dc19
                                                          89-431
                                                          CIP

Production Editor: Amorette Pedersen
Cover Design by: Doliber Skeffington Design
Set in 11-point New Century Schoolbook by Benchmark Productions

    5 6 7 8 9 10-AL-95949392
Fifth printing, July 1992

To the people that made this all possible:

Arthur Mullin
Creigh Wagner
Gene Fucci
and
Maxine Porter

ACKNOWLEDGEMENTS

My personal thanks go to:

my father, for many fundamentals.

Gene Fucci at Dartmouth, for all of his help in starting me off in the right direction, and his continuing advice. And to Dartmouth College for its benevolent attitude about sharing its toys. And to John Kemeny for BASIC, so long ago.

Patrick Maritz, one of my first converts to OOP, and a steady sounding board for esoteric design ideas.

Dr. Shriver. He started the quest that produced this book.

Ron Herold and company, of PH-Associates, for being a guinea pig for the first commercial attempts. Not a policy for the faint of heart.

Steve Levine of ParcPlace Systems, who provided some wonderful dog and pony shows, just when they were needed.

Simon Form, for some very interesting discussions, and to all those OOPSLA attendees who provide the yearly OOP headspace check.

And, to Jerry Allen, who agreed to be the "reader." Jerry deserves credit for whatever is good in this book, whatever is bad is entirely my fault.

My professional thanks go to:

Adele Golberg and her associates, for Smalltalk.

Bjarne Stroustrup for C++.

Apple Computer for the Mac-II. It made writing the book as pleasant as possible.

Finally, I'd like to thank Chris Williams and Amy Pedersen of Addison-Wesley, for putting this book in your hands.

INTRODUCTION

In the last several years, Object Oriented Programming (OOP) has experienced increasing scrutiny and use. Some view OOP as a passing fad and some view it as a real revolution in programming. While both of these viewpoints are a bit extreme, I lean more towards the second than the first.

C++ is a language that implements several key elements of OOP, allowing you to use certain powerful object oriented design (OOD) techniques. A major attraction of C++ is that, in many ways, it is immediately usable by C programmers. C programmers learning C++ are extending their knowledge, not starting from scratch. But C++ has a profound impact on the way that programs are developed. To develop a program in C++ in the same way that the program would be developed in C is self defeating. This is not to say that the program won't work, only that there is little point in using C++ in the first place.

Object oriented programs are structurally and functionally distinct from their non-object oriented counterparts, common features of the language notwithstanding. The focus of this book is to show *how* to use an object oriented language and also to address *why* you should use an object oriented language.

In the past, once you learned the syntax of a programming language, you could usually "translate" your problem solving techniques from one language to another. In other words, if you knew C, and you wanted to use Pascal, you only needed to learn how to translate what you would do in C into its equivalent Pascal form. With C++, or any other object oriented language or system, it is no longer simply a process of translation. An OO system is based on the assumption that the system and the programmer share a common environment, and all programs are defined as extensions to this environment. If you will, C is an atomic language, whereby you can build a house by describing it, atom by atom. Object oriented programming allows you to define things such as bricks, boards, and nails, and then to define your entire house in these terms.

Due to this, an object oriented language's (OOL) main impact on development has relatively little to do with its syntactic properties. Instead, the focus of the system is a structural framework upon which all programs are assembled and through which all program elements communicate. The reason for using an OOL is for the seamless boundary between the design of a system and the implementation of the system. To realize the power of an OOL, it is more important to understand the design philosophy that serves as its foundation than to know the raw syntax of the language.

In fact, if you understand the OO design methodology, you don't really even need an OOL to implement these kinds of programs. All an OOL does is to enforce the constraints necessary to support OO programming and manage some of the mechanical tasks. The primary advantage of an OOL is that it provides the environment in which OO programs need to operate. The most important feature in this environment is the concept of an object, which encompasses data, functions that operate on the data, and communications with other objects.

The Presentation

To clearly illustrate a design process that works well in OO systems, I will go through the complete design of a corporate database, implementing inventory, supplier, customer, and employee tracking, as well as a general ledger. Admittedly, I cannot cover every single aspect of the design of such a system in a single book, but it does allow me to address OO design within a consistent framework. My objective is to show a complete OO design process, from the initial idea through implementation of software based on this design.

In doing this, I have tried to restrain myself from using hindsight to write the book. While I could initially design the entire program, work out all of the bugs, write all of the code, and then write the book, I feel that it would not be very instructive, as it wouldn't exactly be truthful. What I have tried to do is to illustrate the design process as it actually occurs, showing it in its natural form, warts and all. The book reflects the actual process of design that I went through, including missteps and revisions. Although I spend a lot of time discussing it, the design example is only that, an example. It is a vehicle to show how OO design is done, and how code is implemented from this design.

The process starts with the hypothetical customer making a bunch of vague demands and waving their hands around a great deal. From this, some of the basic requirements are deduced, then relationships between these components are clarified, the function of the components fleshed out, and code is written. During this entire process I have tried to illustrate how and why I make the decisions I do, and how these decisions directly relate to the use of an OO programming language.

This book has been written in two distinct sections, Strategy and Tactics. The Strategy section deals with the design of object oriented systems, and is of use to anyone using an object oriented language, from C++ to Smalltalk. It is not a cookbook, where you look in the index to find the three paragraphs that you need. Instead, it is a history of the evolution of the design, showing how the design went from rough specifications to a finished product, and how the inevitable changes and clarifications were incorporated into the process. When you have finished this section, I hope you see the reasons that object oriented systems can aid you in your software development, and exactly how they can be used to their best advantage. In the second section, Tactics, pieces of the program designed in the Strategy section will be implemented in C++. This deals with the decisions that must be made to actually code an object definition and some of the operational considerations.

Throughout the book, I will highlight some of the basic concepts of OOP, such as inheritance, function overloading, and polymorphism, but my intent is not so much to give examples of syntax as it is to explain why these concepts are so valuable. (Therefore, I assume you have a copy of Bjarne Stroustrup's book next to you.) I take these diversions at points in the development where these concepts truly come into play, so that you can see why they are important and how they will help you in your own projects.

STRATEGY

CHAPTER 1

AN INTRODUCTION TO OOP

If you don't know what your program is supposed to do, you'd better not start writing it.

Edward Bancroft, chief executive of the Bancroft Trading Company, has issued a contract to have a coordinated corporate database created. Bancroft is a conglomerate of several enterprises, ranging from mail order operations to stock market brokers; therefore, the new software must both satisfy existing demands and recognize that new ones will continually evolve. For this reason, the software will be developed using object oriented programming techniques. After a consultation with Dr. Bancroft, the following objectives are selected for the initial implementation:

- An inventory tracking system.

- A sales tracking system.

- A personnel database.

- A consolidated general ledger containing relevant data from the previous objectives.

The Bancroft Trading Company

In brief, Bancroft Trading needs a corporate database—they are not satisfied with any commercially available package because of the limits in each of them. It is up to us to develop a package that meets their standards.

The reader may have detected that already we have encountered our first problem, namely that Bancroft's specifications are a bit vague. Most requests for software development are not clearly defined, but are refined over time *as the software is developed*. It is up to the developer to take the information that Bancroft provides, to develop what they can with it, and then to return to Bancroft for further information on how to proceed. This is not a problem with object oriented design, since the design method is based on a continuous process of *specification*, *implementation*, and *refinement of the specification*. While this cycle exists in many standard languages, in OOP it becomes something of an art form. By developing a software package from prototype to final release and by allowing the user to interact with the software throughout its development cycle, the likelihood that the user will not like the final version is greatly reduced. In addition, this development means that all of the programmer's time is spent on enhancing the capabilities of the system, instead of on writing and removing code that is only used for testing the package during development. This benefits both the programmer and the user. The user can interact with the software as it is being developed, identifying what they do and do not like about the behavior of the system before it is too late to change it. And the programmer gets this feedback as a natural element of the development process, instead of having to write specialized testbeds to obtain this information from the user.

The initial step is to begin decomposing the stated requirements, as they now exist. Real requirements usually are not given in concrete terms, instead they are given as overall objectives to be achieved. The first question to ask is: *What does each of the stated objectives imply?*

The first concern, inventory tracking, implies the existence of inventory items. The second, sales, implies the existence of customers who place orders and the third, personnel, implies the existence of employees. The last concern, the general ledger is based on relationships between these items and can be safely ignored for the time being—as it cannot be defined until the other three sections are known. While solving the other three, however, it is advisable to always keep in mind this fourth objective so that it is not impeded by decisions made on implementing the other objectives.

While this may appear to be a trivial set of deductions, it is not. OOP systems deal with objects, which are software analogues of real world things. The key difference between an object in an OO system and any component of a system written in a non-OO language is that objects are self contained, meaning they contain both data and code. Whereas in standard C the programmer is responsible for explicitly connecting functions to the data on which they operate, OO languages such as C++ do this as a matter of course. In standard C, there are functions that are used to do date and time calculations, and it is the programmer's job to ensure that these functions are fed the right data. In C++, there would be **time objects**, which contain the **data** that represents a time, and the **functions** that know how to operate on this value. Whenever we encounter a time object we can assume that it contains both the data that represents a specific time and the knowledge of how to operate on this data. In a traditional language we must tell the program *what* to do and *how* to do it. In OO systems, we can assume the system already knows how to do things and we only need to tell it what to do. This isn't to say that you will never have to explain how to do something, only that you will have to do it just one time. You will then be able to depend on the compiler to ensure that the instruction is carried along to wherever you might need it in the future.

OOP design is less concerned with the underlying computer model than are most other design methods, as the intent is to produce a software system that has a natural relationship to the real world situation it is modelling. As a matter of fact, a major concept in OOP is **modelling**. The job of the programmer is to build software models of real things. If this job is done well then many of the problems encountered in high level interactions between these objects will become non-problems, which is a much different situation than normally confronted in traditional languages. To understand, consider the fact that all software, OO or not, operates at two distinct levels. First, there are operations that are specific to particular data components, such as computing tax rates for employees or sales taxes on inventory items ordered by customers. Then there are operations that are global to the applications domain, such as computing the organization's total tax bill, including the payroll and sales taxes calculated at the lower levels.

In short, many global features of programs are not new creations in and of their own right, instead, they are based on the capabilities of the system. Instead of writing a huge routine to compute the total tax bill the hard way, we'd write a routine that added the results of all the more primitive tax calculation functions to get the total tax bill.

In object oriented design, if the first level of object specific operations (e.g., computing an employee's income tax) are well engineered, the second level (e.g., the amount of money Bancroft owes the IRS) will be relatively simple to implement. This is because global application operations are built from operations based in specific subcomponents of the application. The easier it is to exploit these lower capabilities, the less work needs to be done to implement the higher level capabilities. If you can't use the lower levels to accomplish these jobs, then you must reimplement them.

This whole situation is most apparent when one considers the standard libraries provided with C compilers. These libraries provide low level functions that are used by the entire application to accomplish primitive operations. In order to work, they must be clearly defined and well documented. When an application is initially developed, definition and documentation tend to suffer. This is not a fault of the developer, it is the nature of programming—especially within time and budget constraints. The C library depends on the investment of a lot of programmer time in order to make it of general use, a cost that cannot easily be borne within the domain of a single application. OOP systems solve this problem by shifting much of the structuring workload to the compiler so it can ensure that functional capabilities may be easily shared within a single application, without the traditionally high overhead costs.

Returning to Bancroft Trading's software, you can take each of the three sections and start to decompose them. To do this, make a cursory examination of the requirements of these sections, and the relationships between them.

First, the inventory tracking system is basically a container of inventory items. When discussing it, we are either talking about the set of all items in inventory, or a particular item in inventory. Therefore, the inventory tracking system is an object that contains many individual inventory items, and provides some means by which specific items may be accessed. Each inventory item is also an object in its own right, with some, as yet unknown, associated data. The following can be safely assumed:

- There are a certain number of items in stock for every item.
- Every item has an inventory code or part number.
- Every inventory item is purchased from one or more suppliers.
- There is a history of purchases and sales for each item.

Secondly, the sales model is a container of individual sales. For each sale, there must be:

- A customer order.
- Information about the final delivery.
- Information about payment.

Finally, the employee database is another container, this time holding a collection of individual employees. It will contain, as a minimum:

- Address information about the employee.
- Tax information.
- Job description and employment history.

At this point, one of the primary rules of object oriented design comes into play. During the entire process of constructing a program, similarities between objects in the system must be recognized and immediately exploited. In this particular case, there are certain components of each of these sections that share a common concept. The inventory system knows about suppliers, the sales system knows about customers, and the personnel system knows about employees. Each of these objects (*customer*, *supplier*, and *employee*) is a person and they all share common traits, namely they have names and addresses. Therefore, there must be a more general type of object in the system, an object that defines the **general** characteristics of each of these elements, the characteristics that they all have in common. We can say that these elements are all **kinds of** another, more general object, which we will call an **Entity**.

In OOP, every object is defined by a class, which can be viewed as a template for creating specific objects that behave in a similar fashion. Classes are grouped together into a hierarchy, going from very general characteristics that apply to many specialized classes, to very specific characteristics that apply to a single class. When we use classes, we are grouping objects together based on their similarities. Classes in OOLs are based on the same concept we use to divide animals into related groups. For example, when we talk of carnivorous animals, we aren't specifically dealing with dogs or lions. Instead, we are dealing with the things that dogs and lions have in common, such as a taste for meat. When we get to the level of detail of a dog or a lion, they are very different indeed, but when we discuss them in the more general terms of being carnivores, they are identical. This is what the Entity class allows us to do with customers, suppliers, and employees. Although these three objects are quite distinct, they are all kinds of Entities, in exactly the same way that dogs and lions are kinds of carnivores. By doing this, we don't have to describe every aspect of each new object we implement, instead, we only have to describe how this new object is *different* from the classes we have already defined. We don't have to specifically state that a customer has an address, any more than we have to specifically state that dogs eat meat. Customers have addresses because they are specialized kinds of Entities which already have addresses—just as dogs are specialized kinds of carnivores which we already know eat meat.

At this point, a structure is becoming apparent for how the Bancroft corporate database is modelled. This structure contains at least three distinct collections of objects, one each for inventory, sales, and personnel. Each of these collections operates the same way, by managing a list of components of its respective types, and by providing a uniform means of access to them. Each of these subtypes has a unique organization suited for its individual purpose, however, all use the Entity class to maintain information about the various kinds of people they must track.

This allows two vital assumptions to be made about the actual operation of the system. First, since all three of these information groups are collections of data, they should all operate in the same way. Regardless of whether an inventory item, customer record, or employee record is being retrieved from a collection, the mechanism for retrieval should be the same. At the top level, the application can be expected to know that these are collections and to understand how to access their contents. To expect the top level to treat a collection of inventory items as something totally distinct from a collection of employees is to needlessly complicate the program. Second, there is an object class, Entity, that tracks persons such as customers, suppliers, and employees. This class defines things common to all persons, from companies to real people. Therefore, it would contain things like:

- The name of the person or company.
- The address of the person or company.

A point to remember is that an Entity object cannot determine whether it is looking at a real person or a company. It is up to more detailed kinds of Entities to make this distinction. The Entity object itself not only doesn't know, it shouldn't know. Objects always behave in a uniform fashion, therefore Entity should behave the same way, regardless of whether it contains a person or a company. The easiest way to guarantee this is not to put information into Entity that differentiates between the two. Object oriented programming allows the development of software in a top down form, without the nagging fears about the final integration of the modules that often accompany this method in more traditional languages. It is apparent that the system will need a general object called **Collection**, which must behave in a uniform way. All accesses to the three specialized databases will be made through these collection objects and all accesses are guaranteed to perform in the same fashion. We can now ignore the top level and begin a more detailed decomposition of each of the databases.

Prior to solving Bancroft's problems, some of the programmer's tactical problems must be addressed. These are not really problems, but boundaries that the programmer must operate within and which define exactly what the programmer is and is not responsible for doing at this time. The first area is what information the programmer should address and what information the programmer should not address. The second is what functionality the programmer can assume is required at this time and what may be safely shifted elsewhere.

Generalization vs. Specialization

Before beginning to design the specialized database components, the programmer's responsibilities must be clearly delineated. As stated, this phase of design can be described as a *search for similarity*. For example, in the case of inventory items, they all have a part number and a description. They *all* do not have a color or a size. OOP systems allow designers to clearly distinguish between what is common to all cases and what is specific to just a few. More importantly, OOP systems allow designers to defer specialization until the general structures have been built. Therefore, a basic rule of thumb vital to designing an object oriented program is *to ignore special cases until they can be ignored no longer*.

Some programmers, when beginning a design, immediately begin searching for the most detailed information they can find. In short order they find themselves overwhelmed by a mass of unconnected information, consisting primarily of exceptions, rather than a coherent collection of information that has no exceptions. This is exactly what OOP is supposed to prevent. Specialization is the last step of development, done after all similarities within the system have been exploited. After the general design has been done and the known exceptions have been implemented, a continuous process of introducing rarer and rarer exceptions continues until clients exhaust their budgets! If you generalize well, you then can constantly add specialization to the system without affecting any work you have done previously.

Deferred Functionality

When traditional programs are written, data structures are created and functions to manipulate them are created directly afterwards. In OOP, this is not the case. When a new data structure, or object, is created, that marks the end of the programmer's current responsibility. For example, many accounting systems use time stamps to mark each transaction as it is processed. In conventional design, the programmer defines the accounting record with an internal time stamp field and then defines the operations that manipulate the time stamp. In OOP, the programmer's responsibility ends with the inclusion of the time stamp object in a **Transaction** object. Since the time stamp object is an individual object, the Transaction object is not responsible for performing operations *within* it. Those operations are confined within the time stamp object and can therefore be ignored until a later time. In the simplest terms, objects are never concerned with the internal details of other objects, only with their own. Therefore, objects communicate with other objects in terms of *what* they want to accomplish, assuming that the object they are communicating with knows *how* to accomplish this. If objects communicated with each other in English, their most common remark to other objects would be: *"Don't ask me how to do it, just do it. You're the expert. I told you what I want."* The Transaction object assumes that its request for a time stamp object will give it the time stamp that it desires. How this actually happens is of no concern to it.

When a Transaction object is defined, the internal mechanics of the time stamp it contains can be ignored. This is not to say that no code for time stamp operations needs to be written, only that this code is of no interest when designing the Transaction object. When the design of the Transaction object is completed, the **time stamp** object can then be defined or even be left for a much later date.

Inventory

What can be said about every item in inventory, regardless of if it is a dress, a computer, or a book? This is the question that must be answered at this stage of the design, as we are trying to identify the *similarities* between all items in inventory. These are properties that any item in inventory is expected to have. Once again, we are searching out the similarities of inventory items, seeking to first define what is true about all items in inventory, before we begin to identify the differences between some items in inventory. This cannot be stressed enough, as this is an essential concept in OO design. In standard design methodologies, exceptions to the rules are the driving force behind many design decisions. In OOP, objects are defined because they obey the rules. If they don't, then they *must* be a new kind of object. To identify the similarities between all the possible kinds of inventory items, a list of possible properties is constructed. This list might include:

- Part number
- Quantity on hand
- Price per item
- Suppliers of item
- Sales history
- Description of item
- Color of item
- Voltage of item
- DOS version of item

This list is then examined and each property is tested by the following criteria: *Is there an item that does not have this property?* If the answer to the question is yes, then the property is discarded, as it is too specialized for an inventory item object. We cannot include the property unless it applies to every possible inventory item. For example, Color only applies to items that have a color, such as a shirt that can come in red, white, or blue. Voltage applies only to electrical products, and DOS version applies only to computers. Part numbers and text descriptions, however, apply to any inventory item, from an awl to a zinnia. This is where most conventional programs acquire a nasty complexity. Some programmers will create a structure, something like:

```
typedef struct {
    int part_no;
    char *description;

    .

    .

    .

    int type;
```

```
    int color;
    int size;
} Inventory_Item;
```

They will then proceed to scatter specialized tests through the software in order to check the type field of the structure. If it is a 1, they will assume that there is a valid color; a 2, and there is a valid size; and a 3, there is both a color and a size. While they are at it, they might make 0 mean that there is no size or color. And some, in order to save space, might even replace the size and color fields with a single field, whose contents are defined by the type field. Unfortunately, this little stunt, no matter how well documented, adds an enormous burden to the work of the maintenance programmers who come aboard after the program is released. As is too often the case, they are not aware of this coding scheme and their modifications tend to make the software uncooperative.

This is an anathema to object oriented design. Objects represent themselves in only one way. They do not behave in different ways depending on their internal contents. Objects are always consistent—the preceding mechanism is anything but consistent. Our entire intent in using objects is that we can depend on them to behave in a regular, uniform, fashion. To deliberately subvert this reintroduces all of the problems we are trying to avoid. We want to be able to say that a certain object acts a certain way in all cases, not that the object's behavior depends on some peculiar control variable.

At this point, you may be wondering how things like color and size are represented. Color and size are both properties of *some* inventory items, but not of *all* inventory items. We can assume that inventory items that have a color are more specialized *kinds* of inventory items, as dogs are more specialized kinds of carnivores. However, you should not begin to describe specialized cases of something before you have defined the something of which they are a specialization. We shouldn't define what the properties of a colored inventory item are until we know what the properties of all inventory items are.

One of the inventory item properties deserves special consideration. The Price per item is a property that can reasonably be associated with any inventory item. But, what about items that come in singles, dozens, and grosses? At issue is the difference between the property itself, and how that property is computed. That any inventory item has a price per item is an acceptable statement. How that value is computed is up to the specific inventory item itself, therefore it can be safely ignored at this point. Consider, if Bancroft sells knit sport shirts in red, white, blue, and puce, they might have had the puce shirts in stock for quite a while. They may compute the price of a red, white, or blue shirt at twice what they paid for it, while they might compute the price of a puce shirt at half of what they paid for it. And for something like a wooden table, which has no color at all, they might compute the price another way entirely. But, regardless of the means of computing the price per item, it is a property associated with all inventory items. Therefore, the distinguishing factor is not how a value for any given property is arrived at, it is whether that property is applicable to all occurrences of that object.

Some elements of the design, such as the fact that inventory items have a sales history, are a little vague. How can an item have a sales history, when there is no clear definition of what a sales history is? This illustrates how the process of OO design tends to lead the programmer along by the nose. When you cannot clearly define a property of an object, but you know it is a property of the object, you can safely assume you are talking about a new object, of one kind or another. In cases such as these, you aren't required to come to a screeching halt and completely define the new object, because the simple fact is you can't. You don't have enough information. You do know you need a new object, therefore as the design proceeds, you keep this in mind, waiting for the rest of the pieces to fall into place, so that you can clearly define the new object.

Sales

The first thing that becomes apparent is that there is no such thing as a lone sale. It doesn't make sense by itself. A sale is always made to a customer. For this reason, the sales database is really a database of customers. When a question like *"How many copies of this book were sold last year"* is asked, there are many ways that it can be answered. The most obvious is to look in the inventory and see how many have been sold. A sales database in the purest sense could be nothing more than a subset of the inventory database. What Bancroft really wants, insofar as a Sales database is concerned, is to know *who* bought the copies of this book. Therefore, the sales database is really a database of customers, which are represented by **Customer** objects.

The Customer object is used to track information about individual customers, such as where they live, what they have ordered from Bancroft in the past, and what kind of junk mail Bancroft has sent to them. Once again, similarities are searched out, producing the following list of properties:

- The customer's name and address.

- The customer's ordering history.

- Drop shipments made for the customer.

- Mailing history for the customer.

First, notice that the customer's name and address have been treated as a single item. Previously, it was determined that there was an Entity object in the system, which defined general information about customers, employees, and suppliers. It is apparent, therefore, that every Customer object is a kind of Entity object. From the definition of the Entity object, a name and an address are guaranteed to be available. Because of this we know we can lump the name and address together at this level, because we really don't have to deal with them, they are managed already at the Entity level.

This is the process by which we construct the **class hierarchy**. A Customer is a kind of Entity, specifically it is a **derived class** of Entity. Entity in turn, is the **base class** of the Customer class. And this is where one of the central concepts of OOP becomes invaluable. **Inheritance** is when a derived class uses data and functional capabilities (C functions) from its base class to accomplish certain operations. In this case, the Entity class provides the name and address data elements and the means by which they are accessed and manipulated. By defining Customer as a derived class of Entity, it can immediately work with these two data items, as it uses the facilities of its base class to do the work. Customer has inherited these capabilities from Entity.

Inheritance arises from the fact that objects consist of both data and the functions that operate on this data. Recalling our previous discussion of a hypothetical **Date** object, it contains the data that represents a specific time *and* the functions that operate on this data. For example, a function that returned the day of the week for any given date would be *bound* to the date object. While we will leave the exact mechanism by which this is accomplished to later chapters, it is important that you remember this fact. Certain functions, called **member functions**, do not exist in and of their own right, as do standard C functions. Instead, these functions are defined strictly in the context of a particular object, such as the **dayOfWeek()** function being defined in the *context* of a Date object. Because of this, we can define new derived classes of Date and we can assume that these new classes inherit the original capabilities of the Date class. Returning to our animal example, this is the same reason we do not need to explicitly state that dogs or lions eat meat. Since dogs and lions are carnivores and carnivores eat meat, then dogs and lions *inherit* this characteristic.

The three remaining data items are used only by the Customer class, and are not available to the Entity class. Inheritance is strictly one way to move down from general to more specialized levels. As all three items represent complex data, the design process has indicated, once again, the requirement for new objects. We will leave the actual definition of these three items for future chapters, for now it is only necessary to realize that they indicate the requirement for new objects to represent them.

Employees

Finally, there is the employee database. Once again, an employee is a specialization of an Entity object, like a Customer object. But, employees are not customers, and they have different data associated with them. However, we reach the definition of an employee in exactly the same fashion that we defined all of the previous classes. We identify those properties of our proposed class that apply to each and every specific example we can think of, thereby continuing our quest for similarities. By thinking about characteristics of the average employee, the following properties manifest themselves:

- Name and address (as in Customer)
- Job classification

- Current salary

- Tax information

- Benefits information

- Employment history

In defining an employee, we were already fairly certain that it was a kind of Entity, or more technically, a *derived class* of entity. Notice that our definition includes a name and address for an employee, which we know we will inherit from the Entity base class. When you are defining a new class, and the class is derived from an existing class, then the new class *must* contain all of the elements of the base class. If we had managed to prove that our new derived class did not contain one of the elements of its base class, then we have a clear indication that either there is something wrong with the definition of the base class, or that our new class is not really derived from this base class. In this example, if we managed to come up with some reason that not every employee has an address, then that would imply that either the **Employee** class should not be derived from the Entity class, or that the Entity class should not contain an address property. From this, we can see that the search for similarity is not simply a holy grail for the OO programmer, but instead, governs their every action.

We cannot establish a clear relationship between the tax information for an employee and any class we have defined so far, so we can safely assume that it is implemented in a new class, **EmployeeTaxInfo**. We make this assumption for the simplest of reasons, namely that there are no similarities between this new data and objects we have previously implemented. Our general experience in the real world tells us that there is more to tax information than a simple number or keyword. Remember that we are building models (objects) of things that exist in the real world, therefore our knowledge of the real world is very helpful in making design decisions. Simply speaking, we can assume that tax information has to be represented by at least one specialized object, because it's so complicated! We do know that there is most likely only one **Tax** object per employee and it contains such things as the number of exemptions for that employee and more complex data understood by CPAs and IRS employees. This does illustrate another powerful aspect of OO design, namely that we can depend on the fact that objects are analogous to the real world objects or concepts that they represent. If it's complicated in real life, it's most likely going to be a complicated object, or set of objects. In any case, we know that if it's complicated, we sure aren't going to represent it as an ASCII string, unless we simply have no other choice.

The Job Classification is another object class, **EmployeeJobClass**. For simplicity's sake, there is only one job classification per employee, but in the real world this might be a collection for those employees that wear multiple hats in the organization. If it could be either a single object or a list of objects, a test would definitely have to be made every time this property is accessed. This example serves to illustrate another important feature of OOP. Since only an Employee object can actually access this data, only an Employee object would have to determine whether there was one or a series of job classifications. Compare this to most programs where every reference to this element would have to perform the test. This is called **encapsulation**, where bizarre characteristics of the program are confined within individual objects and not scattered through the system. All other objects in the system would simply ask an Employee object for its job classification. Whether there was one classification or a collection of classifications wouldn't matter to the object requesting the data.

The Benefits information is another specialized object. This object contains information on insurance, sick leave, and other benefit information. The Employment History record is a more complex object. It contains reviews of the employee, previous employee job classifications, and previous employee benefit information. Since both of these will be new kinds of objects, their definitions can be deferred.

Summary

1. Remember that this is model building. There is a direct relationship between the objects you create and the objects they represent in the real world. They should function similarly. The computer's point of view is not important, the real world's is.

2. Objects behave in a uniform fashion, without regard to the data they contain. A building is a building, whether it is a church or an office. If a church and office are two different kinds of buildings then say so.

3. Recognize and exploit similarities. Don't handcraft three identical copies of the same data structure.

4. Ignore special cases as long as possible. Special cases and exceptions to the rules are implemented after the standards are established. In order to be a special case, it must deviate from a defined common standard.

5. Don't let one object tell another how to do its job. Every object is self sufficient.

6. Always distinguish between what something is and how that something was arrived at. They are not necessarily related. There are many cases where an object can arrive at a particular value in more than one way. The value is still common, even if there are multiple paths to it.

7. Don't scatter the little bizarre details of the application all over the place, because if they change, you will have a great deal of editing to do. Keep them where they belong, provide limited access to them, and treat them like radioactive waste. They will hurt you.

CHAPTER 2

OBJECT PROPERTIES

When you open a can of worms, the only way to recan them is to use a larger can.

In this chapter, more of the internal architecture of the database will be revealed. This is good, as no design is complete until all of its components are complete. This does not mean that the deferral of definitions to a later point in the development is bad, it is also good. Remember that some programmers who were taught traditional design methods share a common weakness. When these programmers are asked the time, they proceed to give a detailed explanation about the construction of a watch. This is primarily due to their shared experience with the computer. They must remember that telling time and understanding how time is kept are two different areas of knowledge. I own a watch and I have often responded to the requests of others for the current time. This does not imply I know anything about the internal workings of my watch. The watch is an object, one that satisfies my requests for the current time. It does not need me to tell it how to do its job!

At this point, a basic structure for the Bancroft Trading Company's corporate database has been defined. This structure is *very* basic, as it consists of a great deal of handwaving and a small amount of concrete data. Experienced programmers may have already taken issue with this approach, wondering how definitions can be deferred at the drop of a hat. As stated previously, in designing object oriented systems, *one deals with a single object at a time*. Other distinct objects, while they may be used by an object currently being defined, do not need to be defined right away. There is always a clear distinction between *using* the capabilities of an object and defining precisely how these capabilities operate, or *implementing* them.

Collections

The design laid out in Chapter One depends on a concept called the **Collection** object. This object serves to group other objects together, so that they can be referred to as a single entity. In the case of the Bancroft database, these collections all contain objects that are indexed by some element. Inventory items are retrieved by part number, customers are retrieved by customer IDs of some sort, and employees are retrieved by their name and job description. This does not preclude doing such things as a search for a customer by name, it just dictates how the individual customers will be coded in the collection. The objective is to use a key index used by the widest segment of the "user" objects, since if they cannot provide a value for this key index, these objects will have to search manually through the customer records to locate the information they desire.

Because of this mechanism, the type of collection actually required is some type of *indexed* collection. Those who have previous experience with object oriented languages may have encountered Collection classes that have a host of derived classes, from arrays to strings. Those lucky enough to have such a system available to them will probably be able to use an existing indexed collection class that came with their system. For others, a Collection class will have to be developed from scratch. Reflecting upon our discussion of the animal kingdom in the previous chapter, notice how we are already assuming the presence of two *hierarchically related* classes, specifically the base class Collection and an **IndexedCollection** class derived from this base class. Once again we are searching out similarities, in this case, the fact that we will need to make generic collections of other objects. We also know that not all collections are necessarily indexed, some may be viewed as simple buckets into which we dump a number of distinct objects. By using the class hierarchy to separate the concept of a collection in general from the concept of a specialized kind of collection that supports indexing, we can manage to clearly delineate the various kinds of collections we may encounter. We know that all collections contain things, regardless of the specific behavior of the collection. However, we also know that a certain kind of collection, the IndexedCollection, also contains keys for locating specific elements in the collection. Therefore, we use the class hierarchy to support our claim that:

- All collections contain a list of elements.
- Some collections also contain a list of keywords.

The hierarchal relationships between classes allows us to do this because we have said that the base class, Collection, contains an arbitrary group of objects. Since we have said this is true for the base class, it is therefore true for any class derived from the base class. Also, we have said that some collections contain keywords that can be used to access specific elements of a collection, implementing this capability through the derived class IndexedCollection. Therefore, we need only specifically state that the IndexedCollection *is a derived class* of Collection, which contains a list of keywords. IndexedCollection *inherits* the behavior of collections in general and extends this behavior to support keywords.

This brings up another point that the object oriented programmer must consider. When constructing a class, is the class being constructed to solve a particular problem for the application or is the class satisfying some weakness of the underlying system? For example, the Customer object is definitely associated with the Bancroft database. While other programs may have a customer definition, they will most likely interact with it quite differently. The Collection class is different. It is a general purpose class, designed to collect together a group of objects, regardless of their individual types. Regardless of the purpose of individual applications, from inventory control to word processing, their concepts of a Collection object are identical.

As most books available today on OOP say, one of the major benefits of objects is that they are *reusable*. So are C functions. The difference is that objects, representing both data structures and operations that can be performed on these structures, represent functional packages, requiring no additional work on the part of the programmer to use them. The packages are always uniform and they interact identically with other objects, regardless of the purpose of a given object. The data definitions and member functions are tightly coupled, the use of the data automatically guaranteeing the ability to use the functions that operate on it. In order to support indexed collections in the Bancroft database, we will have to implement indexing algorithms, data structures, and a host of other minor details. Once this operation has been completed, the entire mess can be packaged into a nice, neat black box called "Collections." When it works, you will never be forced to look inside of it again—neither will any other programmer who needs to use it. This is similar to using C library functions such as **printf()**. While all C programmers are familiar with this function, not many of them understand its internal operations. They don't have to, it works, so they use it. This is what objects provide for you. You get exactly the same effect and you don't have to work nearly as hard as did the developers of **printf()**. Instead of working hard to ensure something is usable by a large group of your peers, you can allow the compiler to provide this capability.

The collections that will be developed for the Bancroft database will come in two flavors. The base class, Collection, is essentially an unordered container of objects without a mechanism for keying it. Objects can be added to and deleted from this collection at will and elements of it may be retrieved in the order they were inserted. Searching for a specific element would require that one start at the beginning and search forward through each object until the desired element is found or until the data is exhausted.

The derived class of Collection, IndexedCollection, adds a crucial capability to the base class. IndexedCollection allows for the addition, deletion, and retrieval of elements in the collection by the use of keys. This allows for the retrieval of specific items from the collection without requiring the requesting object to actually perform the search.

In order for the Collection object to function, it needs the following data items:

- Number of items currently in the collection.

- Number of items the collection can hold at this time.

- A reference to where the collection data is stored.

- The current working position.

Notice there is no provision for saying what the items are that the collection contains. Again, this is a central premise of OOP and good designs will always reflect it. It is not the collection's job to understand what types of objects it contains, since as far as it is concerned, one object is just like another. A collection collects objects. If it is necessary to make a collection of widgets, you do not alter the function of the Collection class itself. You make a new derived class, **WidgetCollection**, specialized for collecting widgets. Remember, Collection can be used to collect any arbitrary group of objects. If you build only collections for specialized objects, then you will spend a great deal of time building collections, when you could be doing more interesting things. Rarely will you find yourself creating a new kind of Collection class that is particular about what kinds of objects you place in it. Collections are meant to be general purpose and they are supposed to collect objects. They are not supposed to dictate what kinds of objects you can actually place in them.

Most languages force you to specify clearly what you are putting into an array or list, with some exceptions such as LISP. C also would like you to do this, but will allow you to circumvent it by declaring something as **void** * and using casting operations to convert the reference to another form. Unfortunately, this means you don't really have a way of telling, aside from blind faith, to what you are actually referring. This tendency of computer languages is a basic limitation requiring the use of **homogeneous structures**, structures that contain items of only one type. In OO systems, because all objects have the same basic behavior, **heterogeneous lists** can be constructed containing all sorts of different kinds of objects. And because each object still retains its identity, you don't have to know *a priori* what kinds of objects you might encounter. This is because, at the top level, one object looks just like another and each object is capable of identifying its specific type to other objects. A collection states that it contains objects. Regardless of the specific type of object you place in the collection, in the most general terms, it is still an object. While a collection of Employee objects might seem to be quite distinct from a collection of Customer objects, from the Collection class' point of view, they are identical because they both contain objects. This arises from the fact that in a pure, or **first class** OO system, the most base class, or ancestor of any specialized class you may create, is the **Object** class itself. Since collections deal with their elements as members of the Object class, they aren't concerned with the more detailed pedigrees of these elements.

Up until this time, only the data associated with individual objects has been discussed, although some type of associated functionality has been implied. In this case, we have defined *what* a collection is, but we have not described *how* a collection behaves. No object is complete until both of these properties have been completely defined. This is the advantage of objects, they serve to package information about what something is (its structure) along with how it behaves (its functionality). However, this also means that no object can be defined as either data or code, it must be defined as data *and* the code which operates on this data.

In order for a collection to be useful, it must understand how to perform the following operations:

- Insert an item after the current item.

- Go to the next item in the collection.

- Return the current item.

- Delete the current item.

- Go to the first item in the collection.

- Tell if the collection is empty.

These represent functional capabilities and could be represented by the following functions:

- insertAfterCurrent(aNewObject)

- object * goToNextElement()

- object * returnCurrent()

- deleteCurrent()

- goToFirstObject()

- BOOLEAN isEmpty()

The actual definition of these functions will come later in the form of real C++ code. The algorithms themselves are fairly standard; any computer science textbook should provide examples. The internal organization of these functions is not at issue here, only the fact that these functions represent the capabilities of a collection. One common characteristic of the functions is that none of them accept the collection itself as a parameter. They are directly associated with the collection and; therefore, already have the capability to access it. This mechanism is one of the main contributors to the overall reliability of OO software—functions can only operate on data for which they were specifically designed. No special checking needs to be done at the time the function is called, as it cannot operate on the wrong type of structure in the first place. No more wondering what would happen if someone called your new string fiddler with an array of floating point numbers. It can't happen.

IndexedCollection

Now that the Collection class has been specified, it is time to define its derived class, the IndexedCollection class. The design of this derived class should bear in mind another of the central goals of an OO program, namely that uniformity is a prized characteristic of a program. Uniformity has a direct impact on the costs of developing and maintaining the software, the more uniform the software is, the cheaper and easier it is to develop and maintain. The IndexedCollection class should behave in a similar fashion to its base class. Another basic rule of thumb is that the programmer has deliberately selected this particular class and therefore, they will have some preconceived notion of how it must differ from other classes they might have selected. For example, if one were to select an IndexedCollection, it is reasonable to assume that it must know something about indexing. However, actual retrieval and storage of items should function like all other collections.

In defining the IndexedCollection, the five operations defined for Collection would be inherited automatically by the IndexedCollection, thus providing it with the means to add, delete, and retrieve data items. The only thing truly necessary to make it behave like an indexed collection, is some function that could perform indexing, like:

```
selectObject(objectKey)
```

This function could be used to set the current object to an object in the collection associated with the supplied key. After this function completes its job in locating the desired element, the standard Collection functions can be used to operate on the collection to retrieve or delete the selected object.

The definition of this function implies that an IndexedCollection must have a list of keys for the collection, with each key matched up to a particular object. Advanced OOP systems, like Smalltalk, include a standard object class, called an **Association**, that serves to link together keys and the objects to which they refer. Both the key and the reference of an association are objects, leaving the lucky programmer with a whole range of choices. For our case, we will simply say the keylist contains two values, the first a pointer to the key and the second an index to the object in the collection. This would produce the C structure:

```
typedef struct {
char * elementKey;              /* can be recast as needed */

int itemIndex;                  /* position of object in collection */

} indexKey;
```

Be aware of the fact that this design requires that the collection be re-indexed every time an object is added to or deleted from the collection. While this example might not be satisfactory in all cases, there are particular reasons it has been selected. After all, it will work, it just doesn't rate highly in the efficiency department. Also, the adding of elements to the collection with their associated indices has not been discussed yet. Fear not, this issue will resurface later. Remember, the intent is not to radically change the behavior of a collection just because it is indexed. For that reason, you don't need a new function, you only want IndexedCollections to act differently when they perform the analogue of the **insertAfterCurrent()** function. Also, you want the user of the object prevented from using the inherited insertAfterCurrent() function on an indexed collection.

The design of the IndexedCollection class shows another aspect of the OO design method. In this case we knew what function we need performed—searching for an indexed item—and this implied the existence of an index table. This is the inverse of the example given in Chapter One, where we knew what data was required and it implied the functions that had to be available in order to manipulate it. Objects are binary organisms, consisting of both data and functional capabilities. Knowing about one side of the object will usually imply something about the other; therefore, the idea is to start off with the side about which you know. It is unlikely you will be trying to create an object where you know nothing about either side.

Interestingly enough, there is a distinction between system level objects and application level objects. For those not familiar with the distinction between system and application oriented capabilities, consider string operations for a second. Converting a string to all lowercase letters is a system capability, as it is likely to be used in many applications. Determining if a string represents a legal inventory part number is an application capability, of little use to any other application.

Although it is not always true, it is often the case that you will initially know about data when dealing with an application's type objects and you will know about functionality when dealing with a system's type objects. Remember, when you are dealing with a system's type objects, you want to make them reusable. You really aren't adding capabilities to the applications with them, you are adding capabilities to the system, because the application has indicated that they are omitted. If they are designed in a general manner, without being bound to the application, then you can use these capabilities in every new application you develop, without a single bit of extra work.

In summary, two general purpose classes will be created: Collection and IndexedCollection. IndexedCollection is a derived class of Collection and, correspondingly, Collection is the base class of IndexedCollection. Collection will implement functions to move through the data and to retrieve and alter the collection contents. IndexedCollection will extend these capabilities to allow access to a particular element in the collection by a keyword.

Address

The next object to examine is the address component of the Entity object. In Chapter One, it was said that any Entity and any derived class such as Customer, has an address. That address referred to is another object, which serves to manage all of the data associated with an address.

In the modern world, an address is more than just a postal address. For example, someone's phone number is also part of their address because it provides a means for reaching, or addressing, this person. When designing objects, relationships such as this should always be considered. Although there is nothing wrong with associating a postal address and a phone number with each entity, packaging them together provides more flexibility.

For example, Bancroft has both domestic U.S. addresses and international addresses. This means that postal codes (ZIP) and telephone numbers have different formats, depending on whether the address is domestic or foreign. If the address and phone number were stored individually within the Entity class, then the Entity class would have to know about these relationships and enforce them. OO programmers should consider this extra work, and avoid it at all costs. By building a single, uniform address class, the burden of managing these differences has been shifted from Entity to the **Address** class, where it belongs.

Yet again, the OO design method has illustrated how new classes are derived from existing classes. In Chapter One, it was said that entities had addresses. After examining Address, it becomes apparent that there are really two kinds of addresses, **DomesticAddress** and **ForeignAddress**, as well as subcomponents such as phone numbers and street addresses. In this case, both addresses deal with the same information, they just deal with it differently.

The DomesticAddress and ForeignAddress object classes are both derived from the Address class. The address itself contains the following elements:

- Street address
- Local phone number
- City

The DomesticAddress contains:

- State
- Zip
- Area code

The ForeignAddress contains:

- Province
- Postal code
- Country
- International access code

In this example, first consider the fact that the local phone prefix is contained within the generic address class. Secondly, consider that the phone numbers for foreign countries differ greatly and it is desirable to be able to check them for validity. These cases illustrate one of the very few times when you can make an object behave differently based on its contents. The reason for this is simple, it is pointless to create objects for every foreign country you wish to support, since you cannot determine beforehand which countries would have to be defined. Bancroft Trading will balk at paying for Fiji's phone numbers to be validated, as they currently do no business with them. However, they will balk equally as much if you tell them to forget Fiji because the software can't handle it!

In this case, you are confronted by an object that can legitimately have different behavior patterns, ones that you cannot clearly define at this time. In this case, the object must be intelligent enough to manage the change itself. This is not to say that it can simply absorb the means for validating a phone number in Fiji, only that it will do the best it can and will not frustrate the user.

When the Address classes are implemented, the DomesticAddress is set up to validate its private data and the generic address data in terms of legal U.S. zip codes, states, and phone numbers. Given the appropriate zip code database, it could accept only the zip code and then determine the appropriate city and state. The ForeignAddress will be set up so that it uses specialized logic for testing addresses and phones in Britain and France (known customers of Bancroft), and simply assumes all other foreign addresses are legal. Once again, logic could be added to cross match between the country, city, and the international access code, in the case of phone numbers. DomesticAddresses will always ensure that their contents are legal and ForeignAddresses will do the same, when they can. When they can't, they will assume the data is legal.

Should Bancroft start doing a large volume of business with Fiji, then the ForeignAddress could be modified to support checks without affecting any other operations. This is another important feature of OOP—the ability to modify running code without running a high risk of rendering it non-running code. In later chapters, the exact C logic for how this is accomplished will be shown, now it is simply necessary to make sure the design reflects this requirement.

Suppliers

One of the elements in the InventoryItem class is a supplier of a particular item. As suppliers tend to supply more than one item, some form of cross linked data structure needs to be created, linking InventoryItems to Suppliers and vice versa. To do this, the **Supplier** class needs to be created. If this class is to be created, it implies that there is a collection of suppliers within the system. OO design is done, primarily, by starting off with a rough idea about the software and then beginning to establish links between the various objects that will exist. Although the path generally moves from the top down, there are times, such as this one, where lower levels indicate the need for data storage at a higher level. In the majority of cases, lower levels may indicate the need for collections at higher levels. In this case, while it is not necessary, a collection of suppliers would be useful at the top level of the application. It is relatively painless to provide it, as the Collection class to hold it is already available, and the individual suppliers themselves are mandatory. Not much new code has to be written; instead, existing abilities will be exploited. The top level of the application will be modified to include a collection of suppliers, in addition to the other collections already defined.

The Supplier class will itself be a derived class of Entity. In addition to the name and address provided by Entity, it will contain:

- Supplier ID

- Contact Name

- Contact Address

- Supplier Inventory

The Supplier ID is a unique string, generated by Bancroft, that serves as a shorthand way of naming the supplier. This value is used primarily to index references to the supplier in other collections.

The Contact Name is also a string, holding the name of some responsible party at the supplier, one who tells the truth at least half of the time. The contact address is another Address object, the Supplier Inventory is a collection used to index into our inventory by our part numbers and also by theirs. See Figure 2-1 on the next page for a graphic summary.

In referencing the Contact Address, certain considerations must be taken into account. The address might be identical to the address inherited from the Entity base class. Also, only the phone might be different. Finally, the whole thing might be different, e.g., the salesperson's home phone and address for times that require extreme measures. Although the Supplier does have these three separate cases to consider, it really shouldn't have to do anything. If the Supplier class is modified to make specific provisions for each of these cases, then this adds overhead to the class. At all times, you should strive to avoid these situations.

To solve this particular problem, think of the old phrase *"The buck stops here."* In OOP, if you don't know exactly what to do to the buck with a minimum of fiddling, don't overload your program with a lot of tests. Do what you know you can do and pass the buck off to an object that knows more. In this particular case, whenever the user creates a Supplier, they are going to supply an address for the address element inherited from Entity. This address is a fine starting point for the contact address. If changes are desired, communicate with the address directly. This means the only actions required of Supplier is that it copies the supplier address into the contact address when the particular supplier is created and that it returns this address on demand. Further modifications of this address can be performed by communicating with it directly.

Figure 2-1: Entity and Supplier

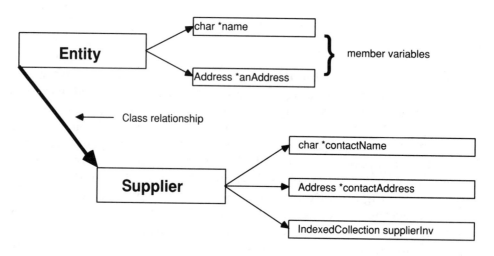

Entity is the base class, with two member variables. Supplier is the derived class, with three new member variables, plus two that are inherited from Entity.

The supplier inventory is a collection, containing references to items in our inventory, information about price and delivery time, and supplier part numbers. The supplier inventory items are interlocked with the internal Bancroft inventory items, each referencing the other. The Bancroft inventory collection lists suppliers who can supply a particular item and the supplier's collection lists Bancroft inventory items that individual suppliers can provide.

Prior to this, individual objects were discussed, along with static class relationships developed at the time the software is written. The relationship between suppliers and inventory items is dynamic, developed as the system is loaded with data, and as suppliers fall in and out of favor. Formally, the generation of derived classes represents the development of static **hierarchal** information, while the relationships established between suppliers and inventory items represents dynamic **closures** on sets of information.

For example, the Bancroft inventory item for a specific book would list a publishing company and its part number as supplier information. In turn, the publisher supplier record would list this Bancroft inventory item, as well as all other products of this publisher that are stocked by Bancroft. This relationship between objects allows the generation of very powerful query tools. If a user is looking at a particular item in inventory, they can move directly from that single item to the supplier information, and then produce a list of all items in inventory that the supplier can provide. This capability is provided without any extra work on the programmer's part, as it is a natural byproduct of the way in which objects operate.

This arises from the **encapsulation** of both data and functionality within specific objects. While a traditional language would have to implement an entire query architecture to provide these same features, working from the total set of raw data contained within the system, an OO system can simply shift from one object to the next, by following the links between these objects. Traditional programs will deal with all of the data available and will then use internal logic to select particular subsets of that data, based on user commands. OO programs, on the other hand, are never dealing with all of the data in the first place. In the previous example, the program would first deal with a subset of the data representing an item in inventory. By following the link to the supplier, the OO system replaces this entire subset with a new one representing information on the supplier, but it does not have to provide any logic that actually performs this separation, as it arises from the fact that each object represents a self-contained part of the total system. All the OO system has to do is to replace the reference to the inventory item with a reference to the supplier. By doing this, it has changed both the data on which it is operating and the set of functions that are available to operate on this data. Because of this, there is no need for extra logic to determine which actions are or are not appropriate in a given context. The use of objects guarantees that whatever data or functions you can access are legal. If they don't apply, you can't get at them anyway!

Finally, each inventory item has an associated sales and purchase history. Each sale is associated with a customer and each transaction is associated with a supplier. The inventory item itself contains a collection, into which all of these various transactions are loaded. Each individual transaction is referenced at two points within the system. The inventory database lists both purchases and orders, the supplier database lists the orders, and the customer database lists the purchases.

To implement this capability, two new classes need to be provided. They will be derived from a common base class, Transaction, which also needs to be implemented. The base class will contain shared similarities:

- Transaction start date

- Transaction complete date

- Transaction ID

- Transacting entity

- Line items of the transaction

Notice that this definition supplies the requirements for both purchases and orders. Purchases would list the customer's order code as the transaction ID and would list the customer themself as the transacting entity. Orders would list the purchase order as the transaction ID and would list the supplier as the transacting entity.

If this was all of the information that was to be provided for either transaction, would there still need to be the two derived classes: **PurchaseTransaction** and **OrderTransaction**? Yes. The reason is that the two transactions behave in quite different ways. In terms of simple reference, the PurchaseTransaction is tied into customer information and the OrderTransaction is tied into supplier information. Both of these classes provide no new data, but deal with the data in the base class in different ways. Additionally, if these two derived classes were not provided, then we would have an object, Transaction, whose behavior is context sensitive, something that should not be done without a very good reason.

Given this definition, Transaction is not really capable of functioning on its own. It simply provides a common frame of reference that is used by its derived classes. Compare this to the Collection class, where the IndexedCollection class is used to further specialize the behavior of the Collection class. In the case of the Transaction class, it has no behavior of its own. Its behavior is implemented by its derived classes. The function of the Transaction class is to provide a common abstract model for which the derived classes then implement specialized functions.

The Transaction class is an example of an **abstract class**. The function of an abstract class is to group together related classes, providing a common root from which a series of more specialized classes may be derived. The abstract classes serve to group together the member functions and data elements that are common to all of the subclasses, but they do no real work, and they are not truly complete enough to operate as independent entities. The easiest way to tell if a class is abstract is if you use it. If it was necessary to create a class, but you only use classes derived from it, then that class is an abstract class. Returning to our animal world example, the designation carnivore is an example of an abstract class. Carnivore represents a concept, of which their are many concrete derivations, such as dogs and lions. You will never encounter an animal that is simply a carnivore, but it will always be a specific kind of carnivore.

Although abstract classes are most clearly illustrated when the derived classes provide no new information, this does not mean that the derived classes are barred from adding new data to the abstract class.

It is now apparent that the Supplier class is the most complex class developed so far. It contains multiple references to other objects and the inventory references are circular—between the supplier and inventory items. To summarize, there is the Supplier class, derived from the base class Entity, which can contain multiple embedded references to specific instances of the Address class, and multiple references to objects in the Inventory class. Figure 2-2 on the next page illustrates this summary.

Sales

The definition of sales, as laid out in Chapter One, is:

- The customer's name and address.

- The customer's ordering history.

- Drop shipments made for the customer.

- Mailing history for the customer.

Figure 2-2: Reference Flow

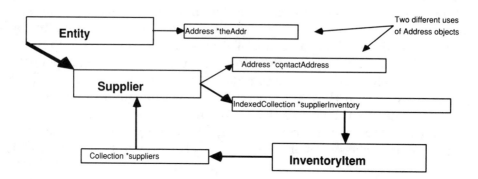

The circular flow of references covers all references from the supplier inventory to individual inventory items. Each of these items refers back to the Supplier via the Supplier's collection. These links differ from all the others in that they are all dynamically established by the system at run-time.

The name and address are already defined, name being a component of Entity and the address being another object referenced in Entity. This leaves the last three items needing further definition.

When designing an OO program, always remember what objects you have already implemented, for this project or any previous one. The goal is to avoid re-inventing wheels, so if you already have an object that will provide a needed feature, use it. In the case of a customer's ordering history, the Transaction object defined for Supplier is also usable within the context of a customer order. In this specific case, the customer's ordering history is really an IndexedCollection of PurchaseTransactions made by the customer and indexed by the customer's purchase order number. No new work needs to be done at this time.

The drop shipments made by the customer is another indexed collection, containing an arbitrary mixture of Address objects and other Customer objects, for reasons laid out in the previous chapter. Because the objects necessary to create this structure have already been specified, once again there is no new work to be done.

The customer's Mailing History records what kinds of promotional mailings have been sent to the customer. By using this data and comparing it to the customer's ordering history, the value of direct mail campaigns and the customer themselves can be ascertained. This also is a collection of objects, containing zero or more **Promotional Mailing** objects.

A promotional mailing is described by:

- What literature was sent.

- What items were being promoted by this literature.

- When the mailing was done.

Because our objective is not to provide Bancroft with a system to analyze the effectiveness of their promotional campaigns, there is no need to further refine this definition, although we can always come back and extend it at a later time. In many cases, OO designs do not have a clearly defined stopping point, there is just a fuzzy boundary where the increase in specificity is not needed. It's as important to know when to stop making objects as it is to know when to make them. A detailed reduction of a problem into a large number of distinct objects is not per se bad, it just isn't always necessary. Basically, not everything worth doing is worth doing well. In conventional programming, it is very hard to go back and retrofit an existing program. In OOP, this is not the case. You can stop making more and more detailed objects at any time and just release what you currently have. If this proves to be insufficient, you simply extend the system to support these new requirements, without affecting its overall function. The worst scenario would be that your extensions will not work, but these extensions can't break the software that is already functional.

Summary

Collections   Collections are general purpose objects, of use to many other applications than the Bancroft system. For that reason, they are defined in a general context, without reference to any Bancroft specific data. Collections are implemented through the base class Collection and its derived class, IndexedCollection.

Addresses   Addresses are also general purpose objects, defined in a general context. The base class Address provides two distinct derived classes, DomesticAddress and ForeignAddress. As the Address class itself will never be used to hold any real data, it is an abstract class. Instead, its derived classes will be used to represent addresses within the system. You would never see the definition:

```
Address cityHall;
```

You could, however, expect to encounter either:

```
DomesticAddress cityHall;
```

or:

```
ForeignAddress cityHall;
```

Suppliers   Suppliers are derived from the base class Entity and are used to represent external people or companies that supply Bancroft with products. Suppliers implement circular links between themselves and objects in the inventory to provide a reference mechanism allowing the Bancroft system to easily switch between Bancroft's part numbers and the part numbers used by suppliers.

Transactions   Transactions are an example of a utility class. A Transaction provides supplier and customer objects with a means for tracking purchase and sale transactions with Bancroft. Like Address, the Transaction class itself is an abstract class, as its two derived classes, Purchase-Transaction and SaleTransaction are the ones actually used to record the transaction information.

Promotional Mailing   In order to finish the definition of the customer class another object, called a Promotional Mailing, has been constructed. This object is used to represent information about specific promotional mailings so that the system can determine exactly what mailings have been sent to the customer and can possibly identify relationships between a customer's orders and mailings they have received.

1. If something is of general use by other applications and projects, don't stick application specific things into its definition. It will still work fine for the application and it can be used in a lot of places without a single change.

2. You don't always need to know everything about the data being manipulated. You can depend on the ability of the data to understand itself. If you don't know what you are looking at, don't try and figure it out. Just ask whatever you are looking at to tell you what it is.

3. Don't worry too much about data verification. The system won't let functions operate on data that is not their own. Syntactical verification is the compiler's responsibility, semantic verification is your responsibility.

4. Uniformity is good. If two objects are related, then they should do the same things in the same way. To do the same thing two different ways is to have to learn two different ways of doing the same thing.

5. Differences are good too. They should however, be obvious. If two classes are related, then the differences between the ways in which they operate should have a one to one correspondence to these differences.

6. If two objects are always found together, they might not be two objects. They might be two pieces of one object.

7. Objects may behave differently because of their contents.

8. There are two distinct ways in which objects may be related to each other. They may be related statically, by derivation. This says that one object is a special kind of a more general object. The other is by establishing relationships between objects at run-time, which implies that two distinct objects are joined to form a larger, more complex, object.

CHAPTER 3

CLASSES AND INSTANCES

The inevitable result of improved and enlarged communications between different levels in a hierarchy is a vastly increased area of misunderstanding.

In the previous chapters, many different objects were defined and linked together. For example, the Supplier object was defined to include other objects, specifically Address objects and InventoryItem objects. What happens when two suppliers sell Bancroft the same InventoryItem—are there two copies of the InventoryItem, one for supplier A and one for supplier B?

Happily, the answer to this question is no. Although the programmer can enforce deliberate exceptions, the rule is that objects *refer* to other objects, they do not *contain* other objects. To understand this, a more detailed explanation about the nature of objects is in order.

Creation of Instances

An object is an **instance** of a class, and usually referred to as an object of the class **aClass**. Classes themselves are not really things, so much as they are rules, or templates, for *making* things. The class of an object determines:

- The name for what **kind** of object this is.
- The **data** associated with this object.
- The **functions** that can operate on this object.
- The class from which this object is **derived**.

For example, the InventoryItem object class describes what any InventoryItem looks like, and how it behaves. It does not describe characteristics of an individual inventory item, it simply states what those characteristics are. A class can't really do anything, as it isn't a concrete entity, it is instead a **template** for constructing concrete examples, or **instances** of itself.

In an OO system, a distinction is made between the class of an object, and an instance of an class, although this difference is not always directly stated. Instead, it is often implied by context. This is an issue that confuses most novice OO programmers, as they can never figure out whether the class of an object is being discussed, or a specific, real instance of that class is being discussed. Writers of OO books often use the word object to refer to both class descriptions and specific instances of an object. The reason for this is simple, if we had to add the word class or instance everywhere we used the word object, we would cause entire forests to be decimated. A simple test can be used to determine if we are discussing a class or an instance of an class. When discussing the behavior of an object *in general*, its internal data and behavior, we are discussing the class of the object. Whenever we are referring to an object that *contains specific data*, such as a unique part number, then we are discussing an instance of an object. As OOP evolves, an attempt is being made to standardize references, so that when we are talking about the behavior of classes, we say class, and we use the term object to refer only to real physical instances of a class. However, the terminology is still evolving so as you read this book and others, you should always be examining the context in which we are discussing classes and objects, or instances of classes. For example, *the partNumber of an InventoryItem object* means *the partNumber field of the InventoryItem class* and *the InventoryItem object with partNumber X0059* means *the specific instance of an InventoryItem object class with partNumber equal to X0059.*

When dealing with objects, context is always an important issue. If you are discussing the behavior of every possible case of an object, you are discussing the object's class description. If you are discussing the unique characteristics of a specific object *that contains real data*, you are discussing an instance of the object.

In starting the process of design, you must first define the classes. You cannot discuss a particular instance of a class, such as the InventoryItem Part Number X0059, until you have first described what an inventory item looks like. You must create the class description and then use this class description to construct instances of the inventory object.

Also, you cannot modify the data of any object by external means. To alter any data within an object, or to get it to perform any function at all, you must send a request to the object asking it to perform the desired action. To define the Address of a new Customer, you must have an instance of Customer available with which to work. How can you load data into a new object? How do you get from a class description of an object, to a specific instance which represents a single object of that class?

The mechanism differs across many OOP systems, but the concept is the same. If you were to generalize completely, there are two distinct contextual viewpoints relating to the class description of an object. First, there is the point of view of the objects which that class describes, or instances of that class. To them, a class description is not an object, it is a template that describes the basic structure and functionality that each of the instances have. It serves as a total definition of their world, both what it looks like, and how it behaves. From the OOP system's point of view, a class is actually an instance of a class object, which is an object used to represent templates that describe classes. In some OO systems, such as Smalltalk, the class exists as a physical instance; in others, such as C++, it is simply a concept.

This is the means by which classes are used to manufacture specific instances of the objects that they describe. This is done through a common capability shared by all classes. Specifically, this is the ability of the class to respond to a request to create an instance of itself. In C++, this is done using a compile time variable definition:

```
MyFirstClass myFirstObject;
```

Using the *new* keyword:

```
myFirstObjectPtr = new MyFirstClass;
```

The returned value is a brand new instance of the class, different from all other instances you may have created. Its organization and functionality are described by its class, which is shared by all the created instances. Change the behavior or organization of a class and you change the behavior and organization of every instance of that class.

Strictly speaking, the exact implementation of classes varies from one OO system to another. Smalltalk implements Class objects, MetaClass objects, and a host of other, even more complicated objects, to dynamically represent class definitions. C++ on the other hand, uses class descriptions to generate standard C code or to directly produce machine code in some cases. It does not actually place descriptions into the code, it simply uses them to control generation of the code. Whatever the representation, instances are constructed using the same basic mechanism. It is the function of a class to create instances of itself and differences arise primarily due to when this is done. In Smalltalk it's done at run-time, so the system must know how to dynamically install new classes. In C++, the compiler uses the class description to generate code, and the run-time system doesn't need them at all—instead, it is a **product** of the class descriptions.

C++ distinguishes between two major kinds of object creation. It can create objects in the normal C fashion, by building them on the stack or in memory based on the occurrence of static or automatic variable declarations. For example, a function might define a temporary object, as in:

```
someFunction()
{
    InventoryItem anItem;
    <some code>
}
```

The *anItem* variable has a **local scope**, meaning that it comes into existence each time this function is called and is destroyed each time this function is left. For that reason, it would be difficult to install a locally scoped object into the inventory database because it would keep disappearing right after you left the function that installed it. Yes, the reference would still be in the database, but it would now point to empty space. Some systems would politely tell your user that you had a segment violation if you attempted to use this reference at a later time, others might simply go south for the winter. In any case, doing this is an excellent way to lose your data.

Not all objects have a local scope—the above definition could be moved outside of the function and it would then have a **global scope**. It would still be next to useless for loading new items into the inventory database, as you really only have one object. The inventory database would contain a large number of references to the same object. If you tried to use this definition to create new objects in the inventory, you would end up with every object in inventory containing whatever you had loaded last.

Additionally, if you have a globally scoped object **anObject**, and a locally scoped object (defined within a function) anObject, while you were in the function, the local definition of anObject would hide its global definition. Any alterations to anObject within this function would affect the local object only, leaving the global object unchanged. After leaving the function, the globally defined object, anObject, would no longer be hidden. Be careful when you play games like this, as you can get quite confused about which scope applies to a given variable name, leaving yourself playing the old *Who's on First?* game. There are reasons for deliberately hiding variables, but they are only found in programs that are extremely complex and usually unmaintainable.

How do you create new instances of InventoryItem, where each instance is unique and the program can control each object's life? By doing just that. C++ provides two keywords, that are similar to **malloc()** and **free()**, but are functions designed to create and destroy new object instances. Actually, they are replacements for using malloc() and free(), but they are of special interest in dealing with creating and destroying objects. The two keywords are **new** and **delete**, and they are used in conjunction with constructor functions, which we define a little further on in this chapter. Due to this split definition there is a mechanism available for arbitrarily creating and deleting objects, a mechanism driven by the program at run-time, instead of at compile time.

A basic rule is that you will *use objects with a known scope as temporary holders and working areas for data manipulation*. These objects are all defined at compile time. You will *use new and delete to create and destroy objects used to collect information while the program is running*.

Referring to Instances

In the case of the Supplier object, it contains references to various InventoryItem objects. These references are to specific instances of the InventoryItem class and were obtained by querying the inventory database collection. These very same references are stored in the Supplier object. The collection of InventoryItems that constitutes the inventory database, and the set of all inventory items referred to by all suppliers therefore, refers to a common pool of inventory items. See Figure 3-1 on the next page.

Because of this, you can expect the system to have certain standard capabilities in dealing with references between one object and another. The central capability is that changes made by one object to another object which it references are automatically available to all other objects that reference the changed objects—as they are all looking at exactly the same instance. When a Supplier object is told to mark a PurchaseTransaction completed, it can tell the inventory items referred to by the purchase transaction to modify their in stock counts, and can do so with a high level of confidence that the inventory database will automatically reflect these changes. This is an important aspect of OO programs, the sharing of physical information between the many different users of that information. By making each inventory item responsible for managing changes to itself, the collection of inventory items that constitutes the inventory database, and users of inventory items—such as suppliers and customers—are absolved of this responsibility.

This is why OOP systems do not allow anything outside of an object to arbitrarily modify the private data of that object, without very clear instructions to the contrary. Any instance of any object is limited to making changes to its own, private, data. If that objects feels that another instance of another object also needs to be modified, it can request that the other object modify itself appropriately, by asking it. It is barred from modifying the other object directly. By doing this, anyone can change an object and know that all other users of that object will also see the changes. Contrast this to straight C, where this is a function of the programmer's skill, instead of an underlying characteristic of the programming system itself. In straight C, this is often the stated objective, but there are no technical means for enforcement. If you cannot enforce something, you cannot guarantee that it will be the case, you can only hope. Many program crashes occur because section A modified some data and section B never knew about it.

Figure 3-1: Links

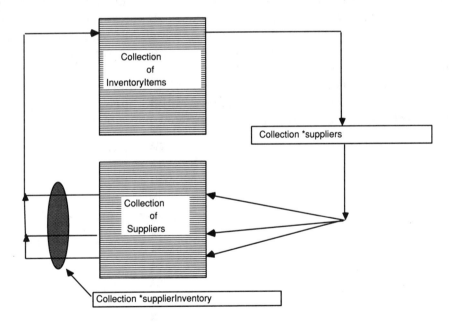

This shows the links between an InventoryItem and the three suppliers that provide it, and the corresponding links back to the InventoryItem database.

Object to object links are established by reference, instead of by value. This ensures that changes to any object are immediately apparent to all objects that use it. And this behavior requires no work on the programmer's part, instead it requires them to go through a great deal of work if they wish to violate it!

Interobject Communications

So far, the issue of communications between any two objects has been described in very general terms. An object "requests" that another object perform some operation, much like a computer on a LAN requesting that the server on the LAN give it a file. As a matter of fact, this is quite similar to the ways in which objects communicate.

Technically, one object (A) communicates with another object (B), by sending it a **message**, and possibly some parameters to go along with that message. If object A wants object B to tell what it contains, it might send the message **contents** to object B and the data returned from this message would be the answer to that request.

This is the cause of a fundamental coding difference between OO languages and non-OO languages. A normal language, such as C, could implement the functionality of the contents message by the code:

```
char * contentsofDataStructureAlpha (alphaDataStructure)
DataStructureAlpha * alphaDataStructure;
{
        <try to be sure this is kind of structure we want>
        <code to convert structure to a string representing
            its contents>
        return(contentsString)
}
```

Notice that this function is specialized for returning the contents of a specific structure and that it requires the structure itself as a parameter. It also requires code to check that the correct structure is passed as a parameter, otherwise the system might not be reliable.

In an OO system, when the class was defined, the function **contents()** would also have been defined as a **member function**. This means that any object could get the contents of this object by sending it the message contents. In C++, if object A wants the contents of object B, then the code to do this would be:

```
aFunctionOfObjectA()
{
    .

    .

    contentsOfB = B.contents();
}
```

Upon execution of the contents message, the result of sending the message would be placed in the variable *contentsOfB*.

In this case, the raw data structure is not required as a parameter. This is because messages are sent to instances of objects; therefore, the information is already available. You aren't calling a function, you are talking to the data you want. You have sent a message to an object requesting that it re-represent itself in a new form. The data is already there, you just don't like the way it's represented.

There is no need for the actual contents function, defined in the class description of object B, to bother with validating the data on which it will operate. Since the message is bound to the data itself, the function implementing the message can assume that whenever it runs, it is always referring to legal data. Instead of inserting extra code to check for valid parameters, or rigidly defining all the parameter types and using a tool such as lint, the compiler itself guarantees that messages are only invoked for objects with which they have been specifically associated. If you are here, the data is correct!

One other characteristic of messages is that they represent requests, not guarantees of actions. For example, the DomesticAddress object might have a function implementing the message **newZipCode(aNewZip-Code)**. Part of the code for this function would be:

```
DomesticAddress::newZipCode(zip)
```

```
char * zip;
{
    if(strlen(zip) != 5 && strlen(zip) != 9) return(*nil);
    if(allNumbers(zip) not) return(*nil);
    <put zip into the zip field for this object instance>
    return(*this);
}
```

Now, the first thing the function does is check the parameter to ensure that it does represent a legal zip code. Since this function is coupled to a DomesticAddress object, no consideration needs to be made for international addresses. If the function feels that the supplied data is incorrect, it can elect to ignore the request to change the zip code.

In returning a result, the function has two choices. If the zip is not acceptable, then it will return a special object called *nil*. If the zip code is acceptable, it will return a reference to the DomesticAddress object itself. This is a traditional coding mechanism in OOP, returning the nil object on an error condition and returning the receiver object itself on a successful exit. For example, if a Supplier object S wanted to send this message to its main address, it would do so in the following manner:

```
someSupplierFunction(aNewZipCode)
char *aNewZipCode;
{
    .

    .

    .

    if(address.newZipCode(aNewZipCode) == nil)
    {
        < the message failed>
    }
    else
```

```
     {

          < the message succeeded>

     }

}
```

As you have seen from this and previous examples, the C++ syntax which deals with objects is quite similar to straight C code which deals with structures. As stated earlier, objects contain functions that operate on their data in addition to the data itself. C++ expands upon the standard direct (.) and indirect (->) structure reference elements by allowing you to address the functions bound to an object, its member functions, in the same way that you address the data it contains. If you examine the previous example, you will see that the member function **newZipCode()** is called using the same C structure references you have already encountered. C++ simply allows you to refer to the member functions of an object the same way that you would refer to the data elements it contains.

Taking this one step further clearly illustrates the great power of OO programs. If there is a screen manager, used for entering data into various objects, it will receive input from the user, input which is not always valid. For this reason, most commercial screen managers incorporate validation functions where the programmer can link functions that validate input to the generic input drivers. However this is done, the fact remains that the screen driver is responsible for validating applications data, which places it firmly in the applications domain. The only exception to this rule is if the screen programmer can be dynamically programmed with validation functions, which entails a lot of setup work on the application's part.

In an OO system, the screen manager can depend on the abilities of objects to decide what data is and is not legal for them. Validation is done at the object level, which is where it belongs. The screen manager will simply send a message to an object, stating that there is a new value for it. All the screen manager needs to know is that if any object returns nil as a result of one of these messages, then the data was unacceptable. Why it was unacceptable is only of concern to the object; the screen manager only needs to know if it should ask the user the same question again. While it would be nice if the object said why it didn't like the input, the fact remains that the decision about the validity of data resides within the object itself. External objects only need to know whether or not a value is acceptable, they don't need to know anything about the criteria that actually determines the acceptability of the data.

Unfortunately, messages are often another area of confusion for the OOP novice. This is due to the fact that once again, the OOP gurus have a less than totally precise lexicon. In C++, a message is a function call. Sending a message to an object is the way you call one of that object's member functions. Therefore, whenever you see a reference to a message being sent to an object, remember that this is simply the mechanism by which member functions are called. The message itself is identical to the object's name for the function and the message will always provide the parameters required by the function. When you see a reference to a member function of some object, remember that the only way it can be called is by sending a message. Sending messages causes their correspondingly named functions to be invoked, invoking functions implies that a message must have been sent to cause this to happen. As an aside, you can still define and use standard C functions, although you will find that in designing an OO system, only the most primitive things are defined as C functions. Everything else is done by sending messages. You only call a C function when you have nowhere else to go. The golden rule about using straight C functions (and functions invoked by sending messages to objects) is: C function calls twiddle bits, messages twiddle data structures.

Initialization and Destruction of Instances

In determining what messages an object needs to implement, guidance comes from the nature of the class to which the messages are sent. In the case of an InventoryItem object, it needs to respond to messages in order to access and edit characteristics of inventory items. While accessing and editing data elements is a common requirement of all messages implemented for any class, the exact means by which this is done is based on the characteristics of a particular class.

The first messages that need to be defined are the **constructor** messages, those messages which are responsible for actually initializing new instances of this object, whether they are created because of statements in the original source code defining the new instance, or by functions dynamically creating the instance by using the **new** keyword. OOP has added a new word to English to describe this process, calling it the **instantiation** of an object. To create a new object from a class, you instantiate an object of that class. For inventory, a basic fact would be that anyone creating a new inventory object would already know the following parameters:

- The part number

- The description

- The number on hand

The constructor function, **InventoryItem(partNo**, **description**, **numberOnHand**) would have to be implemented. The responsibilities of this function would be:

- Make sure the part number is legal.

- Copy the parameters into the new instance.

- Put "empty" into all the other InventoryItem fields.

- Update the inventory database with this new item.

Notice that the InventoryItem constructor function is responsible for ensuring that newly created items are placed into the database. This allows the rest of the system to ignore the maintenance of the inventory database, at least as far as adding new items to it. Through this, the programmer can be absolutely certain that each new inventory item will be installed in the database, because there is only one mechanism by which to create them in the first place, and this mechanism is responsible for ensuring the database is up to date. In many cases, debugging OO programs is easier than debugging other programs, because if something doesn't work, you usually have a good idea of who messed up.

Notice that the name of the constructor function is the same as the name of the class itself. In C++, this is how you indicate that a particular function is a constructor. The exact syntax of constructor functions sometimes has a few more twists, but these embellishments are to be discussed later.

The next function is the **destructor**, which has the same name as the constructor (or class) with a tilde (~) in front of it, and no parameters:

```
~InventoryItem()
{

}
```

Now, the job of the destructor is to do just what its name suggests, to destroy a specific instance of a class. The specific responsibilities of the InventoryItem destructor are to:

- Destroy the objects to which it refers.
- Tell all objects that refer to it to delete their references to it.
- Destroy its reference in the inventory database.
- Destroy itself.

The first concern is: what if an object referred to in inventory is used by another object? This happens to be the case, as the inventory items will log transactions which we might want to keep, and the transactions in turn refer to customers and suppliers which we definitely want to keep. The solution to this problem depends on the relative sophistication of the system you are using. If the system tracks references between objects, a request to delete an object will not necessarily result in the physical deletion of that object. The object in systems such as this, will only be deleted if this is the only reference to it. Unfortunately, C++ does not track references between objects; therefore, our destructor must do this job itself. The logic actually used in any destructor is going to be object specific, using some programmer-defined heuristic technique to determine which objects, referenced by the object being destroyed, should or should not be deleted. To delete an object that is still in use by other objects, is the surest way to kill your program.

If this sounds like trouble to you, you are not mistaken. However, you most likely will have experienced the same difficulty in standard C. The problem arises from the fact that you may have multiple pointers to a single area of memory, where you are holding some value you wish to share with a number of different functions. In straight C, whenever you have more than one copy of a **pointer** in use, you know that you should not be too cavalier about deleting the physical storage this pointer refers to just because *one* of the users of this pointer wants to do so. For if you do, and then some other function uses its own copy of the pointer to reference the data, a tragedy is guaranteed. OO programs simply raise this risk to a higher level, because it is quite natural in these systems to have many different objects sharing a reference to a common object. Before this common object can be deleted, *all* of the references to it must be cleared. However, OOP systems also simplify this process because the only functions that need to deal with this problem are the destructor functions, as nothing else can destroy objects. Instead of scattering logic to manage this through your entire program, it can be confined within the destructor functions.

Constructor and destructor functions are called whenever an object is created or deleted. This applies to objects with a **fixed scope**, meaning they were defined at compile time and to objects that are created and deleted by the program at run-time. For compiler-defined objects, the constructor function is called when the object is created, either by starting the program (global and static declarations) or when a function is entered (automatic declarations). Destructors are called for these objects when the program terminates (global and static) or when a function terminates (automatic). For objects you wish to create yourself, the constructor is called when you invoke new, and the destructor is called when you invoke delete. The actual syntax of the calls on new and delete would be:

```
newItem = new InventoryItem("PNX0059","A widget",15);
```

and:

```
delete newItem;
```

Notice that the new keyword is followed by a constructor function, while the delete keyword is followed by a variable referring to the object to be deleted. Remember, the new keyword doesn't have an object to work with, it needs to make one. This is why it needs information on which constructor function it should use. In the case of delete, there is a specific instance of the object to be deleted; therefore, that's what we will provide as a parameter. The compiler figures out which destructor to use by checking to see what we have defined **newItem** to be.

The programmer makes calls on constructor functions whenever they define an object. One of the classic causes of program bugs is uninitialized data. In OO systems, this isn't so much of a concern, as you can't create a new object without using a constructor function, and it is the job of the constructor function to ensure that the new object is correctly initialized. As far as destructors are concerned, the compiler will handle this for you. To help in producing less buggy code, you never want to be destroying objects using multiple functions, there is just too much of a chance for introducing bugs. While an object may have multiple **shutdown** functions—functions that help prepare it to meet its maker—there should be only one function that actually handles the zapping of the object. Although the explanation here may seem a little complicated, it really isn't. The simple fact is that: *only destructor functions should handle the physical deletion of an object.* If this is a multistep process, involving several different functions, then the destructor function should be responsible for performing the necessary calls on these functions. We will leave the actual mechanism by which destructors remove objects for the next section, for now simply remember that this is an area strictly reserved for them. If there are special considerations involved in destroying any object, make sure that the destructor function *alone* is responsible for accomplishing these objectives. This isn't to say that destructor functions can't have helper functions, only that if they do, they should be the only ones to use them.

To summarize, every single class must provide functions to initialize itself (constructors) and a single function to handle its deletion (destructor). These functions are responsible for managing operations that are needed to create and destroy this particular object, and they are helped by the run-time system, which will handle allocation and deallocation of the actual object storage area.

Object Specific Messages

All other functions that support messages received by the object, can be lumped together as object specific messages. These are the messages sent to get an object to perform its function, whatever that function may be.

These messages therefore, tend to be defined within the context of the class for which they are being implemented, sharing few common characteristics with other messages for other classes. There are three basic types of messages, regardless of the function of the specific class with which they are associated. These three types are:

- Requests for internal data within the object.

- Requests for the object to accept new data.

- Requests for the object to perform some specialized operation.

Requests for data usually don't supply parameters, but they expect a specific answer back from the object. Requests for the object to accept new data usually have parameters that carry the new data, but they usually don't produce any specific data in reply, other than a general indication of whether the update was successful or not. (See the preceding example on zip code verification for the DomesticAddress class.) Finally, requests for the object to perform some specialized operation have a definition that is a function of what the object does. Other than the fact that most objects spend a good deal of their time asking other objects to do something, there is little more similarity in the arrangement of these messages and their parameters.

Public vs. Private Messages

There is an unspoken rule in OO programming that says if the length of a function implementing a message is more than can be displayed on a single screen, it is probably too long. The idea is that most of the work in an OO system is done by very small functions that are hooked together into larger composite functions by sending a series of messages. For example, suppose that every object in the Bancroft system responds to the message **stringForm** by returning a representation of its data as an ASCII string, suitable for display purposes. Now, the print message for a Supplier object could be written as a single function that constructs a string by directly formatting the contents of the Supplier object. As Supplier contains a lot of data, this method could become quite large.

Instead, what you do is look at the Supplier object and say, "Well, there are three major pieces of information that need to be printed. First there is the supplier's address information, then there is the supplier's inventory, and finally there are all of the transactions we have done with the supplier." You would define a **public** function called **print** for the supplier, and then three **private** functions called **printAddress**, **printInventory**, and **printTransactions**. The difference is that a public message may be sent by any object, say for example, an instance of InventoryItem could send the message print to an instance of Supplier. The three private messages however may only be sent by Supplier to itself. No other object is allowed to send Supplier these messages.

Why is this important? As stated earlier, functions should be small. They are much easier to debug that way. If they are large, they are trying to do too much. The second reason is that some messages are just not meant for public consumption. Supplier knows all about its internal workings; therefore, it may fiddle with its data without being too careful about checking the parameters that it uses. This is often the case when a high level, public message to change a value in an object, actually means that quite a few values will be recalculated and changed. These private messages may all be designed with the assumption that only a certain function or functions within that same object are ever going to call them. By declaring that these particular messages are private, the designer can get the compiler to enforce these rules. The compiler will never allow another object to send a message to an object when the receiving object has declared that that message is private.

Summary

1. Objects do not copy each other, they refer to each other.

2. The Class of an object is a blueprint for creating an instance of that class.

3. Objects can be instances of the same class. Objects of the same class are treated identically to each other, but each contains its own set of values.

4. Object is a loaded term. To determine whether class or instance is meant, pay attention to the context in which the word has been used. If there are no specific values for the object, the class is being dis-

cussed; if there is a specific object with specific values, an instance of the class is being discussed.

5. The point of view of an object is very important. To an instance of a class, its class description is a blueprint for the instance itself. The instance is a specific copy with specific data. To the system, a class is an object that uses a template to manufacture new objects *which are not class objects*.

6. Objects defined at compile time have a definite scope and may only be accessed within this scope. For this reason, they serve primarily as temporary holders and working variables. If you want to collect a group of instances together at run-time, you need to dynamically create them.

7. Objects may only modify themselves. Other objects make polite requests by sending messages to invoke member functions.

8. Messages know to which instance they have been sent. You don't need to make it a parameter.

9. Just because you ask another object to do something, there is no guarantee that your request will actually succeed. That's up to the requestee. There is no harm in asking an object to do something which you aren't sure will be legal. If it isn't, it won't.

10. All objects can respond to requests for initialization (constructors) and destruction (destructors).

11. All other messages handled by objects come in three basic flavors:

    • Return some internal data.

    • Change some internal data.

    • Do some specific operation.

12. A function implementing a message should be small enough to fit on a single screen. If it doesn't, it's too complicated.

13. Private member functions can only be used by other member functions of the same class. Public member functions can be used by anyone.

CHAPTER 4

INTERACTING OBJECTS

There comes a time when one must stop suggesting and evaluating new solutions and get on with the job of analyzing and finally implementing one pretty good solution.

In the first three chapters, some of the essential objects required to build the Bancroft database were laid out with special attention given to the proper care and feeding of a design destined to create an OO program. In this chapter, we will begin to specify the basic messages that each of the objects in the system need to handle. The focus will be on messages used to support operation of the system from the application's point of view. This will provide a definition of the capabilities of each object, for what operations it is directly responsible, and on what operations it depends in other objects. This will be done by discussing the elements contained in each object and by showing what messages are provided in order to support **queries**, **retrievals**, and **manipulations** of these elements. As stated in Chapter One, the overall objective of the Bancroft Database program is to implement:

- An inventory tracking system.
- A sales tracking system.

- A personnel database.

- A consolidated general ledger.

Once again, the general ledger will be ignored. As soon as we have completed the design of the three sections, we will have enough information to define the general ledger. First we must complete the internal definitions of these three structures and the web that connects them.

Inventory

The InventoryItem class provides the functions and data structures necessary to manage all of the items in Bancroft's inventory. All of these items are collected together in the **InventoryDatabase**, an Indexed-Collection of InventoryItems. The contents of this database are managed only by the InventoryItem constructor and destructor functions, with the constructor responsible for adding newly created items to the database and the destructor responsible for removing deleted items from the database. The physical InventoryItem objects are dealt with by reference, which means that there is no need for any kind of database **update** logic. This guarantees that our only responsibility is to ensure that the database contains the correct references.

Part Number

The part number is a field that contains, of all things, a part number. This part number is generated by an unknown gnome at Bancroft, and is unique to each part stocked in inventory. This element is also used in the inventory database collection to index particular inventory records, providing a convenient means for checking data integrity during run-time. If you retrieve a record from the collection of inventory objects using part number X0059, then the inventory object you get should have the same part number. While this may seem to be a rather trivial observation, it is very useful during program debugging. If all of the objects you create respond to the message **consistencyCheck**, you can check the integrity of your system at any time simply by sending this message to any object or objects that are available to you. In this case, the object message would use the part number to attempt to retrieve itself from the inventory database and see if it got itself back. This test is very simple, as the reference received from the database must be *equal* to the reference we started with. If it isn't, the time to crash gracefully is now.

Because of the fact that the part number is both a field within a specific inventory object and a key in an indexed collection containing this object, there are special twists to the messages that must be defined.

TYPE	MESSAGE NAME	DESCRIPTION
PUBLIC	partNum()	This message, sent to any inventory object will return the part number assigned to that inventory item.
PRIVATE	setPartNum(pn)	Accepts a char* parameter and sets the part number for this object. If the part number is not empty before the change, the existing inventory item will be renamed in the inventory database. The part number will be rejected if it is not legal.

The request for a part number, **partNum()**, is a public message—one that any other object can send to an inventory object. The message to set the part number, **setPartNum()**, is private to the inventory object itself and cannot be used by any other object. This is done to control changes to the part number, as we will be using these values to index our collection of part numbers and do not want the indices changed on a whim. Although we are not currently dealing with them, many of the private messages are used by the object constructor functions that were discussed in Chapter Three, and serve as helpers for object initialization.

Quantity On Hand

This is an integer value that contains the number of items currently in stock. It must respond to messages from the Customer and Supplier objects in order to update the value for items sold and received, respectively.

TYPE	MESSAGE NAME	DESCRIPTION
PUBLIC	onHand()	Return the number of items currently on hand.
PUBLIC	sold(numSold)	Decrement the number on hand by amount sold. *Do not decrement if stock goes below zero!*
PUBLIC	received(nRcd)	Increment the number on hand by amount received.
PRIVATE	inStock(quan)	Used to initialize the item or to adjust for the inevitable mistake. Sets quantity on hand to the passed value.

Notice that the **sold()** and **received()** functions are both publicly accessible, and can therefore be used by any other object. Direct manipulations of the quantity on hand through **inStock()** can only be done by the inventory object itself. Again, this private message is for the use of the InventoryItem constructor functions. The reason that these private messages are provided for use by the constructors is to keep the constructor functions as small as possible. In many cases, constructor functions will issue a flurry of private messages to initialize a newly created object. As these messages fiddle directly with the object's data, it is a good idea to prevent other objects from using them. You don't know and cannot necessarily trust the sender of a publicly available message. Because an object can only receive a private message from itself, the guilty party is easy to identify if something goes wrong. The sold() message presents a host of possibilities as to what might be done if there are 14 units of part# X0059 on hand and the inventory item for part X0059 has just received the message: sold(100).

For example, if we wanted to be truly sophisticated, we could have the sold message automatically send a **reorder(soldQuantity-onHand())** message to this object **(part#X0059)** and then continue. We could complicate the issue by writing the sold message onto an external disk file after issuing the reorder message and by then resending this message when the order is received from the supplier three weeks later. With OO programs, you can take a lot of liberties with messages, even to the point of arbitrarily delaying them on external events. I am not saying you can do this without hassles—for you would have to write a fair amount of code. It would be for general use and could be used to support a lot of similar operations. There are many ways to implement message behavior, from the extremely simplistic to the hideously complex. Because they are self contained and well behaved, you don't have to decide in advance what you are going to do and then be stuck with that should you come to dislike it. In building an OO program, you have entered an environment where constant revision is the norm. Start simply, by complaining vigorously if someone tries to sell what they don't have. Later, you can go back and implement even more sophisticated behavior. Since you will only be dealing with specific object/message combinations in the clearly defined area of *things you want to modify*, you don't have to worry too much about breaking something in which you weren't interested in the first place!

Price Per Item

This gives the unit price per item. It serves to illustrate here that you never really know when a new object will hatch. Specifically, about whose price are we talking? Bancroft's, or the customer's? *In building an OO program, you should not be surprised to discover that you need new objects through all phases of the design process.* You *should* be surprised, however, if the objects you need have a scope covering a larger area than what you are currently designing. In this case, a new object that understands both wholesale and retail pricing is going to have to be created. That's alright. The object being created fills a specific weakness in the design within the scope of supporting the "price per item." If we were working on price per item and decided we needed a completely new kind of inventory item; that decision would illustrate that our design should really be labeled a kludge. OO design is a tree building process, first the trunk, then the branches, and finally the leaves. Small branches sprouting from larger branches are fine, trunks sprouting from branches are a great indicator of a very sick tree.

Returning to the specific problem, we need a new object that handles pricing for inventory items. It needs to hold retail and wholesale prices, and needs logic to determine how to get from one price to the other. This is the responsibility of the pricing object and can be dealt with when we are interested in implementing that object. Remember the golden rule, just because you've decided you need a new object does not mean that you must now define it. Truthfully, if you just realized you need a new object, you probably still don't understand it very well.

What is known is that the pricing information will be handled by the **InventoryPrice** object and that every inventory item will have an associated InventoryPrice. Because the InventoryPrice is an object, it is responsible for manipulating itself, and conversely, the InventoryItem object is not responsible for manipulating it. Technically, it isn't allowed to manipulate it; therefore, we only need to make two methods for dealing with the price, regardless of what final responsibilities are assigned to the InventoryPrice object.

TYPE	MESSAGE NAME	DESCRIPTION
PUBLIC	priceInfo()	Return the InventoryPrice object to the sender. The sender has to know about the capabilities of this object. The InventoryItem object could care less.
PRIVATE	setPriceInfo(p)	p is a reference, or pointer, to an InventoryPrice object. Put the pointer into the pricePerItem field. Whine loudly and refuse if the passed object is not really an InventoryPrice object.

In this case, there are no methods for handling a change to the information contained within the InventoryPrice object. This is because there is no need for one. By returning the InventoryPrice object on demand, we allow the object sending this message to directly communicate with the InventoryPrice object and to perform whatever modifications it deems necessary. This is an approach often taken in OOP, delegating an object's responsibilities to both the original sender of a message and to more specialized objects that this object references.

However, it does come at a price. If the InventoryItem class does not understand how to manage pricing information, then the InventoryPrice class and users of its instances will have to. In cases such as this, you will often find that the more globally known object is used to manage the sending of messages to the lesser known object. In the case of Inventory-Item, which is definitely used by more parts of the system than is the InventoryPrice object, we may find later that we will be adding new messages to the InventoryItem to handle communicating with this object. This is not to say that the InventoryItem object will become capable of directly managing pricing information, only that it will serve as a sort of switchboard, accepting messages and parameters and redistributing them to the InventoryPrice object, so that the rest of the system can pretend there is no such thing as an InventoryPrice object. Even though everybody else is assuming that InventoryItems directly manage pricing information, in truth they aren't. They are just serving as messengers.

Suppliers of Item

Suppliers have already been examined in some detail. We know that Bancroft is opposed to single sourcing their inventory items, so they usually have more than one Supplier for any given inventory item. We also know that there is a supplier object and that it is responsible for many things, one of which is cross referencing supplier part codes to internal Bancroft part codes. This element will contain an IndexedCollection of the suppliers who can provide this part. The Supplier ID will be used as the indexing field within the collection.

TYPE	MESSAGE NAME	DESCRIPTION
PUBLIC	suppliers()	Returns the IndexedCollection of suppliers.
PUBLIC	suppliedBy(s)	Returns TRUE if supplier s is in the collection, FALSE otherwise.
PUBLIC	dropSupplier(s)	Remove supplier s from the collection
PUBLIC	addSupplier(s)	Add this supplier to the collection.

Because of the self-contained nature of objects, it is easy to implement sophisticated automatic verification with little work. In this particular case, it would be a horrible event if we started loading suppliers who don't actually supply this item into this list. Now we can say that verification is the responsibility of the sender of the message, but that implies that we must trust the sender to accurately verify this fact. Trust is usually what kills programs. It would be nice if we could painlessly verify that a supplier really does provide this part within the **addSupplier()** message handler.

This isn't that difficult. Assume for the moment that suppliers respond to a message such as **parts** by returning an indexed collection of InventoryItems that the supplier provides. We can send this message to the Supplier that was passed in the parameters and then we can search the part list returned by this message, looking for this inventory object. If its not there, we can refuse to add the Supplier to the list or we can send more messages to the Supplier, causing it to add this part number to its list of supplied parts.

Objects are somewhat unique when it comes to the chicken and egg problem of circular references. In this case, we have the Supplier that references items in Bancroft's inventory and in turn, Bancroft's inventory items reference back to the suppliers. In traditional software design, you have three choices. First, make one element, inventory or supplier, responsible for managing the links and depend on that element to do its job correctly. Second, you can duplicate a large amount of code on both sides to enable either side to update the other. Finally, you can implement a set of service functions to handle the various parts of the update, and make each side call the appropriate service functions. In OO design, you have the best of both worlds. If there are no code duplications, each side can update the other and each side is totally oblivious to the requirements of the other side. Why? Because the actual code stays within the object it is associated with, and the other object just sends messages to accomplish its desires. The OO approach gives you the most control over your code, by encapsulating the various supporting functions within each object that requires them. This means that to locate a faulty part of the code, you need only examine the object that implements this part. In any of the examples given for standard development, you would have had to search through a great deal more code to accomplish the same thing.

Sales History

Now things start to get a little hairy. The sales history for any particular inventory item is composed of zero or more customer orders; however, we don't want to use the customers themselves as components of the sales history, because they tend to order more than one item. The customer who places many repeated orders for a single inventory item is a rarity and will probably end up ordering directly from the manufacturer before much time has elapsed. If we can't tie the sales history to customers, to what do we tie it?

Customers do place orders and they just don't order the same items from inventory each time they place an order. But sometimes they do. What we are really interested in are specific orders the customer has placed where they did order this particular inventory item. What should be used; therefore, are the SaleTransaction objects that contain orders for this particular inventory item. We could even go so far as to make sales transactions a composite object containing a list of specific transactions, one per inventory item, but for now we won't. At least we know for any given purchase transaction, one of the line items will be an order for this inventory item. If we used the Customer object, then we might have to search a lot of SaleTransactions before finding this order.

This is all well and good, but what does it really tell us about the requirements for manipulating the sales history? Not much! When designing an object oriented system, the programmer *should always consider delegation of the responsibilities of one object to more specialized objects that are referenced by that object and/or to the users of that specialized object*. In this case, regardless of what the collection of sales for this item contains, the fact remains that it is a collection. The only real concern at this level is providing access to it. We couldn't care less about loading new customer transactions into the collection or removing them because the customer's check bounced. The only issue at this level is that we have a collection which we wish to manipulate. Since collections know how to manipulate themselves, why should we do it for them? The method to manage the sales history at the InventoryItem level is:

TYPE	MESSAGE NAME	DESCRIPTION
PUBLIC	salesTrans()	Return the collection of sales transactions to the sender.

To add or delete sales transactions, one would send this message to the inventory item and then send "collection" type messages to the returned object in order to achieve the desired results. As a matter of style, many OO programmers will implement **relay** messages that allow the InventoryItem to do this for them. This is what we were discussing previously, when we were dealing with the fact that InventoryItems might *manage* the sending of messages to InventoryPrice objects. Remember, it's not really for the system's benefit, it just makes the code more readable and it reduces the number of distinct objects the system has to deal with on a general basis. Such relay messages for this case would be:

TYPE	MESSAGE NAME	DESCRIPTION
PUBLIC	addSale(t)	Add this sale to the transaction list. Do this by first checking to make sure that t is a SaleTransaction and if it is, sending a message to the sales history collection that will make it add this element to itself.
PUBLIC	deleteSale(t)	Delete this transaction if it exists.

Essentially, this is a kind of **meta-message** in an OOP. It serves to group together a series of messages, and to give these messages a name that is sensitive to the context in which they are used. However, it doesn't actually *do* anything, so much as it issues a group of messages to get something done. As stated earlier, the concept is analogous to a telephone switchboard, with the object playing the receptionist.

Purchase History

While this element was not initially specified as an element of the InventoryItem, it is now apparent that it would be nice to have this data available within an InventoryItem. As a matter of fact, if you carefully re-read Chapter Two, you will see that the Purchase History's existence is implied by several statements. In designing an OO system, there are times when you will discover that it would be nice to insert another element into an object. Sometimes, it's not so much of a new discovery as it is a realization that you must now define something you had previously assumed. Since objects are packaged in a uniform fashion, such a discovery does not mean that you have invalidated your previous design, only that you have extended it. While I do not recommend that one begin writing code as soon as possible, I also do not feel that designs should be frozen in stone prior to writing code. These days, if you can clearly describe a problem, with no holes, then the problem has probably already been solved. Design is an ongoing process of refinement and extension and OO systems allow this to progress in a natural fashion. The central issue is growth of the design. If you alter your design, ask yourself whether you are *extending* it, or *changing* an existing part. If you are extending it, the new section should drop painlessly into place. If you are altering its existing behavior, then the design probably has flaws.

The Purchase History is intended to complement the sales history, allowing an inventory item to be queried about its purchases from suppliers as well as about its sales to customers. It is going to look a lot like a sales history on the surface. This element would contain a collection of individual purchase records, called PurchaseTransactions. We know these objects already exist, they were defined previously for supporting the Supplier object. All we really need to do is to define how these objects are linked to the inventory item.

TYPE	MESSAGE NAME	DESCRIPTION
PUBLIC	purchTrans()	Return the collection of purchase transactions to the sender.
PUBLIC	addPurchTrans(t)	Add purchase transaction to the list of purchase transactions.
PUBLIC	deletePurchTrans(t)	Delete this purchase transaction from the list.

Once again, the **purchTrans()** is the only message function that must be provided; the other two serve as relay messages to make future code more readable, and also to save us the trouble of directly manipulating the collection for every update to it. Figure 4-1 shows the relationships between the mentioned objects.

Figure 4-1: Object Relationships

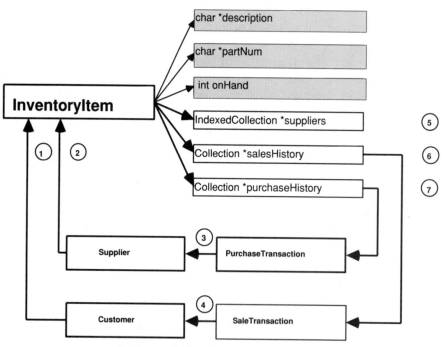

1. **Through the Customer's order history.**
2. **Through the Supplier's inventory list.**
3. **Filed directly in the transaction.**
4. **Filed directly in the transaction.**
5. **See Figure 1 in Chapter Three for linkages.**
6. **Shows only one element relation.**
7. **Shows only one element relation.**

Description of Item

Finally, an easy one. Traditional design methods take over. This is a text description of the inventory item, just as you would find in any other language or commercial database product. Contact the client, determine how concisely they can describe their average inventory item, and triple that estimate to account for everything they forgot.

TYPE	MESSAGE NAME	DESCRIPTION
PUBLIC	description()	Return the text description of this item.
PUBLIC	setDescription(d)	d is the new string containing the text description of this item.

Planting Trees

At this point, much of the high level functionality of the InventoryItem object has been defined. We know basically how the InventoryItem operates, what facilities it makes available to other objects, and on what facilities it depends in other objects. We have also established the dynamic relationships between the InventoryItem and other objects, as shown in Figure 4-1. There is still some work to be done, but much of that is mechanical and more involved with demands of the computer than demands of Bancroft.

You have seen that *throughout the design process, new requirements for objects and data items keep popping up*. This is not a sign that your initial design is bad, it is just a natural component of the design process. The question to ask each time this happens is: *"Am I changing something bigger than what I am dealing with right now?"* If the answer to this is no, then you are simply extending your design. If the answer is yes, you probably should review your design carefully. Designing a program in an OO framework is a natural process, much like the growth of a tree. If you can describe what you are doing in terms of the growth of a tree, then everything is good.

For example, consider the implementation of the Entity class, and its three derived classes, Supplier, Customer, and Employee. From Figure

4-2, you can see how the Entity class forms the trunk of this tree, a tree with three branches, one for each of the derived classes.

Figure 4-2: The "Entity" Tree

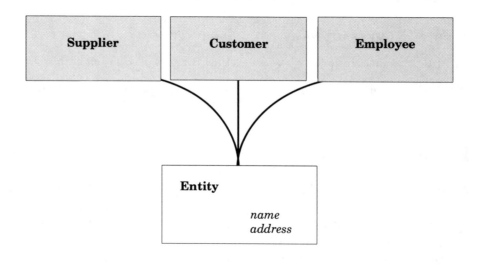

Customer

As stated in Chapter One, the Customer object contains the following elements:

- The customer's name and address.
- The customer's ordering history.
- Drop shipments made for the customer.
- Mailing history for the customer.

Each of these elements is itself an object. This means that direct manipulations of the data contained within any one of these elements is the responsibility of the item defining the particular data item, assuming we intend on delegating these responsibilities. To limit confusion, we will not call this an assumption. In this case it is a fact. So for what exactly is the Customer object responsible?

Not to beat a very dead horse beyond recognition, but, direct manipulation of an object's contents is the responsibility of the object itself. The Customer object is not responsible for manipulating the specific entries in a customer's ordering history, as the ordering history is an Indexed-Collection and is quite capable of manipulating its own contents. It does not even *allow* a Customer object to directly manipulate its contents. When an object contains references to other objects, it can safely delegate its responsibilities to these "sub" objects, as they are supposed to know more about what they are doing than does this object itself. Customer knows it contains a collection of customer orders, but it doesn't know anything about working with collections, per se. And since it will be delegating its responsibilities, it doesn't care about the contents of these collections, as long as they are all collections of customer orders.

The relationship between objects, in terms of both their static definitions and their working relationships, has been an area of much work in the OO community. On one hand, there is inheritance, where statically defined objects can inherit capabilities from their base classes. On the other, there is delegation, where an object depends on another object to accomplish something for it. In this case, sales inherits certain capabilities and data elements from its base class, Entity—such as the ability to manipulate the customer's address. Customer doesn't need to know how to access or to alter the address, because Entity already does. Entity, in turn, depends on the address object itself to actually perform manipulations of the address. In other words, Entity delegates its responsibilities for address manipulation to the address itself.

Although there are those who say there is no real difference between inheritance and delegation, I must respectfully disagree. Inheritance is a static relationship, established at the time the program is written. Its primary function is to separate areas of specialization in objects that are related by function. It is as immutable as your genetic inheritance. After you are born, you cannot decide you don't like the genetics your parents gave you and switch to someone else's. Delegation is a more complex relationship, as it is defined both statically and dynamically. Its primary function is to distribute the workload of an object to more specialized objects linked to that object.

Returning to the Customer object, it can effectively delegate all of its physical data manipulation responsibilities to each of the four objects it references. It is; therefore, a gateway between objects that send it messages and the objects to which it delegates these various functions. If you will, Customer is a manager object, it doesn't know how to do anything, but it does know who knows how to do things. Customer has no direct functionality and that allows the argument to be made that it is not really necessary—any object referencing a sales object could simply incorporate these four items directly. This is true, but look what would happen in that case.

First, we lose the Sales database, which Bancroft considers mandatory. Customer objects are actually customer records and to discard them is to discard the customer records. Even if this was not the case, the effects on the InventoryItem would be quite painful. Where it now has a collection of Customer objects that track the history of sales of the item, it would have to use a collection of collections, each subcollection containing the four elements mapped by a Sales object. InventoryItem would have to contain logic to know about each of these four items, what they contained, and what they were capable of doing. What's worse, is that if we decide to use the Customer information anywhere else in the system, we must reduplicate all of the code managing these four elements.

There is such a thing as over-delegation. In real life, managers are expected to delegate. However, should they ever reach the nirvana of delegation, where they do nothing more than direct 100 percent of the requests they receive to their subordinates without any translation, they will have rendered themselves useless. Interoffice mail could accomplish the same thing, and at a much lower cost. Customer will delegate most of its work to the objects which it encompasses and to the objects that actually use them. It should provide a little guidance, however, to ensure that the overall "rules" of being a customer are not broken by users of Customer objects or by internal components of Customer objects.

A customer object does not actually manage the guts of a **Sale-Transaction** object for a given order of that customer, as it isn't really responsible for what goes on in sales transactions. It can, and should delegate that responsibility to the SaleTransaction objects themselves, and to other objects that are interested in SaleTransactions. Does this mean that the Customer object should just blindly return the collection of customer orders every time some other object asks for it? Unfortunately, the answer to this question is yes and no. There are going to be those objects that require the entire list. However, Customer should provide relay messages to add and remove SaleTransactions from the Customer-Orders collection. It doesn't need to look into the internal data of the SaleTransactions themselves, but it should ensure that only SaleTransactions are added to this collection. Total delegation is a certain guarantee that an InventoryItem is going to be stuffed into the Customer-Order collection at some point.

Name and Address

The Name and Address elements of the Customer object are really components of the Entity object, which means that they are also used within the Supplier and Employee objects. In defining the capabilities of an object, *you must always remember where the data really resides.* Having remembered that Customer is not the only user of this data, we can proceed with its definition. This is a definite benefit of OO programs, as we will do the definition now, and we don't have to do it again for suppliers and again for employees.

TYPE	MESSAGE NAME	DESCRIPTION
PUBLIC	name()	Return the name of this Entity.
PUBLIC	address()	Return the address of this Entity.
PRIVATE	setName(n)	Copy string n into the name.
PRIVATE	setAddress(a)	Link address element to the passed address object. Complain if the class of a is not an address.

Order History

The ordering history of a customer is kept in an indexed collection, with the key of the collection a transaction code that Bancroft has assigned to the order. The methods implemented here look like they really do something, but remember, they don't. They just issue another set of messages to the collection object to accomplish the actual work.

TYPE	MESSAGE NAME	DESCRIPTION
PUBLIC	addOrder(o)	Add this order to the collection. It must be a SaleTransaction object and needs to be queried to get the transaction code. Then the transaction code will be used, along with the SaleTransaction itself to update the order history collection.
PUBLIC	getOrders()	Return all of the customer's orders.
PUBLIC	getOrder(tc)	Return the order referenced by the transaction code, or nil if it can't be found.

Deep vs. Shallow Copies

At this time, a little digression is in order. As stated, the Customer objects delegate most of their responsibilities to other objects, but they also try to ensure that inappropriate things aren't stuffed into their data elements. In the case of the **getOrders()** message, a Customer object will obligingly return the collection of customer orders. This could be quite dangerous, especially in an OO project being developed by more than one programmer. The reason is that whomever receives the CustomerOrder collection as a result of this call, can then modify it at will and there is nothing that the Customer object itself can do about it. The changes will most definitely affect the Customer, because it's one of its own data structures that is being modified. For example, if a routine sends a getOrders() message to customer A, as in:

```
orders = A.getOrders();
```

and then proceeds to delete everything in the list, a later request for the customer orders might not produce what is expected. If a ways down the road, another message is sent to customer A:

```
orders = A.getOrders();
```

customer A is going to return an empty collection. After all, it just gave it out a while ago, and the object that got it deleted everything.

If this situation strikes fear deep within your heart, you are not alone. In single person tasks it is easily controlled, but in a large programming effort it can cause very painful things to happen, like putting your career in a nose dive. But, there is a cure. In a language such as Smalltalk, sending the message **deepCopy** to any object will produce a clone of that object. You may then destroy the clone without fear. In C++, you are even safer. C++ will *always* duplicate objects that are passed as parameters to a function (normal or message) and will also duplicate all objects returned by any function. You actually have to do extra work to prevent this.

But in any case, delegation and paying attention to whether you are using the original object or a copy of it go hand in hand. In many cases, delegation requires that you *do not copy the object*, as you are expecting the act of delegation to alter data underneath the object that did the delegation in the first place. You must be careful. A good rule is that if you are simply answering another object's request for data, then give it a copy of the object it has requested. If you are expecting that object to do work for you *because you have intentionally delegated the work to it*, then let it have the original.

Some core elements of our design affect how you will do this. As stated, C++ will automatically duplicate any object which you *pass by value*. In our system, we are primarily passing objects *by reference*. This means that you must explicitly copy a referenced object to new storage if you want to make sure the receiver can't alter the original copy. While this does cost us some extra work, we must do it. If we were to pass everything by value and take special steps when it came to delegation, we would have a serious problem insofar as the reference we would then use would not necessarily be to the original object. The bottom line is that you can convert from calls by reference to calls by value without affecting the operation of the system. To convert from calls by value to calls by reference is very difficult because you would have to add a great deal of extra logic to the system to figure out which copy of the object was the one that should be modified. However, in using statically defined objects, you will find this automatic duplication helpful.

Drop Shipments

This is another indexed collection. It contains an arbitrary mixture of Entity objects and Customer objects, depending on whether or not the drop shipment was made to another Bancroft customer. The reason that an Entity is used instead of an Address object is that an Address does not hold a name and Bancroft wants to keep track of it. We already made the decision that an Address object would not contain a name, and changing it now would have wide ranging repercussions. While there have been times where we decided to extend the design without being concerned about impacts on what has already been done, this is not such a case. If we were to incorporate the **Name** element into the Address object, we would have to go back and significantly alter the existing design. For example, Entity itself would have to be changed to remove its Name element and all of the messages to Entity that dealt with the name would have to be changed. This operation is just as risky in OO design as it is in any design methodology because if you forget to change everything involved with name, you are guaranteed problems further on. Deciding to do something like that is an open admission that your design is wrong. *You must always pay attention to the difference between things that augment your existing design and to things that change your existing design.* OO systems take very well to the former, they are no better than any other language at dealing with the latter. In the first case, you are simply providing more information in an existing framework, in the second you are changing the rules in the middle of the game.

TYPE	MESSAGE NAME	DESCRIPTION
PUBLIC	addDropShip(o)	Add a drop shipment to the list. Allow any Entity or derived class to be used. Note that this allows us to list drop shipments to our suppliers, should we be so inclined.
PUBLIC	dropShipments()	Return a list of all drop shipments made for this customer.

Notice in this case that we have not provided a relay message for deleting drop shipments from the collection. This has nothing to do with OO design, it just wasn't necessary. Remember, OO design is not a replacement for traditional design, it is an extended form of it. There is no need to worry about OO design considerations when traditional experience tells you it's a moot point.

Mailing History

This is a collection containing PromotionalMailing objects—the details, catalogs, and ads that the customer has received. In this particular case, the collection is not indexed.

TYPE	MESSAGE NAME	DESCRIPTION
PUBLIC	mailing(pm)	Add this promotional mailing to the list.
PUBLIC	mailings()	Return the list of promotional mailings that have been sent to the customer.

Supplier

In doing the initial design of the SupplierClass, it was created as a derived class of Entity. This means that it already has a name and an address. At the Supplier level, the following elements were added:

- Supplier ID

- Contact Name
- Contact Address
- Supplier Inventory

As far as the name and address go, we've already done that. When we specified the messages handled by the Supplier objects, another derived class of Entity, we defined the messages used to manage name and address operations. We can therefore forget about it until the inevitable time when we feel we must change it.

Supplier ID

The SupplierID is analogous to the PartNumber of an InventoryItem. Once again, it's a unique code created by some crazed Bancroft employee and serves to uniquely identify Suppliers. Rumor has it that the code has some internal meaning used by the accounts payable staff, but that's no concern of ours. Seriously, in designing any new system, regardless of the language or technology, you will get a great deal of information from your clients. You *must* know how to separate the wheat from the chaff.

TYPE	MESSAGE NAME	DESCRIPTION
PUBLIC	supplierID()	Return the ID code of the supplier object receiving this message.
PRIVATE	setSupplierID(sid)	Copy the sid parameter into the supplier ID data element of this supplier and load this object into the Supplier's collection under this key. If there was an ID there previously, don't load the item into the Supplier's collection, just change the index key to reflect the new ID.

Contact Info

The contact information comes in two pieces, the **ContactName** and the **ContactAddress**. The name is just an ASCII string, providing the name of the individual at the supplier's organization that Bancroft feels is the most trustworthy. The address can contain many things, from the contact name's departmental address to the home phone of the supplier company's president. We can assume that when Bancroft initially starts doing business with a supplier, they may believe in their honesty and integrity for some bounded period of time. They may not actually acquire more detailed information until later in the relationship with supplier, when schedules slip and orders are lost.

We are confronted with two distinct problems because of this. First, we have the standard requirements of accessing this data as we would any other data. Since this is the simple issue, we will dispose of it now. The messages for accessing and manipulating existing supplier contact information would be:

TYPE	MESSAGE NAME	DESCRIPTION
PUBLIC	contactName()	Return the name of the contact at the supplier.
PUBLIC	contactAddress()	Return the Address object for the contact at the supplier.
PUBLIC	contactName(s)	Copy string s into the contact name for the supplier.
PUBLIC	contactAddress(a)	Put the Address object a into the supplier's contact address.

The second problem involves what to do when there is no contact information filed for a supplier. In the case of the contact name, returning an empty string seems an adequate response. But the contactAddress may be used by other objects for such things as sending mail to the supplier; therefore, returning an empty string or NULL could cause problems.

We could document it to death and hope that everybody who ever wants a contact address reads the document, and more importantly, follows directions. Over time this is not likely. Our problem is that while returning an empty string for a contact name is not likely to cause anything more serious than a letter that starts off with "Dear :", returning NULL to someone expecting an address object can cause the system to crash when they start sending messages to the NULL. A better alternative is to alter the behavior of the contactAddress() message so that it will always return an Address object when asked for one. Returning a brand new empty address is a small improvement. Although the system might be more stable, the fact remains that there isn't an address. When designing an OO program, you always want to be aware of objects that can help you out of dilemmas you may find yourself in. In this particular case, we know that the Supplier object itself contains an address, one that was loaded when this instance of Supplier was initially created. So let's use that one.

Once again, we have several choices:

- Copy the reference to the address from the Entity level Address to the ContactAddress.

- Duplicate the Entity level Address and put a reference to it in the ContactAddress.

- Modify the behavior of the contactAddress() message so that it will return the entity address if it does not have an address available.

The first two options have problems, which is why the third option is usually the preferred way to do things in an OOP. In the case of sharing the same reference, what happens when someone really does want to load a supplier? There is no quick way to tell that this is really the supplier address and because of that, the contact address is likely to overwrite the supplier address—believing it to be a contact address, distinct from the suppliers address. Never share a reference to an object between two objects when one believes it is fixed for all time and the other is likely to change it. If you are talking about two distinct objects, in this case the supplier and contact addresses, make sure you are always referencing two objects. The second alternative is not bad, but it wastes memory for little good reason. In this case not much is wasted, but when you are dealing with an object whose size is measured in Kbytes, this can cause you some pain. You don't want to duplicate objects if you don't have to.

This leaves the third approach, to modify the behavior of the function that implements the contactAddress() message so that it will return the Entity address if no contact address has been defined. This ensures that there is a clear separation between these two addresses, so changes to one don't affect the other. And it doesn't use extra memory unless it needs to.

Function Overloading and Polymorphism

Messages that set the value of an element, X, in some previous object have been named:

```
set()
```

Messages that retrieve the value of an element X from an object have been named:

```
get().
```

In the preceding example for manipulating contact names, functions with the same name were used to retrieve and to set values within the contact name. This book was written with the assumption that you have read, or at least have access to, Bjarne Stroustrup's book on C++ or one of the other books about the language. One of the primary objectives of this book is to explain why experienced OOP programmers would sooner die than give up **function overloading**, which is related to one of our favorite things, **polymorphism**. First, here is an explanation of why function overloading is so wonderful.

Up to this point, we have been well behaved, traditional programmers, using unique names for each of the message functions discussed. To indicate that a function accesses the contents of an element in an object, you give it the same name as the element in that object. To indicate that it sets the value of an element, you precede the element name with **set** to build the function name. You have seen examples of this in earlier code.

In working on a multiperson project, what happens if other programmers, equally as well behaved come along and set the following rules for their functions:

- All functions that change elements have the same name as the element they change.

- All functions that retrieve the values of elements have the name of the element preceded by **get**.

In very little time, there is a great deal of confusion, people are calling the wrong function or, at the least, spending more time looking up function names than actually writing the calls themselves. Why? Because we have had to adopt one (or more) arbitrary standards to satisfy the linker's small-minded demands for unique function names.

To confuse the issue even further, we end up with a horde of functions that do things like print records. We have **printEmployeeRec(), printInventoryRec(), printYetAnotherRec()**, and so on, until our heads spin.

Function overloading really means that specific functions are not differentiated by name alone. *What makes a function unique is its name and the parameters it accepts*, with attention paid to both the order and type of the parameters. In other words, if you had a function that fetched a record from a database, called **fetchFromDatabase()**, and you wanted this function to be able to return the data either in a passed structure or a brand new one it created on the fly, you could define two *overloaded* functions:

- fetchFromDatabase(key)
- fetchFromDatabase(key, receivingStructureAddress)

You would leave it up to the compiler to figure out which function you wished to use by looking at what parameters you passed to the function. This means that you don't have to arbitrarily make new names for the same function, just because you want it to accept different kinds of parameters.

The second guarantee an OOP compiler gives you is that message names are tightly bound to the objects with which they are associated. For example, in the Bancroft database, we are going to end up having to implement messages that will cause various objects to be printed in a readable form. We could be traditional and create a number of unique function names, one for each type of object that we wished to print. Unfortunately that would also mean that when we wanted to print an InventoryItem, we would be sitting there muttering, "was that **prinfInvItem()** or was that **InvItemprintf()**?" In an OOP, you simply implement the message print(), and define it for each object you wish to print.

Now, this means that there are a whole bunch of functions named print(), each tied to the specific object that it prints. Each of these functions behaves differently, there being little similarity between printing an inventory record and an employee record, other than they produce

ASCII output. Welcome to the wonderful world of polymorphism. Polymorphism, from the Greek *poly* (many) and *morphos* (shape) means, many shapes. In the context of an OOL, it means that the same message can behave many ways depending on what object it is sent to. In teaching this concept to programmers over time, I have often been confronted with: "What's so special about that, I do it all the time—you know, pass anything to a function and switch on whatever got passed to the function." This is an incredibly dangerous thing to do. How do you know what you're getting? What if the pass isn't what you think it is? In an object oriented language, you have mechanisms available to you to avoid this, so why risk almost certain death for no reason?

By binding the member function to the object, you never have to worry about things like that. The function won't be invoked unless the message has been sent to this object, meaning the computer knows exactly what the object is. Therefore, if the routine works for the object, it will always work and it will never cause trouble. To cause trouble it would have to operate on another object, and the *compiler will not allow that.*

The bottom line is that *function overloading and polymorphism shift much of the burden of determining specific cases onto the compiler, leaving the programmer responsible for knowing only the general case.* When someone asks you, "how do I print a so-and-so?" you can tell them to send it a print message, trusting the compiler to figure out exactly which print function is needed to do the job. If someone wants to use a function with a certain set of parameters, they no longer have to remember which function name corresponds to this particular set of parameters, the parameter's type and order actually constitute part of the function name. As far as the text on the left side of the parenthesis goes, it can now remain consistent, regardless of the particular organization of the parameters.

Supplier Inventory

The Supplier Inventory is more of a mapping schema within the Bancroft system, than a true data management facility. This is due to the fact that individual inventory items track their own purchases and sales, and the Supplier object maps all the relevant supplier data, including the supplier inventory. The data that must be provided is:

- The Bancroft inventory number.

- The Supplier's inventory number.
- The delivery lead time from the supplier.
- The minimum order quantity from the supplier.
- The supplier pricing information.

The intent is twofold. First, an effective means of translating between supplier and internal inventory codes must be provided, as we already know that Bancroft uses their own internal codes for inventory identification. Secondly, information regarding supplier pricing and delivery times must be implemented for inventory ordering purposes. To accomplish this, a SupplierInventory object will be implemented, containing:

- Supplier Inventory Number
- Delivery Lead Time
- Minimum Order Quantity
- Pricing Information

This object contains all of the relevant supplier data except for the Bancroft inventory number. This is because the contents of the Supplier-Inventory object within the Supplier object will be an IndexedCollection, indexed by the Bancroft part number. This decision really has little to do with object oriented design, it simply reflects the fact that the system internally uses Bancroft part numbers. To index the SupplierInventory collection by the supplier's inventory number would mean that the collection would have to be searched each time the program needed to access a SupplierInventory object.

The first three elements of the collection are quite straightforward, simply containing fixed data that gives the values in question. The first would be a string, and the second two would be numbers. The Pricing information is a little more complex. Most suppliers try to encourage Bancroft to order as many items as possible. They do this by providing a series of quantity price breaks. Because these breaks are the result of a great deal of haggling with the supplier, there is not always a simple function whereby one can simply compute the cost per item based on the quantity ordered. This data will be represented by a brand new type of collection, called an OrderedCollection. Even though we have a bona fide requirement for a new collection and we are not adversely impacting the existing design by implementing it, we do want to ensure that the new class is not tied to this application. Remember, when you have to create a new general purpose object, make sure it really is general purpose. Then you never have to create it again, and you can use it in every new program you do.

Ordered Collection

An ordered collection is simply one where the items are put into the collection in a certain order, are maintained in that order, and can be retrieved by their position within the collection. A vector is an excellent example of an ordered collection, where you can load ten items in some order and then get item 7 back simply by asking for it. Now, the collection class already collects things together, why can't we just use it? Because the collection class is not required to keep things in order and it provides no facility for retrieving things from itself by their internal position. It could be modified to do so, but consider what would happen if we decided to implement a new kind of collection, a **SortedCollection**, after doing this to collection. The SortedCollection, which orders its contents in some sorting order, would not only have to specialize the collection class by providing sorting methods. It would also have to undo the effects of the collection class itself—an impossible feat. When you are building a hierarchy of related objects, growth in specialization is a goal. But this is accomplished by enhancing the capabilities of your base class. Never create a hierarchy where more specialized levels operate in direct conflict with their base class. Even if you were to get the code to work, it would be quite inefficient. Not only are you asking the computer to perform one specialized operation, in this case sorting, you are also forcing it to do another specialized operation, indexing, and then you are making the SortedCollection undo the effects of this indexing. *If a base class does something that a derived class must undo, then the base class is doing too much.*

Summary

In this chapter various methods for the application level objects have been presented. Although the presentation has been far from complete, it has touched on the requirements of each application object, illustrating what kinds of methods an object provides for its own internal use and what methods it provides for public consumption. The relationships between objects have been discussed, showing how objects attempt to avoid reduplicating capabilities by delegating tasks to other objects. As the definition of various methods progressed, we found that other new objects were required to support these methods, primarily to provide them with capabilities to make their jobs easier. Although many of the new objects could have been avoided by implementing the functionality within the various methods that use them, it is obvious that doing this would create large sections of similar code throughout the messages, as they attempted to do something that really should be done for them.

Some specialized concepts of OOP have been presented, such as function overloading and polymorphism. These capabilities are needed to construct systems that behave in a uniform manner, rather than a giant collection of special cases. The objective is to distribute computation evenly across the system, allowing each object to implement things that it needs to do, instead of building a single monolithic "computing engine" that knows how to do all things for all objects.

1. Constant, stepwise revision of a program is the objective of OO design.

2. If you break something, the breakage will be contained within the scope of what you were trying to do. Side effects are very rare, and reflect flaws in the overall design.

3. You can only damage what you modify.

4. It's normal to discover you need a new object. OO systems grow like trees.

5. If you are working on the branches of your tree (program) you have a big problem with the design if you have to modify its trunk.

6. Modifications involve the addition of new sub-branches, and once in a while, the dirt the tree is growing in. This reflects the enhancements of existing application and systems capabilities, respectively.

7. If an object contains references to other objects, then it can delegate certain responsibilities to these sub-objects. Don't make one object do something another object was already designed to do.

8. Extending designs is good, changing existing premises is bad!

9. Pay attention to scope. You should always be moving towards further specialization in the applications domain. You should always be able to define your work in terms of the growth of a tree.

10. There is a big difference between the original of an object and copies of it. Only hand out the original if you want the recipient to modify it. Remember, changes to the original are permanent and globally seen.

11. Functions in two objects that do the same thing should have the same name. Polymorphism is there for a reason. Do you want a 40 page list of functions, or a 4 page list?

12. Don't overspecialize classes. Don't make yourself have to undo things. Derived objects do new things, they do not undo old things.

CHAPTER 5

DESIGN SYNTHESIS

If builders built buildings the way that programmers write programs, then the first woodpecker that came along would destroy civilization.

This chapter provides the final design example for the Bancroft system. Although the system is not defined sufficiently to be a commercial package, we have covered the major components of the system, showing how the OO design methodology affects both the design of the application and the underlying system structure. This chapter will coalesce the principles of the previous chapters, showing how a uniform design approach comes as you gain familiarity with OO programming systems.

The specific intent here is to define the Employee object and any ancillary objects necessary to support its existence. In some areas, such as taxes and benefits information, we will deliberately gloss over the details, as this is a book on program design and not a tome on corporate accounting. As before, each part of this chapter deals with a particular element of the Employee object, and is followed by text that relates the design decisions made in that part to topics discussed previously.

Employee

In order to fully represent an employee record within the system, we must provide the following information for each employee:

- Employee Name
- Employee Address
- Job Classification
- Salary Information
- Benefits Information
- Tax Information
- Employment History

We came up with this information simply by asking ourselves, exactly what components define an employee from an employer's point of view? In OO design, we are building computer models, usually of things that exist in the real world. Defining objects is a process of description, one that can be as vague or as detailed as you feel necessary. Object definition is a process of stating what you know, not an attempt to figure out what you do not know. If you don't know anything about the object, you shouldn't be making it. If some of the details about the object are unclear, don't worry, just defer the definition of these parts to a later time. Stick with what you do know and the rest will become clear as you move through the design. You are illuminating a real entity for the computer. You will first light the exterior details and describe them and then the process will become a synergistic one, where the computer model *will help you* to see what interior sections of the model next need to be shown.

Name and Address

The name and address of an employee have been implemented already at the Entity object level and we defined the messages that handle the setting and retrieving of the name when we worked on Customer and Supplier messages in Chapter Four. This serves as yet another example of how OOP is a constant building process, where the work you do today takes full advantage of the work you did yesterday. In any case, we don't need to worry about the name and address elements of employee, since they are completed already.

When doing the initial high level design, in this case specifying the requirements for objects such as Employees, Suppliers, and InventoryItems, you should always pay attention to the concepts that are common to these objects. We decided back in Chapters One and Two that Employees, Suppliers, and Customers were all manifestations of the same basic concept. You can now see exactly what benefits this decision has brought us, as we don't have to do anything to enable Employee objects to handle names and addresses, it is a capability that they already have. Exploit this ability of OO systems at any time you can, as it will save you an immense amount of work. Programming becomes much easier when you can work on programming new capabilities into the system, instead of continuously reprogramming the same capabilities. One caveat does apply: in your quest to search out and exploit uniformity, do not begin to make non-uniform things uniform. For example, in dealing with apples and oranges—they are both fruits and share some similarities because of this. However, an apple and an orange are still two distinct entities and should not be mashed together in a single unit. Once you've made orange juice and applesauce, you are going to find it very hard to get back to the original apple and orange. If you go to the extent of mixing the orange juice and applesauce together into a single container, you have then discarded much of what made an apple an apple or made an orange an orange. You have forever lost the original details that apples and oranges represented.

Job Classification

The job classification of an employee describes the jobs performed by the employee, by giving their department(s) and job title(s). Most employees only work in one department doing one job, but Bancroft does have some employees who wear more than one hat. We must account for this fact within the job classification—if we don't, these employees will need more than one employee object to describe them appropriately. A new record would be needed for each job an employee has. This is undesirable because it is the only information that would differ across the records, thus requiring the system to go through some serious contortions when it modified data within an employee record. It would have to ensure that all of the other objects describing this employee, specifically those giving other job classifications, were also modified.

To satisfy all these criteria, the job classification of an employee record would have to contain an **OrderedCollection**, as defined in Chapter Four. This OrderedCollection would always contain a minimum of one element, but could contain more elements for those employees with multiple job classifications. Each element in the collection would be an instance of the **EmployeeJobClass** object, which looks like this:

- Department Name
- Job Title

Each of these elements is a string that contains text for the department name or job title, respectively. We could embed the intelligence to manipulate the codes within the EmployeeJobClass object, it's just unnecessary within the context of this example. If you do try this on your own, you might find the general purpose objects you would need to create in order to support this, useful in the future.

Messages handled by the EmployeeJobClass object only need to be able to access and to alter these two fields, therefore they would be:

TYPE	MESSAGE NAME	DESCRIPTION
PUBLIC	department()	Return the string contained in the department element of this object.
PRIVATE	department(name)	Put the string in name into the department element of this object.
PUBLIC	title()	Return the string contained in the job title element of this object.
PRIVATE	title(job name)	Put the string in jobname into the department element of this object.

In defining these messages, two specifics need to be mentioned. First, notice how we are using function overloading to use the same function names for both retrieving and storing the data of each field within this object. This keeps the interface to the object straightforward by not requiring the use of four distinct function names to perform the same tasks. Second, we have marked both storage functions private, meaning that they are not available for use by other objects. Although these functions will serve as support functions for constructors, we don't want to have to destroy and rebuild the object just because we want to change the job title. C++, as well as other OOPLs that enforce public/private message distinctions, provide a mechanism called **friend** that can be used to instruct the compiler to allow certain other objects to access private methods within another object. Although we will be dealing with the use of friends in the tactical section during implementation of the system, you should remember that there are always means by which you can allow access to private messages by other objects. The intent is not to provide global, unlimited access to possibly destructive methods by any other object within the system, but to provide a clearly defined access path for those external objects that have a legitimate need to access these functions. A good rule of thumb is that *methods that return data are usually public, and messages that alter data are usually private.* Private does not always mean that nobody except this particular object can use the method, but it does mean that external access to the method is rigorously controlled. You may have encountered a similar constraint at a higher level if you have ever used or implemented an accounting system. Such systems tend to maintain an audit trail, where all transactions in the system are logged by time and operator. These systems have the same basic goal, to track access to critical sections of data and to prevent this data from being modified improperly.

This goes to show that OO design is not a totally new way of programming; it is an extension of proven techniques. A good OO design should not counter what you already feel is good programming practice, but be an extension of what you do already. Here we have two concrete examples of this. First, we don't want to arbitrarily duplicate large sections of employee data every time an employee has more than one job description. To do so would force us to constantly chase these duplicates around the system each time we modified an employee record. The end result is usually that we miss one and the information becomes corrupted.

This is not a new discovery from OO programming, it's something we've known ever since the first companies started doing payrolls with punch cards—OO design is governed by many of the same basic rules as were those systems. Second, we want to be very careful in controlling access to variables in order to prevent any old function from arbitrarily modifying someone else's data.

This particular form of misbehavior, often called **spaghetti coding**, is as bad in OO design as in any other design methodology. OO design is a sophisticated tool that stands on the shoulders of existing design methodologies, which means it is also susceptible to some of their weaknesses. You must follow the principles of OO design and you must also follow the principles of the underlying design methods on which it is based. OO code should be even more structured, even more modular, than code produced using current structured design techniques.

Salary Information

Bancroft has both salaried and hourly employees and both types are filed in the employee database. Although the employee's job classification is a good clue as to whether the employee is hourly or salaried, it is not a guaranteed indicator. For this reason, we will use the Salary information to determine whether an employee is paid hourly or on a fixed salary. To do this, an **EmployeeSalary** object will be created and the object's **HourlyEmployeeSalary** and **FixedEmployeeSalary** will be derived from it. The EmployeeSalary object will contain one element, **salary**, which will hold a floating point number used in salary computations by the two derived classes. It will implement a single method to allow alterations of the salary value, as shown below, but it will leave salary retrievals and computations up to its derived classes.

TYPE	MESSAGE NAME	DESCRIPTION
PRIVATE	salary(value)	Put the floating point value into the salary field.

It is of no concern here whether this value is an hourly or annual wage figure.

HourlyEmployeeSalary The HourlyEmployeeSalary object supports calculations of salaries for hourly employees. To do this it provides an element called **standardHours**, that defines the number of hours in a pay period for which the employee is paid the standard rate. It also provides a field called **overtimeRate** that defines the rate at which the employee is paid for hours worked after the number of hours given in standardHours has been exhausted.

The HourlyEmployeeSalary object would implement a single method used to compute the employee's gross salary for some number of hours worked during the pay period, specifically:

TYPE	MESSAGE NAME	DESCRIPTION
PUBLIC	grossPAY(hours)	Use the salary and overtime information and compute the employee's pay for the given hours. Return this value.

FixedEmployeeSalary The FixedEmployeeSalary object supports calculations and manipulations of salaries for employees who receive a fixed annual salary, regardless of time worked. Therefore, the exact methodology for computing the salary is **hardwired**, returning the same value for every pay period.

It would be desirable for the FixedEmployeeSalary to respond to the same message format as does the HourlyEmployeeSalary, so that outside objects do not need to modify their calls based on whether the salary is fixed or hourly. In other words, there is no real need for passing the number of hours worked to the FixedEmployeeSalary pay calculator function. If we do pass it, it will work identically to the pay calculator for hourly salaries. External objects will be able to send the same message to both hourly and fixed salary objects. This is just another case where a design decision has been made that will keep the system uniform, instead of providing a myriad of special cases for every action the system must perform. In cases such as this, it is preferable to add a little overhead to one routine in order to make it conform to related routines, than to allow a host of different calling mechanisms to be generated. This would force you to remember all of the individual details, rather than a simple set of rules that applies to all cases.

The definition of the **grossPay(hours)** function for the FixedEmployeeSalary is identical to that of the grossPay(hours) function for the HourlyEmployeeSalary, even though they arrive at their respective results by different paths.

Here we see a decision made to keep the overall function of the system uniform, although at deeper levels it is not. We may compute the salary of hourly and salaried workers by two very different means, but it's unlikely that any object requesting this data, cares. If we provided two different messages for hourly and salaried pay, then we are forcing all objects requesting this information to distinguish between these two cases or to "care" about this distinction. Such actions tend to percolate upwards through the design of the system until, at the top, you have to know a priori whether an employee is hourly or salaried, just to look up their address! Enforce uniformity of behavior at any chance you get, keeping the nasty differences between cases limited within the objects that are truly concerned with them. If you don't, you will soon be overwhelmed by a large number of specialized operations at levels that are supposed to be very general.

Benefits Information

Bancroft has an extremely Machiavellian benefits package, far beyond the capabilities of this book. In real life, you will often encounter situations where particular pieces of data are inordinately complex, given their overall position in the scheme of things. In cases such as this, you must extract the information with which you absolutely must deal, and then put all the rest of the information into some flexible structure (usually a large string) that can be presented to the operator. To attempt to fully computerize Bancroft's benefits package could easily double the cost of the project. The operators already understand it in text form, so we will simply maintain the text and allow them to manipulate it. This is the ultimate deferral of definition, where you simply depend on the user to implement the functionality that you need. In some cases this is just laziness, but in others it's the best possible solution to a difficult problem. Remember, whatever system you operate under, the user is the most powerful peripheral to which you have access. The benefits structure, from our point of view, contains three elements. The first is a large string containing all of the benefit information in text form and which we can't understand or we don't care about. The second element contains the total number of sick leave hours claimed by the employee, and the third contains the total number of vacation hours claimed by the employee. There are three sets of messages provided to manipulate this data:

TYPE	MESSAGE NAME	DESCRIPTION
PUBLIC	benefitsData()	Return the text string containing the benefits data. Start system prayer that the operator understands this, because we don't!
PRIVATE	benefitsData(txt)	Load text into the benefits data. Operate on blind faith that operator has legally changed the data, because we can't distinguish between right and wrong here!
PUBLIC	sickLeave()	Return the number in the sick leave element.
PRIVATE	sickLeave(newVal)	Put newVal into sickLeave.
PRIVATE	takeSickLeave(h)	Alter current sick leave value by h hours.
PUBLIC	vacation()	Return the number in the vacation hours element.
PRIVATE	vacation(newVal)	Put newVal into the vacation element.
PRIVATE	takeVacation(h)	Alter current vacation by h hours.

Notice that we have implemented two methods, **takeSickLeave** and **takeVacation**, that really could be implemented through paired calls to their respective element retrieval and loading functions, such as:

```
#define takeSickLeave(hours)
(sickLeave(sickLeave() - hours)
```

The reason for doing this is twofold. First, and simplest, is that there might be instances where we send a message to take sick leave that isn't really available, which would cause the sick leave value to go negative. But this case is overshadowed by a more important design decision. This is a solution that should be used with great care. In this case, we have elected to simplify the design primarily because this is not a book on how to build an employee benefits database, which it would become if we were to fully define this object. In the commercial world, this decision is usually made in two distinct cases:

- A complex entity must be managed by a program, but the program really doesn't have anything to do with it.

- An entity is so complex that its implementation would radically affect the performance of the system.

In the first case, you will sometimes encounter a system that is cursed with some overly complex piece of data it didn't even generate. For example, in large communications systems, the database describing available lines also contains information used by hardware to "condition" the lines in order to ensure that they reliably transmit data. Now this information is usually generated by other specialized pieces of hardware, in conjunction with a whole series of overly complicated mathematical formuli. In such a case, you might just present the conditioning data in text form, ignoring the mechanism by which it is generated and the actual intrinsic meaning of the information.

In the second case, consider a company that manufactures strangely shaped pieces of metal for use by others. Their database might include a perspective drawing of each piece, which can be retrieved by the operator. This does not mean that you need to put a full perspective geometry package in the system, you can limit them to a single canned drawing. In this case, adding a perspective geometry package would make the software, intended for a salesman's PC, require a multimillion dollar supercomputer.

Tax Information

In the interest of simplicity, and to keep the size of the book manageable, we shall not attempt to implement a totally faithful model of a tax object.

We shall implement the object class **EmployeeTaxInfo** to represent the tax information within the Bancroft system. For our purposes we shall consider a tax object to contain:

- Number of deductions claimed
- Federal withholdings YTD
- FICA withholdings YTD
- State withholdings YTD

All of these elements are numeric values and not much more can be said about them. On the other hand, the methods associated with the EmployeeTaxInfo object are more convoluted:

TYPE	MESSAGE NAME	DESCRIPTION
PUBLIC	deductions()	Return number of deductions claimed.
PRIVATE	deductions(num)	Set the number of deductions claimed.
PUBLIC	fedWithhold()	Return amount of federal tax withheld YTD.
PRIVATE	fedWithhold(amt)	Set the amount of federal tax withheld YTD.
PRIVATE	addFedWithheld(v)	Add v to amount of federal withholdings.
PUBLIC	FICAWithhold()	Return amount of FICA tax withheld YTD.
PRIVATE	FICAWithhold(amt)	Set the amount of FICA tax withheld YTD.
PRIVATE	addFICAWithheld(v)	Add v to amount of FICA withholdings.
PUBLIC	stateWithhold()	Return amount of state tax withheld YTD.

TYPE	MESSAGE NAME	DESCRIPTION
PRIVATE	stateWithhold(amt)	Set the amount of state tax withheld YTD.
PRIVATE	addStateWithheld(v)	Add v to amount of state withholdings.

The first thing that should be addressed is the fact that there are no methods or elements that deal with the amount of tax to be withheld for each pay period. This is because the value is computed by the following methods. Notice that each method uses the Employee object as the first parameter so that the tax calculator can determine the employee's base salary and number of exemptions. Also, we pass the pay period length as a parameter, even though we know that Bancroft pays every two weeks. We can do this because we know that this is not likely to be the only project in which we use this object; therefore, we will attempt to make it as flexible as possible. If it turns out this flexibility has a drastically negative impact on the system's performance, we can always remove it. Remember, it's a lot easier to specialize a general object than it is to generalize a specialized object.

The following messages are sent to a **TaxCollector** object, which exists outside of the normal Bancroft data structure. Every system would contain a publicly available TaxCollector object instance to which all of these messages are sent.

TYPE	MESSAGE NAME	DESCRIPTION
PUBLIC	federalTax(e,payPeriod)	Return the amount of federal tax to be withheld for this pay period.
PUBLIC	FICATax(e,payPeriod)	Return the amount of FICA tax to be withheld for this pay period.
PUBLIC	stateTax(e,payPeriod)	Return the amount of state tax to be withheld from this pay period.

This strategy is based on the capacity of objects to contain private data structures, which are used internally within the object. In this case the

TaxCollector object contains a private data structure called **taxTable**, used to compute the data required to satisfy the three tax calculation functions associated with the EmployeeTaxInfo objects. By encapsulating the tax data within an object, many problems that currently confront tax computation algorithms can be solved easily. For example, some states use a complex algorithm to compute the tax owed, based on a combination of the federal tax, the phase of the moon, and the relative indebtedness of the state. Since an object is a self-contained repository of both data and procedural knowledge, separate TaxInfo objects can be created and installed into the various systems bound for the states in which Bancroft does business. The overall system however, will always function in an identical manner to any other system in any other state, because the differences are packaged within the TaxInfo object itself. On the surface they will all be identical. This makes your job much easier when Bancroft's office in Outer Mongolia calls and says their tax package doesn't work. In situations where multiple tax computations may apply, for instance when a location must deal with employees living in different states, the root TaxCollector object can look at the state in which the employee lives and either select a specific table and algorithm to use, or it can relay the message to another TaxCollector that is specialized for the particular state in which the employee lives. All higher levels are happily unaware of the operations performed within the TaxCollector to actually cough up the correct tax values. And if the IRS complains about your means of computing taxes, you know exactly where to look.

In almost any programming task, you are going to run into a situation where you cannot clearly specify a single design because people are indecisive. Identify undefined areas clearly and bind them tightly within a few objects. When they want a system for Outer Mongolia, you bind the Outer Mongolia tax module into the standard system. When they open a new office in Inner Mongolia, you make a new system, binding in the Inner Mongolia tax package in place of the Outer Mongolia package. The exact mechanism for doing this differs radically across OO programming systems, but this isn't really a major issue because you can make each tax module an object that has exactly the same surface characteristics as every other tax module, because they are all instances of a single class, the TaxCollector class. The rest of your system; therefore, is oblivious to which package you are using. As a matter of fact, unless you specifically provide a message such as **whichTaxPackageAreYou**, the system cannot tell the difference between one tax package and another. This is another direct benefit from enforcing uniform, consistent behavior within any system that you develop.

Employment History

The employment history of an employee can be seen as a gigantic bucket of old salaries, job descriptions, and additional elements containing such things as performance reviews, special projects, and so on. The key issue is that this is an employment history and that implies two things. First, this must be a collection, as history is a collection of facts over time. Second, this collection must be an IndexedCollection, keyed by dates, once again because of what the word *history* implies.

This means that the **employmentHistory** element of an employee object is an IndexedCollection, and data is keyed in it by character strings that represent dates. The collection itself can contain three distinct types of objects, in any order and frequency. These are **EmployeeJobClass** objects describing old job classifications, **HourlyEmployeeSalary**, and **FixedEmployeeSalary** objects giving old salary information, and a new object, **AuxilliaryEmployeeData**, giving specialized information on such things as the employee's annual performance review. The first crucial issue is the keying of these objects within the collection referenced by employmentHistory. We cannot use a simple date as a key, because it is quite probable that more than one item can be added to this collection on a single date and IndexedCollections do not accept duplicate keys at this time. For example, consider someone who gets promoted from a programmer to a project manager. In all likelihood, their salary and job description will change simultaneously.

We have two choices. We can derive a class from IndexedCollection, such as **IndexedCollectionWithDuplicates**, that can handle collections with duplicate keys. Or, we can modify the internal keying of the employeeHistory collection to ensure that all of the keys are unique. In this case, we will add intelligence to the Employee class so that it differentiates between multiple items added on the same date.

To do this, we will restrict access to the employmentHistory element, forcing all access to it to go through the Employee object. We will never return a reference that gives any other object direct access to this collection, as we can't trust them to obey and uphold the specialized keying we will be using. We would then define our own internal keying scheme, and the messages by which users of the Employee object may retrieve elements from and add elements to the collection. To key, or index, the collection we will use a combination of the date on which the transaction was done, and the order of transactions from that date. If Ann Droid was promoted from computer operator to programmer on October 8, 1989, the following specific elements would be logged to the employee history file:

- An HourlyEmployeeSalary object, giving Ann's old salary as a computer operator.

- An EmployeeJobClass object describing her old job as a computer operator.

- An AuxilliaryEmployeeData object describing the details of her promotion.

Now, assuming that the transactions have arrived in the above sequence, our internal keys and the key's associated objects would be as follows:

- 10/08/89:1   HourlyEmployeeSalary
- 10/08/89:2   EmployeeJobClass
- 10/08/89:3   AuxilliaryEmployeeData

In order to provide objects using Employee objects access to this history, we will use two methods, **HistoricalDate(Date)** and **Historical-Data(D,Trans)**. These allow the employee's historical data to be accessed and updated:

TYPE	MESSAGE NAME	DESCRIPTION
PUBLIC	HistoricalData(Date)	Return a simple Collection of all transactions logged for this Date.
PUBLIC	HistoricalData(D,Trans)	Add this transaction to the EmploymentHistory collection, after verifying it is one of the three objects acceptable for this collection.

You may feel that I have overlooked a vital point. Exactly how do we know what the appropriate sequence numbers are for adding new elements to the collection? Back to Ann's case, what happens when she crashes the Engineering computer that very afternoon and then makes pointed comments about the Director of Engineering's probable lineage? Well, we will get three more transactions, since her new job will be in the mail room:

- A FixedEmployeeSalary giving her old pay as an operator.
- An EmployeeJobClass object describing her old job as an operator.
- An AuxilliaryEmployeeData object describing the details of her demotion and just what she called the director.

What's to keep **HistoricalData(Date,Trans)** from reusing the sequence from one to three, thereby destroying the data on her promotion and the company's defense when she sues? A method called **LastHistoryTransactionOn(Date)** will do this for us and we can make the HistoricalData(Date,Trans) method use this method whenever it adds new information to the history list. In order to determine the sequence number to use it will call the LastHistoryTransactionOn(Date) method, and add one to that value, giving it the next number in the sequence, and keeping Ann from becoming a major shareholder. If there are no transactions, the method will return zero, if there are transactions, the method will return the highest transaction number found.

In all of this, we have once again created another object, specifically the **AuxilliaryEmployeeData** record. This object is used to hold various vaguely defined information that someone in a position of responsibility feels should be associated with the employee's personnel record. We will define this object as containing the following fields:

- RecordedData—A big text string.

- RecordedByA—reference to the employee that put it there and implementing the following messages:

TYPE	MESSAGE NAME	DESCRIPTION
PUBLIC	record(data,bywhom)	Load data into the RecordedData element and bywhom into the RecordedBy element.
PUBLIC	record()	Return the name of the employee recording the data and the data recorded.

As a closing comment to the EmploymentHistory object definition, I would like to illustrate exactly how copping out in design can hurt you. In defining the EmploymentHistory, we opted not to make a specialized collection that can handle duplicate keys and instead created a specialized keying system to guarantee that we always had unique keys. This stunt could really hurt a system bound to be used in the real world. Specifically, we cannot make the EmploymentHistory object respond to requests for data that spans more than a single point in time, because we have no way of making a collection handle duplicate entries. While we can return a simple collection giving all of the transactions for a single day, we can't give a list of transactions for more than one day. This is because we can't use the dates as keys to the collection we would return. While there are ways around this little impasse, it clearly illustrates a weakness in the overall system. When you are out there implementing the techniques shown in this book, please remember in a few cases (such as the one here), I have taken artistic license to keep the book a reasonable size. When you have an object that seems to need a system level capability, such as the capacity to manage collections containing duplicate keys, there is nothing wrong with trying to determine if you can avoid implementing the object, if you feel it really isn't necessary. But remember, if it's a system level capability, you can most likely use it to save work in future projects. Even if it isn't that important now, it may be worth doing for the time it will save in the future.

If you go to the trouble of implementing a way around the requirement, as we have done here, and then find at a later point that you must implement the capability anyway, you are going to be one very unhappy designer, looking at a lot of wasted effort. Twice over, as a matter of fact, since you will then have to go back and undo your workaround. If you feel that you must find a workaround, wait to define it until you are absolutely positive that you aren't wasting your time.

Summary

In this particular chapter we have confined ourselves to the Employee object. Be sure to notice the clear connection between the unified design of a single object and the various decisions that go into creating that design. If you understand how you got from the vague idea that you needed an Employee object to the definition you now have, then all is well.

CHAPTER 6

OOP DESIGN DRAWINGS

When working towards the solution of a problem, it always helps if you know the answer. Provided, of course, you know there is a problem.

As we have completed a basic design of the Bancroft system, we could now begin implementing a program based on this design. Before we do this, it would be nice to first construct some road maps that show how the various elements of our design relate to each other. To do this, we will create diagrams of object relationships—both structural relationships between object classes and dynamic relationships between objects that send messages to one another. As far as the structural relationships go, we can expect a fair amount of help from our OO development system, regardless of the one we are using, as object structure and hierarchy are what all OO systems work with. In the case of the dynamic inter-object relationships that exist while the system is running, the degree of support we get from the OO system can vary a great deal. With a system such as Smalltalk, we will get a great deal of support, although we will lose about half of our machine's processing speed because of Smalltalk's monitoring and control activities. At the other end of the spectrum, with C++, we will get absolutely no help, but we won't lose any system performance either. The diagrams we will generate are very important, for three specific reasons:

- Finding flaws in the design, especially those concerning inter-object relationships.

- As a blueprint for actually coding the application.

- For debugging the system when it misbehaves.

Diagramming the Design

When it appears that most of the objects necessary to implement a system have been designed and many of the functions used to access and manipulate these objects have been identified, then it's time to draw some pictures of what has been done. To many, this may seem a little backward, defining the objects first, and then drawing pictures (flowcharts) of them, but it is appropriate in OOP methodology. Remember, during the initial design phase, you are not trying to create a formal design in traditional terms, you are attempting to identify the design of something that already exists. An OOP is not an implementation of something new, so much as it is a representation of something that already exists in the real world. Drawing pictures, however, is useful at many different points.

The reason for this is quite simple and is deeply rooted in the OOP mechanism. At this point, we have defined enough of the system to get started on coding it, if the modules are correctly related to each other, and the messages that link them are sufficient to do what we need. In OOP, deficiencies of a single object, insofar as its internal operations are concerned, are not critical issues. You can fix these deficiencies while actually coding the object, which is most likely where they will become apparent to you. You can even fix them after the system is running, since the effects of the changes you make will be limited to that specific object class. However, deficiencies in the communications between two different objects are usually illustrative of more widespread weaknesses in the design, and can be far more dangerous.

This doesn't mean you can't change or expand messaging between objects after you get the system up, only that if the messaging capabilities are inadequate to start with, you are unlikely to get the system up in the first place. In order to determine if the system design is complete enough and that the objects representing Bancroft's data can communicate and work with each other, we can generate a set of drawings that will graphically illustrate the relationships between the objects which we have defined.

These drawings will help determine whether or not our design is complete. They have a tendency to highlight the particular kinds of weaknesses we are searching for. In addition, the drawings are excellent tools for the coding phase, serving as blueprints for the implementation and testing of the objects. This set of drawings contains three specific types of drawings. The first is a single drawing showing the class hierarchy. This drawing lists all of the classes in an outline form, so that relationships between base classes and their derived classes can be portrayed. The second type of drawing is done for each object defined in the system and shows the types and organization of variables contained within that object, and their relationships to other objects within the system. These drawings illustrate the object dependencies within the system. The final drawing type is done for each object class and is quite similar to the second type of drawing. However, where the second type of drawing was concerned with object dependencies, this drawing is concerned with message flow in the system. It illustrates the messages that each object sends to other objects. The message flow drawings come in parts, illustrating the flow of messages out from a given object and into a given object.

Class Hierarchy

The class hierarchy is an outline that shows all of the classes within the system, in a form where their relationships to their base and derived classes can be easily traced. This drawing is very important for determining what methods and elements a particular class inherits from its base class, or passes on to its derived classes. The outline removes contextual ambiguities that arise, since the definition of an object being a base or derived class of another object can depend on one's point of view. For example, if we implement the three object classes A, B, and C, where B is derived from A, and C is derived from B, text (non-pictorial) discussions about the nature of B are likely to be somewhat ambiguous. When A is the subject of discussion, B is a derived class. When C is the subject, B is a base class. When B is the subject, we can call it either a base class or a derived class, and be right in both cases. But, by displaying the three classes in an outline form and by indenting derived classes under their base classes, we are able to get a clear picture of the relationship between all of the classes. This is clearly a case of a picture being worth a thousand words.

In laying out the class hierarchy, remember that it is a general purpose reference tool, one that you will be using often. A good practice is to alphabetically sort all of an object's derived classes. While the Bancroft system is not too big, some OOPs, such as Smalltalk, have object hierarchy listings that cover many pages. By sorting the data, you make it easier to find a particular class at a later time. Also, it is useful to list an object's public variables in parentheses after the object name, as these variables are often used by classes derived from that object. After all, that was the intent of making them public in the first case.

The addition of the class variable names should done after each class is implemented, as the exact names and organization of the variables are likely to be more stable than they are now, simply because variable names within running programs have a higher informational inertia than do the same elements in design specifications. There's nothing mysterious to this, it's simply a lot easier to change a name in a design than it is in a working program.

Figure 6-1 on the next page shows the class hierarchy for the Bancroft system. This is supposed to be a complete hierarchy and; therefore, it does contain some classes that you have not yet encountered. Fear not, they shall soon rear their ugly heads.

Figure 6-1: Class Hierarchy

```
Object
├──── AuxilliaryEmployeeData
├──── Address
│              ├──── DomesticAddress
│              └──── ForeignAddress
├──── Collection
│              ├──── OrderedCollection
│              └──── IndexedCollection
├──── EmployeeBenefits
├──── EmployeeJobClass
├──── EmployeeSalary
│              ├──── HourlyEmployeeSalary
│              └──── FixedEmployeeSalary
├──── EmployeeTaxInfo
├──── Entity
│              ├──── Customer
│              ├──── Supplier
│              └──── Employee
├──── InventoryItem
├──── InventoryPrice
├──── MailingHistory
├──── SupplierInventory
└──── Transactions
               ├──── PurchaseTransaction
               └──── SaleTransaction
```

Object Dependencies

The next diagram(s) show object dependencies within the system. These dependencies arise when one object uses another, indicated by the fact that the dependent object references the object it depends on in one of its elements. For example, if object A contains an element, e, which is used to hold a reference to another object, B, then there is a dependency between the objects A and B, via the element e. Specifically, object A is dependent on object B, through element e. This is exactly what Figure 6-2 illustrates.

Figure 6-2: Single Object Dependency

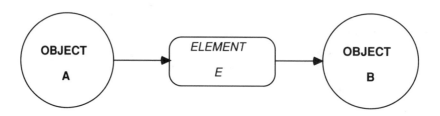

These diagrams illustrate individual object dependencies; therefore, one needs to be produced for every object defined in the system. Although certain objects contain only standard C data types and have no dependencies, they too must be graphed. The set of graphs must be complete so that it can be used to check on the elements of any object and what these elements reference. Also, there are those elements that may reference one of several objects, depending on the state of the program at the time. Returning to the previous example, we know that element e contains a reference to object B. If we complicate the issue by stating that element e may instead reference object C at certain times, then the resulting graph would look like Figure 6-3.

As you can see, all that has changed is that element e has two outbound connections now, one to object B and one to object C. The purpose of these drawings is not to show a particular configuration of references, it is to show all possible references that can be made. The drawings operate on the assumption that while the system is running, the element is referencing one of the objects to which it has been connected. Although it isn't illustrated here, it is not a bad idea to put the conditions that direct the reference to either object B or C at each of the lines that connect element e to these two objects.

Figure 6-3: Multiple Object Dependency

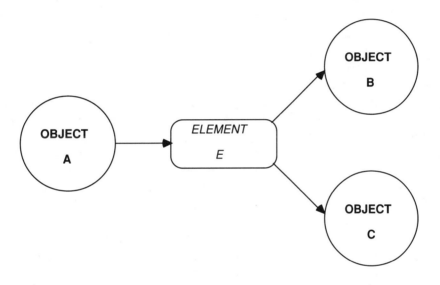

In the case of elements that reference standard C data structures or elements, some description of this still needs to be provided. Replacing the circle around the referenced object with a square around the referenced data item is an easy way to show these references.

Message Flow

The final types of drawings illustrate message flow within the system. The objective is not to illustrate all of the message flow throughout the system, simply the primary messages that are exchanged between dependent objects. This will help in visualizing the way in which dependent objects interact to complete their assigned tasks so that you can detect weaknesses, and strengths, of the design. You will find that these messages are those that are clearly identifiable as unique to this particular application. For example, the message **amountOnHand** is not found in a wide variety of systems outside of inventory management tools. There are two kinds of message flow diagrams, those that show outbound message flow from objects to other objects and those that show inbound message flow to objects. This is a complementary relationship; the same messages occur in both sets of drawings—one showing from where the messages came and one showing where they are going.

Inbound Message Flow diagrams show how a specific object receives messages from other objects. This diagram is essentially a graph of a network with a star topology, representing an n to 1 relationship between the objects graphed. All data flow is from the outside to the inside units. The outside units are the objects actually sending the message and the single inside unit is the object receiving all of these messages. Each message goes through a label defining which element of the object was used to reference the target object, and then goes on to the target object itself. Figure 6-4, gives a simple example of an Inbound Message Flow diagram, where objects B and C each send a single message to object A.

Outbound Message Flow diagrams are the reverse of Inbound Message Flow diagrams, showing all of the messages sent by a specific object to other objects. Technically, they are graphs of networks with a star topology—with a 1 to n relationship between the graphed objects. All data flow is from the single inside unit to all of the outside units. In simple terms, these networks show the exact reverse of what the Inbound Message Flow diagrams show. Figure 6-5 shows the message flow from the object A to the objects B and C.

Summary

These drawings aren't meant to be a concrete form for documenting OOPs; however, the information that each drawing conveys is central to understanding the operation of an OOP. In combination with the fact that the

Figure 6-4: Inbound Message Flow

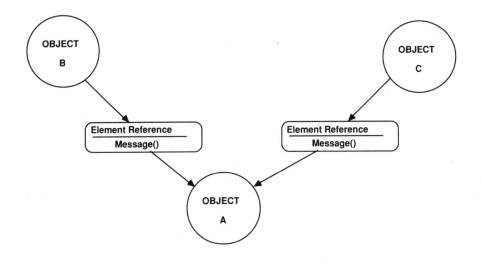

Figure 6-5: Outbound Message Flow

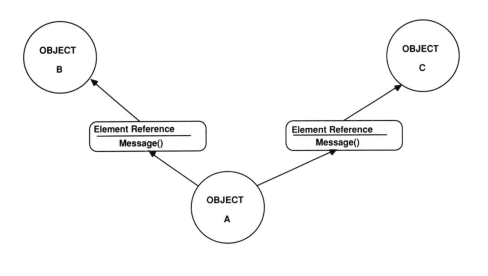

entire concept of a flowchart is meaningless in an OOP, some new form for graphically representing program structure must be used. The method described above is of my own concoction, but I find it has worked well on many projects. Interestingly enough, it has also worked well when applied to existing non-OO programs, but mainly in understanding some anomaly not reflected in the more standard documentation. There are as many ways to generate the object interconnection and message flow drawings as there are OOPs. The design is deliberately non-specific when it comes to such things as how many connections should you show within each drawing, and the physical layout of the drawings. The best rule of thumb is to ensure that the drawings are always comprehensible and usable. This would indicate that such things as drawings on 144" by 144" sheets are not a good idea, and putting 30 levels of message sends in a single drawing is an equally bad idea. My experience suggests the following metrics:

- Hierarchy—As shown above. Documentation of each of the classes can also be provided, indented immediately under the class name.

- Linkage—1 main object on the left side of the page, showing only the immediate links.

- Msgs In—1 Receiving object on the right, showing all the sending objects on the left.

- Msgs Out—1 Sending object on the left, showing the receiver objects on the right.

CHAPTER 7

SCOPE AND TYPING

You can't tell how deep a puddle is until you step in it.

This chapter gives details about the way in which objects are actually constructed by the compiler and the run-time system. It deals with two specific topics: the construction and referencing of objects and the differences between strong and weak typing in an OO programming system. This will help you see how many different frames of reference can come into play when dealing with real objects, whether they are created by an interactive language such as Smalltalk or by a compiled language such as C++. This is related to the issue of scope, which declares what information is, and is not, visible at any given time. The system's concept of typing comes into play because it so strongly affects how objects interact with each other. Essentially, the goal of a weakly typed system is to make the scope of all information as general as possible, whereas the goal of a strongly typed system is to make the scope as specific as possible.

Scope

Consider the case of object classes Class_A, Class_B, and Class_C, where these objects are related in the hierarchy:

- Class_A
- Class_B
- Class_C

This shows that Class_A is the base class of the hierarchy, Class_B is derived from Class_A, and Class_C is derived from Class_B. If we extend this to say that each of these classes includes a single variable, it gives us:

- Class_A
- Variable_A
- Class_B
- Variable_B
- Class_C
- Variable_C

There are some important relationships between these three class definitions that you must remember when dealing with instances of them. These relationships arise from the relationship between the definition for any object you are physically creating or instantiating, and the definitions of all of the classes in its hierarchy.

When we design and implement objects in an OOL, we always appear to be dealing with the definition of an object in terms of a single class. In many cases, the classes that we implement are interrelated; that is, several classes may share the same base class. When an OO design is completed, the entire set of classes can be grouped together as a tree by using the hierarchal relationships between base types and their derived types, as illustrated by the class hierarchy diagram in the last chapter.

The true definition of any object is given, not only by the immediate class of the object, but also by the definition of all of its base classes until the root of the hierarchy is reached. For example, if we were to create an instance of Class_C, the actual instance structure created by the system would be an instantiation of Class_A with an instantiation of Class_B appended to it, and an instantiation of Class_C appended to that. In this case, the object representing an instance of Class_C actually represents three distinct classes, with Class_C being its root context, Class_A being its final context, and Class_B providing a single interim context. Figure 7-1 shows the physical structure of that object.

Figure 7-1: Instantiation of Class_C Object

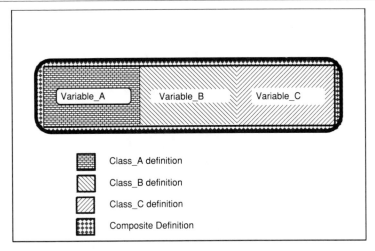

The instantiation of an object is meant to create an instance of an existing object and not an entirely new class. This means it cannot simply merge the definitions of these three classes together and let you treat the three variables as if they were defined in Class_C all along. The definition of Class_C clearly states that it contains a single variable, *Variable_C*. Nowhere does the definition of Class_C mention the variables *Variable_A* and *Variable_B*, even though they are physically present in an instantiation of Class_C. If the system simply were to consolidate the definitions of Class_A and Class_B into that of Class_C, then it would require that Class_C contain all of the code that Class_A and Class_B contain. After all, it would have to do their jobs as well as its own.

Scope, or context, is an extremely important issue in OOLs, more so than in languages such as C. C has very simple scoping rules, such as the fact that you cannot refer to the automatic variable of a function outside of the function in which it is defined. For example, if there was the function **foo()**, such that:

```
void foo(void) {                                    // a variable in the

int fooVariable;                                    //SCOPE of foo

<some code>
```

it would be impossible for the function **bar()** to access this variable. If we were to try this, as in:

```
bar(void) {
    fooVariable++;
}
```

the compiler would balk at our attempt to increment the *fooVariable*.

Scope is critical and much more complex when we deal with objects. Returning to the previous picture of the instantiation of a Class_C object, you can see how the object contains physical storage for the variables that were explicitly defined in Class_C and all of the classes it is related to by derivation. As stated earlier, an OOL differentiates between the variables defined in each level of the hierarchy. This means that although we know that an instance of Class_C contains storage for each of the variables in the classes from which it was derived, we have no idea how to directly access this information. If we have an instance of Class_C, then the only variable we can get at is the variable *Variable_C*. Although we know *Variable_A* and *Variable_B* are contained in the object somewhere, we cannot access them directly. Since we have created a new object of Class_C, the OOL assumes that we are dealing with this new object in the scope of Class_C, because that's what we explicitly stated it was when we created it. If we want to access the other variables, those declared in the hierarchy of base classes for Class_C, we must first explicitly state that we are changing our scope to one of these base classes.

To help in visualizing this, think of an object as a living organism. The entire class hierarchy of that object forms the genetic code of that object. If we had a very large computer, we could define a class hierarchy that was based on the entire evolutionary history of the planet, from primitive one celled organisms all the way down to every form of life that currently exists. The root context of this object's hierarchy would give some organism that was the first step in the evolution of all life forms. A final or terminal context would be the Homo Sapiens class description. Between the base class representing the single celled organism and the final derived class representing Homo Sapiens are many intermediate classes that represent the evolutionary history of human beings, from small mammals on through the ape family. The Homo Sapiens class is a composite of all the phases involved in the evolution of human beings. Not only does the instance of Homo Sapiens contain all of the data specifically related to the Homo Sapiens class (e.g., we have a highly developed brain), it also contains the common data from monkeys, small mammals, and every other entity in our evolutional tree, all the way back to the one celled organism that started everything off: the fact that our body chemistry is based on carbon.

This point is critical to understanding some of the steps we will be taking when we begin to write the Bancroft system. When we deal with an instance of any object, we will not always be dealing with that object at its most specialized level or in its terminal context. Sometimes we will wish to deal with it as if it were no different than any other object in the system. In other words, if we dealt with the consumption of ice cream in terms of the class hierarchy:

Ice Cream
Vanilla
Toffee Crunch

There are times when we wish to eat only Toffee Crunch. And then there are times when we are hungrier and any kind of Vanilla ice cream will do. And finally, there are those times when any kind of ice cream at all will do.

Strong vs. Weak Typing

As stated in the introduction, this is primarily a book about object oriented design and secondly a book about C++. For this reason, some of the decisions we have made conflict with the way that C++ normally operates.

C++ is a strongly typed language, where the exact type of each and every object is explicitly stated in the source code of the program. Many OO languages, such as Smalltalk and Common Lisp Object System (CLOS) are weakly typed languages, where less emphasis is placed on the specific typing of objects at compile time. Instead, these systems depend on the fact that everything is an object and all objects are capable of typing themselves at run-time. For example, in Smalltalk, any object is capable of responding to the class message. When an object receives this message, it will return its class identification to the object that sent the message. If a similar capability was available in standard C, you might be able to determine the type of an arbitrary pointer by executing:

```
whatTypeAreYou(void *).
```

This function would return **int** or **char** or the name of some other type defined by the compiler or a typedef within the source code.

C++ has no built in capability to provide run-time type checking, which is what we must have in order to implement our collection classes. Recall that we have stated in the design of the collection class that a collection is heterogeneous, meaning that it can hold any collection of arbitrary objects, regardless of the type(s) of any of these objects. If we are to use these collections; however, we must have some mechanism for checking the types of objects at run-time, as what we do with individual objects within the collection will most likely depend on what kinds of objects they are.

Our biggest problem is the assumption that type information is only needed at compile time, so that the compiler can ensure that the source code is not trying to do things like copying a ForeignAddress object into a Supplier object. The C++ compiler will check the types of the objects on which we are operating to ensure that any such operation is greeted with an error message. However, C++ will also assume that if the source code does not explicitly attempt operations such as this, then everything is OK, and there isn't any need to keep the type information around.

In strongly typed languages, this is meant to improve the reliability of the produced code, as the compiler can help prevent the programmer from performing actions that would be detrimental to the running system, such as trying to assign a 500 byte structure into an integer value. This capability implies that the compiler is based on a strong typing model, where it expects you to be clear about the type of each variable you are using. On the other hand, many OOLs are built primarily on the concept of weak typing. This means that the system does not check carefully the types of data used in a program, instead it depends on the running system to detect problems that arise from type conflicts. In other words, the compiler would allow you to attempt to assign a 500 byte structure to an integer value, as it assumes that if this operation can't be performed, the run-time system will prevent it in some fashion. This ability of the run-time system to prevent mismatches between data is what allows an OOL to support a weakly typed model.

The relative advantages of strong typing and weak typing are still subject to a great deal of argument in the OOP community. It is unlikely that either of these forms will defeat the other, as they each have complimentary strengths and weaknesses. Weak typing leads to very flexible systems that are easily extended; however, weak typing leads to sloppy coding practices. It also leads to programs whose total behavior is difficult to validate because so much is dependent on the run-time system and so little help is received from the compiler. Strong typing produces programs where the compiler has done a great deal of work to verify that all of the individual operations are legal. It produces a system where all code operates on clearly defined types of data. Strong typing also produces programs that are more difficult to modify, because they are less flexible.

Speed is also an issue, as weak typing requires much of the system be supported by a run-time environment, which takes a percentage of the computer's time to support. Strong typing systems do not introduce this overhead to such a degree because most of these issues are resolved at compile time. This book is based on the weak typing model. The reason for this is OO programs implemented in strongly typed systems such as C++ form a subset of the kinds of programs that can be produced in a weakly typed OO system, as far as the design essentials go. The approach we are using is to design a program for use in a OO environment based on weak typing. Once the developed system is debugged, it can be moved to an environment where strong typing is used by discarding some of the capabilities found in a pure OO environment and replacing them with hardwired logic.

Moving from a pure OOL such as Smalltalk to a strongly typed OOL such as C++, is primarily a process of limiting the behavior of the existing Smalltalk program. Moving from a C++ program to a Smalltalk program; however, could involve a total restructuring of the program logic. In this book, moving from the weakly typed programming model we will be using, to the more natural C++ strongly typed model is also a process of limiting the program's options at various points, rather than any kind of logical redesign. In many cases, after the program has been debugged and standardized, there isn't so much need for the flexibility of a weakly typed design anyway. Conversely, using a strongly typed design while the program is being constructed can often lead to arbitrary limitations and restrictions that would not be encountered if a weakly typed design had been used.

For this reason, this book is based on a style of OO design usually encountered in OO systems such as Smalltalk and CLOS. After the program has stabilized, much of this environmental framework can be removed, which converts the system from a weakly typed model to a strongly typed model.

CHAPTER 8

OBJECT CLASS

The fault lies not with our technologies but with our systems.

In the Strategy section, I laid out a rosy view of Object Oriented Programming and now is the time to put that view to the test. In the coming Tactics section we will use the C++ programming language, specifically the Zortech C++ version, to implement the design produced in the Strategy section. We are going to take a rational approach, even if we are writing code now.

We are still going to put off the actual act of writing code until the last possible moment, at least as far as large, complex functions are concerned. The fact that cut-and-paste editors are used in many of today's OOP environments is no coincidence, it is a result of the design and coding process. Why write something from scratch, when a few changes to something you've written will do exactly the same thing and with much less effort? OOP is a very modular design paradigm, meaning that code is written and used in very small pieces. OOP programs don't consist of five large functions doing all the work, they consist of several hundred tiny functions, each doing a very specialized job. It could be said that OOP programs accomplish their tasks through huge teams of morons, rather than through small squads of geniuses.

In this chapter, we are going to define the Object class, something that was not even mentioned earlier. The Object class is the root of the entire class hierarchy, the class from which all other classes are derived. In all future classes that we implement, there will be a path through the hierarchy that starts with the derived class, moves up through more general levels of the hierarchy, and eventually terminates in the Object class itself. The Object class was not discussed in the Strategy section because it is really a basic component of a pure OOP environment that is based on weak typing. In order to use weak typing with any margin of safety, the system must be able to assume that everything it encounters is either an instance of the Object class itself, or an instance of some derivation of the Object class. The Object class serves as the common root of all classes implemented in such a system, providing the capabilities expected of any object in the system, regardless of its specific purpose. The Object class is a critical component of our design, because it the foundation upon which our design method rests.

Basic Terminology

Before leaping into the actual Object class definition, some basic groundwork concerning the syntax and structure of class definitions needs to be covered. I will discuss aspects that I feel are particularly important; however, this does not mean you shouldn't have another book on C++ available to you, as this book does not pretend to be a programming reference on C++.

Classes are built from **member functions** and **member variables**, both of which are tied quite closely to a particular class by the compiler. A member variable or function is only accessible within the context of the class with which it was associated. This means that you can't arbitrarily decide to call a member function of a particular class or to alter the contents of a member variable, if you don't give the compiler a very good idea about the exact instance of which class you want to access or to alter. Essentially, the terms member function and member variable or element simply mean that these functions or elements are the components of a specific class, or hierarchy of classes in the case of inherited members.

Before you actually code any member functions, you must define the class data elements and the function prototypes for the functions you wish to implement for the class. We will be doing this in the next several chapters, and you should see how, after the class definitions have been coded carefully, writing the actual functions becomes somewhat of a (pleasant) anti-climax.

To define a new class to the compiler, you create a text file that contains a class definition. While you can merge a herd of class definitions into a single file, it isn't advised. Classes are the basic informational unit with which you are dealing, and it's much easier when your filenames reflect this. With C++, you will usually have two files for each class you have implemented, one containing the definition of the class, and one containing the code for the member functions of the class. There isn't anything illegal about merging several different class definitions into a file, it just means you are going to do a lot more searching. And remember, if you decide you want to use one of these great classes you built in your next program, you'll have to go into your herd file, rope the definition and possibly the member functions, and move it to a new herd. If you hadn't herded them all together, you could have just included the class files you wanted.

In order to understand the definitions of classes in C++, consider two different definitions of the class myClass. The outside of the definition comes in two flavors, the first being:

```
class myClass {
    // .
    // .
    // .
    // body of myClass
    // .
    // .
    // .
}
```

The second being:

```
class myClass: public MyBaseClass {
```

```
    // .
    // .
    // .
    // body of myClass
    // .
    // .
    // .
}
```

The difference between the two definitions is that the second definition has the sequence **public myBaseClass** following the name of the class. This is because the second definition is for a **derived** class, specifically, *myClass is derived from myBaseClass*, and the first definition means that myClass is a base class, *from the compiler's point of view*. This final caveat is important, because one class' derived class can be another's base class. For example, if the following class definitions were encountered:

```
class A {
    // blah blah blah
}


class B: public A {
    // blah blah blah
}


class C: public B {
    // blah blah blah
}
```

we can clearly see that A is a **base** class, and that C is a **derived** class. But what kind of class is B? From C's point of view it's a base class, from A's point of view it's a derived class. In any case, the first definition style given above is only used when the class is the top hierarchal class, meaning that nobody thinks it's a derived class. In this book, the only class defined in such a fashion is the Object class itself.

Descending into the bowels of a class definition, you will find it contains a collection of variable declarations and function prototypes, such as:

```
class myClass {
    int myInt;
    char *myString;
    int myFunctionProtoType(int);
}
```

If you look at the class as a structure, then the variable definitions are the elements of the structure. The function prototypes are something you may not have encountered yet, as they are a fairly recent addition to C. Essentially a function prototype gives all the pertinent information about the interface to the function, but doesn't say too much about the actual code it contains. If you start with the function declarations you have seen in older versions of C, for example:

```
char *malloc();
```

a function prototype is an extension of this that also provides **typing information** on the parameters passed to the function. The function prototype for malloc would then be:

```
void *malloc(unsigned int);
```

This represents the appearance of **type checking** in C++, something you can easily subvert by using **void** * with wild abandon, but I would only advise doing this in cases where it is *truly* justified.

Given that we have defined a class, how do we access its members? The mechanism for doing this comes in two forms, the first very similar to the standard structure member accesses you have encountered in C. If you have a variable of type *myClass* defined, through a statement such as:

```
myClass myInstanceOfMyClass;
```

then you can refer to the member elements and functions like this:

```
anyInteger = myInstanceOfMyClass.myInt;

anyString = myInstanceOfMyClass.myString;

anyInteger = myInstanceOfMyClass.myFunction(15);
```

Notice that while the first two statements are accessing variables within myClass, the third statement is actually calling a member function of myClass, the **myFunction()** function. The reason you must use this syntax to call member functions within a class is that the compiler deals with each object as a **closed universe**, meaning you can have many different object definitions, each containing a myFunction() function, and each of these functions performing a unique task. The only way that the compiler can tell exactly which function you are talking about is to treat the function like an element of a structure, specifically an element of a structure that represents a myClass object. In the Strategy section we said objects were manifestations of **intelligent data**, meaning that they carried both raw information, in standard structure variables, and the functions that know how to operate on this data. Think about this for a bit and you'll see that it makes perfect sense to consider the functions themselves as elements of the classes structure. From an OOP's point of view, the only difference is that some data can be executed (functions) and some cannot (variables).

The next item of interest is the **public** keyword that can be placed at any point within a class definition. C++ assumes that until it sees this keyword, nobody except the member functions of a class has access to any of the defined variables or functions. Given the definition of the variable *myInstanceOfMyClass*, at some point in our program, the placement of the public keyword would control exactly what components, both variables and functions, we are allowed to access. In the last example of myClass, since public does not appear at all, we would be unable to use anything within the class, meaning that the last three examples are technically illegal because there is no public access allowed to the elements of myClass. If we tried, the compiler would print nasty errors about an unauthorized function's attempt to access the class' private parts. Let's modify the definition of myClass to :

```
class myClass {
    int myInt;
    char *myString;
public:
    int myFunctionProtoType(int);
}
```

The compiler then would allow us to use the class function via the statement:

```
int result;
result = myInstanceOfMyClass.myFunctionProtoType(15);
```

However, we still would not be allowed to access either of the member variables. If we were to move the private statement immediately underneath the class line, then the compiler would allow us to modify the variables in addition to allowing us to call the member function.

What private provides us with is a means for segregating the dangerous data within a class and restricting access to it. For example, if we have the definition:

```
class ListManager {
    int numberOfElements;
public:
    // blah blah blah
}
```

where the *numberOfElements* variable is used to control the memory usage within the list manager, we certainly don't want to give everyone global access to this value, because they are most certainly going to harm it and crash the software. This is what **private** class elements provide, a means for putting a "No Trespassing" sign on dangerous data and functions. There is another benefit to this, that becomes clear during debugging. If the numberOfElements field does end up with trash in it, you have a very good idea as to which section of code misbehaved, as there can be only one guilty party, (unless you have simply written over a large chunk of your program's memory).

The Object Class

The first class actually to be implemented for the Bancroft system wasn't even discussed in the design. This class, the Object class, is the root of all other classes we will define in the Bancroft application. It is the only real base class we will implement.

Why are we implementing an Object class? The C++ language supports OO design, but it isn't a pure OOL, therefore it doesn't contain one of the more important elements of a pure OOL, specifically a class library where all classes form a single tree derived from a common root. The class library is a large collection of standard classes that implement standard programming **units** which you can use as building blocks to create your own program. Examples of these kinds of building blocks are:

- Collections, such as indexed lists, dictionaries, and arrays .

- Magnitudes, which are extensions to the numeric environment. These can be such things as dates, fractions, and alternate numeric representations.

- Graphics elements such as points, lines, and rectangles.

Languages as disparate as Smalltalk and Objective-C both implement this standard class library, their only real difference being in the choice of names and the larger scope of Smalltalk's class library. In any case, C++ does not implement a class library at all, leaving it up to the individual developers to do so.

We need to have an Object class because there are going to be questions we wish to ask of any object within the system. These might be requests for the exact class of that object, information normally discarded by the compiler after it has finished converting the code. Also, we will want to know when any given object is being referenced, or used, by another object so that we don't free the object's storage at an inappropriate time. These types of capabilities are necessary in order to implement systems based on weak typing. When the system is finished, many of these mechanisms can be discarded, trading the flexibility of weak typing for the higher execution speed and code control of a strongly typed program.

OO design can often be used to create very powerful systems with a minimum of work, especially when weak typing is used. The use of weak typing does require that *all* elements within the system be a specialized version of some common type. To understand this, consider if C++ had a class **Number** and all of the familiar C numeric types such as **int** and **double** were derived from this class. This would mean that we could begin implementing Number functions that would operate effectively on integers and floating point values, instead of requiring that we write separate functions to operate on them. If we extend this idea to say everything in the system is an object, even blocks of code, then we could use weak typing easily. The reason for this is fairly simple. If all elements that the system encounters in the course of its operation are objects, and all objects the system encounters are capable of identifying themselves, then the run-time system can handle all of the type sensitive tests. This means that the compiler does not have to establish the type of any given data element, it can simply assume that every data element is some kind of Object element. C++ does perform strong type checking, and not everything a C++ program encounters is an object. If an Object class is implemented to construct a large unified hierarchy of classes and the Object class provides mechanisms to identify an instance of any of their classes at run-time, we can approach the goal of being a weakly typed OOL. At the same time, when there are any time or hardware contstraints, issues involving the use of data structures must be addressed.

We could elect not to implement the Object class, but this would have an immediate and expensive cost. If we don't put these common capabilities in the Object class, then we will have to duplicate them in every single class we implement in order to achieve the same effect. In duplicating these functions across all of our classes, we are running a risk of making a mistake someplace and leaving ourselves with a lot of functions to debug when we make that mistake. This is what OOP is meant to prevent, as functions are packaged within objects, and then are shared with all the other objects that need them, either through inheritance or by directly sharing instances of objects.

In addressing the design issues, we know that the object class will need to keep information on how many objects are referencing it (actually they are usually referencing an instance of one of its subclasses), what its exact subclass is, and flags that we'll probably need at some time or another. This tells us that the object has three fields:

- flags: An integer with bits to fiddle.
- referenceCount: An integer telling how many users of this object there are.
- subClass: An integer telling the exact class.

By examining these variables and our plans for them, we can begin to determine what functions the object should implement. First, it must provide a mechanism to increment and decrement the reference count; secondly, it must provide functions to set, clear, and test the flag bits; and finally, it must provide a means for retrieving the subclass code. Our functions; therefore, should be defined as:

TYPE	MESSAGE NAME	DESCRIPTION
PUBLIC	incReference()	Increment the reference count.
PUBLIC	decReference()	Decrement and return reference count.
PUBLIC	setFlag(bitNum)	Set the bit.
PUBLIC	clrFlag(bitNum)	Clear the bit.
PUBLIC	tstFlag(bitNum)	Return the bit's value.

One issue of importance is the exact mechanism by which we define the identity of the subclass. C++ is not going to help us much here, we are going to have to do this dirty job ourselves, specifically by ensuring that the run-time system can use some common mechanism to identify the exact type of any object. To accomplish this, we have two choices. First, we can couple in a type element to the object class itself and initialize this type value every time we create a new object. This mechanism, however, is extremely inefficient and somewhat messy. Instead, we can make every new class we create implement the **subclass()** function, a function that simply returns a constant value representing that class to the run-time system. System classes will start out with the constant type index -1, assigned to the Object class, and will count down for the new system classes as they are defined. The application specific classes will start with the index 1, and will count up for each of the application classes as they are defined. This means we can move the system class definitions from one project to another, constantly building on our system class library, making all the system classes implemented for one project available to the next project. One final detail is the actual name we are going to use for the Object class. To avoid offending various compilers that may feel they have a proprietary interest in the word "object," we are actually going to call this the **GenericObject** class. This is simply to ensure that if we move to a C++ compiler that implements the "object" keyword we don't end up with our system in the bit bucket. Here is the real definition of the GenericObject class, as it would be given to a C++ compiler:

```
class GenericObject                    // the root of all our objects

{

    int flags;                         // control flags

    int referenceCount;     //# of objects referencing this object public:
                                       // constructor
GenericObject()                        // initialize the object

{

    flags = 0;                         // zap the flags

    referenceCount = 1;                // referenced by myself

};                                     // destructor

~GenericObject()                       // destroy the object

{

    if(referenceCount > 1 || referenceCount  < 0)
                                       // serious problem
```

```
        systemCrash();                          // go to a fatal error handler
    };                                          // reference control
    void incReference()                         // increment the reference count
    {
        ++referenceCount;
    };
    int decReference()            // decrement and return the reference count
    {
        if(referenceCount  < 0)                 // serious problem
            systemCrash();                      // go to a fatal error handler
        return(--referenceCount);
    };                                          // flag control
    void setFlag(int bitNo)                     // set given bit
    {
        flags |= (int) pow((double) bitNo,(double) 2);
    };
    void clrFlag(int bitNo)                     // clear given bit
    {
    flags &= ~((int) pow((double) bitNo,(double) 2));
    };
    int tstFlag(int bitNo)                      // test given bit
    {
        return((flags & (int) pow((double) bitNo,(double) 2)) ? 1
  : 0);
    };                          // subclass control virtual int subclass()
```

```
int Subclass ()                    // return the subclass code for this object

{

    return(-1);

};
```

As you can see, the two data elements are defined before the **public:** keyword is given, meaning that only the GenericObject member functions can access the values contained in these elements. Following the public: keyword are the constructor and destructor functions that are usually implemented for every class in C++. Following those functions are the functions we originally defined to implement reference counting: **flag control** and **subclass control**. In this particular file, we have placed the code for the member functions **inline** with the class definition. This means that instead of providing only the function prototype, and using another file to provide the function's code body, you provide the code in the class file. For example, you've seen the inline definition of the tstFlag() function. If you weren't going to define this function as an inline function, then you would have the following in the class file:

```
int tstFlag(int);
```

The **implementation file** would have this:

```
int GenericObject::tstFlag(int bitNo)              // test given bit

{
return((flags & (int) pow((double) bitNo,(double) 2)) ? 1
: 0);

};
```

The definition given in the implementation file requires that the tstFlag function name be prefaced with **GenericObject::** so that the compiler can determine exactly for which class you are defining this function. The reason this leading class name wasn't required in the class definition file is because the compiler was already assembling the class definition and; therefore, it knew in what class the functions belonged.

You should only do this for short functions. Longer functions should be defined in an implementation file, so that the class definition does not get lost in large chunks of C++ code. The intent behind inline functions is twofold. First, it allows you easily to create simple functions, without having to alter two separate files. Secondly, it allows some more sophisticated compilers to actually replace calls on this function with the code that implements the function, which cuts down on the function calling overhead.

Constructors and Destructors

The constructor and destructor functions are special creatures within the C++ zoo. Constructor functions are called when objects are instantiated and are responsible for initializing the new instances variables, and allocating any required dynamic memory. Destructors are called when an object is about to be destroyed and are responsible for releasing any dynamically allocated memory and doing any other necessary cleanup. Due to the fact that constructors and destructors are so important, there must be a clear way for the compiler to tell what are constructors and what are destructors. In most conventional languages, this would be done by using keywords to indicate the appropriate functions.

Thanks to the function overloading capabilities of C++, a much simpler rule can be used. Any member function that has the *same name as the class it is a member of* is a **constructor** function. Likewise, any member function that has the *same name as its class and that is preceded by a tilde (~)* is a **destructor** function. In the GenericObject class; therefore, our constructor function is **GenericObject(int)** and our destructor function is **~GenericObject()**. The process that the system automatically goes through in order to execute the appropriate constructors for a derived class, involves the propagation of parameters from the derived class up through its hierarchy of base classes, followed by the execution of the constructor functions from the base class down the hierarchy to the derived class. All the parameters are distributed upwards to the more generalized object constructors, and then the constructors are invoked— first to build the base object, and then to perform a stepwise specialization of the object, resulting in a fully initialized derived class. What this means to you, the programmer, is that you can safely assume that when you are executing your own specialized code for a particular derived class' constructor function, all of your base classes have already been initialized. For the Bancroft system, the GenericObject constructor function is always executed first, whenever a class is defined. This function always receives a parameter from the derived class being instantiated and which gives the identification code for that class. It will place this code in the subclass field, it will set the **referenceCount** to 1—indicating the instance's implied reference to itself, and it will clear all of the flags. Destructors work in exactly the opposite way, first destroying the derived class, and then moving upwards through the base class hierarchy, destroying each of the bases in turn. This means that your destructor functions should concentrate on destroying the data and references unique to the derived class, leaving the destruction of the more general information to the classes which own that information.

The primary job of a destructor function is to release memory and objects that have been dynamically created and linked to the object being destroyed. The destructor functions are the primary users of the **dec-Reference()** function. They use it to determine if they should truly destroy the object in question. If the value returned by this function is zero, it means that there are no active references to the object and it may be safely destroyed. If the value is greater than one, the destructor should not destroy the object, as there are still objects using it. If the value is less than zero, then something has gone very wrong. The reason that a reference count is allowed to hold either a zero or a one value is as a convenience to the programmer. If the reference count is one, it's only counting this object's implied reference to itself. If it is zero, we make the assumption that the object has simply cleared its own self reference. The exact reasons for this will become clear when we get into multiple levels of derived classes. For now, the only important consideration is that the destructor functions cannot directly modify the reference count, because of the way that derived classes invoke all of their base class' hierarchy of destructor functions. The GenericObject destructor doesn't really have any chores to do, as there hasn't been any dynamic data linked to this class. However, it does check to ensure that the reference count is zero, calling a fatal error routine if this is not the case. This is because most of the object has already been destroyed at this time, even though the referenceCount indicates it shouldn't have been because it's still in use or it has already been destroyed.

Summary

In this chapter we discussed the basic syntax used to define classes in C++. We have covered the **class definition** or **class header file**, that contains the structural definition of the class, and touched on the **class implementation file** that contains the definitions for the larger **member functions** that were not placed inline in the class definition file. We then dealt with the GenericObject class, the root of our entire class hierarchy which will help us create a system that approaches a first class Object Oriented Language. The GenericObject class we constructed provides limited support for **reference counting** and, more importantly, provides us with the subclass function that allows us to determine the exact class of any object that we are referencing. This allows us to construct heterogeneous collections, containing many different classes of objects, and then to determine the exact class of any object in that collection. It also allows us to construct functions that may accept more than one class of object as an argument, and to select appropriate logic based on the class of the object the function actually receives.

Further Enhancements

Implement a GenericObject copy function. This function should accept two object pointers. Ensure that they are both references to the same object subclass, and then do a bitwise copy of the object from one object to another. To do this you will have to augment the list of Object Class IDs with a memory resident table giving the size of each object in bytes. If you succeed, you will never need to build a specialized copy initializer in any of your subclasses.

TACTICS

CHAPTER 9

SIMPLE SYSTEM CLASSES

The road to hell is paved with good intentions. And littered with sloppy analysis!

In this chapter we will discuss one of the two system classes needed in the Bancroft system, the Collection class. As we saw in the Strategy section, it is very important to maintain a clear separation between the system classes and the application classes in order to keep application details out of the system class. When this is successfully accomplished, the system classes can be used in your future work without first requiring that you unadapt them from the previous application model and adapt them again to the new application model.

The Collection class is a relatively unsophisticated beast used to maintain collections of data. The most important aspect of the Collection class is that it is heterogeneous, meaning you can stuff all sorts of different objects into a collection—you do not need to restrict collections to containing a single Object class. It can be used to hold any arbitrary collection of objects, including collections of collections. This class also forms the root of more sophisticated collection classes, such as the IndexedCollection we will implement in the next chapter and others, such as sorted collections, arrays, and matrices.

Collections are dynamically constructed objects, which means their contents are not defined at compile time. This is not to say you can't define what goes into a collection in your program, but only that the system actually builds the collection on the fly, so you aren't completely restricted to what the source code said was in the collection. Collections do not do any fancy indexing or sorting of their contents, as this is left for more specialized derivations of the Collection class, such as the Indexed-Collection class.

We therefore need to make a class that provides the necessary variables and functions to allow for the following:

- Creating the collection (Constructor functions)
- Destroying the collection (Destructor functions)
- Getting elements in the collection
- Changing elements in the collection
- Adding elements to the collection
- Deleting elements from the collection

The coming sections will deal with each of these requirements in turn, blending the work that was done in the strategy section with the actual requirements placed on us by C++.

Creating Collections

We know from our design work that the collection needs to have a member variable which contains the list of elements that have been placed into the collection, we will call the *variable*. From the requirement that the collection be heterogeneous, and from our knowledge of C++, we know that this must be a pointer to a list of pointers, and each pointer must be a **void** * pointer. This allows the user to cast it into whatever form they desire, without complaints from the compiler. The actual definition of the *elements* variable would be:

```
void  **elements;
```

This means that the variable is a pointer to a list of pointers to void, which means we have a list of pointers to untyped storage, as far as C++ is concerned.

Here is an important suggestion for when you are dealing with what one might put into a collection. Put only objects into a collection, especially if the collection is heterogeneous. If you put many types of objects into a collection, you can easily determine what object you are looking at by invoking the subclass() function. Subclass() will provide the exact type of the object at which you are looking. If you have mixed objects together with pointers to standard C base types in the same collection, the results of attempting to find the subclass of a non-object will be unpredictable, as the software is likely to jump to some random address when it tries to invoke the subclass() function. Although objects add some overhead to your program, it's only because they are doing a lot of useful work for you. If you must make a collection that doesn't contain objects, don't make it heterogeneous. The contortions you will have to go through to determine what exactly it is you have a pointer to is much too high a price to pay.

We also must deal with the fact that collections can change size during system execution, gaining new elements and possibly having those elements later removed. We should know two things about the element list; first, the number of elements that the list can physically contain and; second, the number of elements that it currently contains (this number will always be less than or equal to the capacity of the list). These variables would be defined as:

```
int currentCapacity;              // physical size of elements list

int numberOfElements;             // number of elements in the list now
```

We would assume that the following relation always holds true:

```
0 <= numberOfElements <= currentCapacity
```

Given the nature of the elements list, creating a collection requires at a minimum, the initialization of the two variables defining the current state of the elements list and the allocation of some amount of storage for the elements list. There are three foreseeable ways in which we might choose to instantiate a collection: by simply asking for a "standard" empty collection; by asking for an empty collection of a specified size; or, by asking for a collection to be created from a list of pointers that we just happen to have lying around. In accordance, there would be three constructor functions:

```
Collection()                    // make standard empty collection

Collection(int)                 // make empty collection of int size

Collection(void **,int)         // use int elems from list to make it
```

Assuming that a statement such as:

```
const int  collect_dflt_size = 100;          // std collect size
```

is found somewhere in our class definition, we could implement the first constructor function, **Collection()**, through these steps:

```
numberOfElements = 0;                                // nothing in it

currentCapacity       = collect_dflt_size;
elements = new char *[currentCapacity];
```

These steps would result in an empty collection with the capacity to hold **collect_dflt_size** objects. Note: *for the use of the keyword (new), you may want to reference Stroustrup for the exact usage. Basically, it is a replacement for malloc().*

For the second constructor, **Collection(int)**, we are going to do almost the same thing, but instead of using the **collect_dflt_size** value to determine the initial size of the collection, we will use the first integer value passed to the constructor as the default size. The only change to the steps for creating the standard sized collection would be in changing:

```
currentCapacity = collect_dflt_size
```

to:

```
currentCapacity = <the first integer argument>
```

As for the third collection, where a collection is constructed from a list of character pointers passed by the caller of the constructor, things will be a little different. The essence of this particular constructor would be:

```
numberOfElements = 0;                    // nothing in it

currentCapacity      = list size argument;

elements = new char *[currentCapacity];
//loop to copy the provided pointers into the elements array
```

.

.

.

One issue we have avoided discussing thus far is the fact that the Collection object is a derivative of the GenericObject class and therefore it also contains all of the GenericObject member variables, although it cannot access them. It is required that each of the three constructors we have outlined must call the GenericObject constructor prior to actually initializing the variables that are unique to the Collection class. When C++ creates a static or automatic object, it must call all of the constructors in that object's definition hierarchy. For instance, if you simply wanted a GenericObject, then the statement:

```
GenericObject myGenObj();
```

would create the instance **myGenObj** of a GenericObject with the reference counters correctly initialized. The following statement would be necessary to create an instance of a Collection object:

```
Collection myCollection();
```

The first job of a derived class' constructor function is to call the constructor function for its base class, so that all of the variables that it has inherited from its base class are correctly initialized. The following constructor function, used to create Collections with a default size, shows how this is done:

```
// make MT collection with COLLECT_DFLT_SIZE units
Collection()
{
    numberOfElements = 0;                        // nothing in it

    working = 0;                                 // working points at base

    currentCapacity = COLLECT_DFLT_SIZE;         // standard size

    elements = new char *[currentCapacity];      //allocate storage

};
```

Although you can't see them in this code, all constructor functions call the constructor function for their base class. This process continues recursively until the top class in the hierarchy is encountered, in this case the GenericObject class. In future code we will deal with constructor function calls you can see, because they require parameters to be supplied by the constructor function for their derived class. Here, since Collection is derived from the GenericObject class, the call is on the GenericObject constructor. But, borrowing an example from the next chapter on Indexed-Collections, a fragment of an IndexedCollection constructor would be:

```
IndexedCollection(int size) : (size)
```

This would result in the Collection class' constructor being called with a size parameter, *which in turn would result in the GenericObject classes constructor being called*. What is important to realize here is that these calls occur before the actual *local* constructor code is executed, therefore giving us this sequence of events when an IndexedCollection is created:

- IndexedCollection constructor starts.

- IndexedCollection constructor calls Collection constructor.

- Collection constructor starts.

- Collection constructor calls GenericObject constructor.

- GenericObject constructor executes its local code.

- Collection constructor executes its local code.

- IndexedCollection constructor executes its local code.

- The new IndexedCollection object is now completely initialized.

From this example, you can see how constructor calls pass up through the hierarchy to the final base class context, which is always the Generic-Object class in this book, and then move back down through the hierarchy executing each of the constructor bodies in turn. This shows that objects are built recursively, based on their class hierarchy. A more common example of this kind of operation is the standard factorial computation algorithm. By initializing an object in this fashion you can see how, at each level of initialization, the constructor function within that context can depend on the base classes already initialized. Using multiple inheritance, this process becomes even more complex as the search for constructors branches out to cover all of the base classes from which the current class inherits, but we shall leave the problems of multiple inheritance for some other time.

This finishes the rough definitions of the constructor functions for the Collection class. As you have seen, the Collection class constructors couple the static initializations that you saw in the GenericObject class with dynamic memory allocation of the collection element list itself.

Destroying Collections

Whereas most statically sized collections require a simple check to make sure that their imminent destruction is not some horrible mistake, the Collection class destructor must go further by actually releasing the storage that was allocated for the list. It is not responsible for deallocating the actual members of a collection, as these members might be in use someplace else, but it does need to release the storage for the element pointer list. This isn't too difficult, after checking the referenceCount to ensure the destruction is warranted, the following statement will do the job nicely:

```
delete[currentCapacity] elements;
```

It releases the memory used by the elements list for future use by some other object.

Accessing Collection Elements

A collection is a list of object pointers with no clear definition as to the ordering pattern of these pointers. This is not to say that a collection randomly reorders information it receives, only that it allows the user to treat the collection as an indexed array, not being directly concerned with why the user places data at some arbitrary location in the elements collection. The collection does need to have some idea as to where the user is working in the collection—this is mainly as a convenience to the user. For this reason, we will add another member variable to the Collection object class. The variable will be used to keep track of the current user selection within the collection, specifically:

```
int working;                          // current user selection
```

And where working is bound by the constraint:

```
0  <= working < numberOfElements
```

Given this definition of working, there are two functions that can be used to access members of the collection. They are:

```
char *selection() char *selection(int)
```

The first function returns the current element selected by *working* and the second function sets *working* to the passed value and returns that selection.

From here, we can define more sophisticated functions that resemble those used to move through sequential records in a database. These functions allow the user to move forward through the collection by one or more records and also to move to the first and last elements of the collections. These functions all treat the collection as a **closed loop**, meaning that if either end of the collection is encountered, the next element accessed will be the opposite end of the collection. The functions provided are as follows:

```
advance()                              // advance by one

advance(int)                           // advance by int

first()                                // go to the first element

last()                                 // go to the last element
```

Finally, given that we are doing most of this movement through the collection by using the *working* variable, it would be nice to get the current value of *working*. The following function will do that:

```
int current();                         // return value of working
```

Changing Elements in the Collection

To change elements within the collection we will provide a single service function defined as:

```
void changeItem(void *);
```

It will replace the existing pointer at the working index (*working*) within the collection, with the pointer that this function receives as a parameter.

Adding Elements to the Collection

Adding elements to a collection is slightly more complicated than getting them back out. Adding elements to a collection can be a simple operation, or it can be a somewhat complicated operation. The complexity arises from two specific issues, whether there is room in the collection to add the element, and whether we are adding the element to the middle of the collection, or tacking it onto the end. The second consideration comes from the fact that there are two ways to add to a collection:

```
int addItem(void *)          // add ptr to end and return index

int addItem(void *,int)      // add ptr at position int and return int
```

The first thing we need to know is if the collection can hold the element to be added. As long as **numberOfElements** is less than **current-Capacity**, we can add the element to the collection without worrying about running over the end of the elements list. This test for remaining capacity is so important that we will add a function to compute this on demand to the class. We will define it as:

```
int remainingCapacity();
```

So, the first question is, what if we don't have room in the collection to add the new element? Well, we could be user hostile and reject the request to add the element with some kind of cryptic message. Unfortunately, this would encourage users of the collection class to always construct gigantic collections to avoid this, and this leads to trouble. What we need is a mechanism to "grow" the size of the collection, making room for new elements to be added. The **grow** message would increase the size of a collection by some fixed amount. In fact, two versions of grow would be nice, the first growing the collection by some default size, and the second accepting an integer that tells it by how much to grow the collection.

```
void grow();              // grow collection using default parameters

void grow(int);           // grow collection by specified size
```

Now, grow would operate by taking the following steps:

- Add growth to old size to determine new size.

- Allocate storage for new sized array of pointers, calling a system error manager if the request for memory is denied.

- Copy the old pointer list into the bottom of the new pointer list, putting NULLs into all of the new unused pointers.

- Release the storage held by the old pointer list.

- Adjust currentCapacity to reflect the new collection size.

What the grow function has just done is to take advantage of the **encapsulation** provided in all OOP systems. Since an object can be viewed as a closed system, you can make a lot of changes to the internal organization of an object, and you don't need to worry about telling everybody who uses it of these changes. Remember, everybody else just uses the collections, they don't try to tell them how to do their jobs.

We have now defined the first step of the process of adding new elements. Before we actually attempt to add an element, we must see if the collection can hold the new element and if it can't, we call the **grow()** function to get the collection to increase its size.

Now that we have a collection that we know can contain the new element, our next question is whether we are adding the object to the end of the collection, or into the interior of the collection. The first case is quite simple, the second is complicated. When we add an object to the end of a collection, we simply place the new object pointer we have been given at the last position in the collection and increase the numberOfElements by one. When we are adding an object to the interior of a collection, we must first move the element currently occupying that particular index out of the way by shifting all of the pointers in the collection forward one unit from that point. After this is done, the index we want to use can be loaded with the new object pointer without losing the one that was originally there. This particular function which shifts collection elements forward, is very dangerous. As if the collection does not have enough room, it will consistently place the last element of the collection into electronic wonderland, most likely making the system behave bizarrely. This function will be declared as a private member function of the Collection class, so that only member functions of the Collection class can access it:

```
void xpand(int)          // shift collection fwd from position int
```

This is an excellent solution because the add functions are the only ones that truly need to use this function. We do not expect users of a collection to directly handle all of the resizing and moving that needs to be done in order to add elements to a collection, since they might make a mistake.

Deleting Elements from the Collection

There are two specific kinds of deletions that can be done in a collection. First, the deletion of the current working element and second, the deletion of an arbitrary element. These cases are embodied by the following two functions:

```
void deleteItem()                          // delete working selection

void deleteItem(int)                       // delete indexed selection
```

In either case, the delete operation is fairly straightforward, first checking to ensure that the item to be deleted is already in the collection, and then deleting it. The actual means by which the item is deleted depends on whether the item is the last element in the collection. If it is, the pointer to that item can simply be overwritten with a NULL pointer, and the numberOfElements can be decreased by one. However, if the item to be removed is not the last element within the collection, then there is a more complicated procedure to go through. When we delete an item from the interior of the collection, we must move all of the items above it down by one, and then overwrite the last object in the collection with a NULL pointer. Essentially this is the inverse of the **xpand()** function, and is equally as dangerous. It is also suitable for being made a private function:

```
void krunch(int);                   // shift collection down over int
```

We can make this function private for the same reason that the xpand() function was made private, namely that it is a function that supports another publicly available function, in this case, **krunch()** supports the publicly available **deleteItem()** functions.

Writing the Collection Class Header

Now that we have finished detailing the various responsibilities of the collection class, and the means by which it will meet these responsibilities, it is time to group all of these facets together into the class definition.

This class definition is similar to the one presented for the GenericObject class, as it defines the variables contained within the class, and the simpler member functions of that class:

```
const int collect_dflt_size = 100;
class Collection: public GenericObject {
    void **elements;        // a list of pointers to the collection elements

    int numberOfElements;
                            // count of the number of elements in the collection

    int currentCapacity;
                            // current number of elements the list can contain

    int working;            // current working position in collection
                                                               // grow

    void grow();            // increase capacity by default amount

    void grow(int);         // increase capacity by specified amount
                                   // compaction and expansion

    void krush(int);
                    // pack collection by shifting down one starting at int
    void xpand(int);        // expand the collection by shifting up at int
public:
//constructors
// make MT collection with collect_dflt_size units
Collection()
{
    numberOfElements = 0;                           // nothing in it

    working = 0;                             // working points at base

    currentCapacity = collect_dflt_size;        // standard size

    elements = new char *[currentCapacity]; // allocate storage
```

```
};
// make empty collection with n units
Collection(int cSize)
{
    numberOfElements = 0;                              // nothing in it
    working = 0;                                // working points at base
    currentCapacity = cSize;                          // standard size
    elements = new char *[currentCapacity];   // allocate storage
};
// make collection from int elements in supplied list
Collection(void **elementList,int cSize);
virtual ~Collection();                      // DESTROY the collection
                                            // subclass information
virtual int subClass()
{
    return(collection_classID);
};
                                                       // size queries
int numberOfElements()          // number of elements in the collection
{
    return(numberOfElements);
};
int capacity()              // number of elements the collection can hold
{
    return(currentCapacity);
};
int remainingCapacity()
```

// number of elements that can be added before next grow

```
{
    return(currentCapacity - numberOfElements);
};
```

// element access

```
virtual void *selection()
{
```

// return selection indexed by working

```
    return(elements[working]);
};
virtual void *selection(int newWork)
{
```

// set working to int and return that selection

```
    if(newWork >= numberOfElements)
        newWork = numberOfElements - 1;
    if(newWork < 0)
        systemCrash();                          // really bad reference

    working = newWork;
    return(elements[working]);
};                                              // working pointer adjustment
virtual void advance()
{
```

// move to next element , wrap around at end

```
    if(++working >= numberOfElements)
    working = 0;
};
virtual void advance(int advAmt)
{
```

```
// advance by specified amount
    working = (working + advAmt) % numberOfElements;
};
virtual void first()
{
// move to first element
    working = 0;
};
virtual void last()
{
// move to last element
    working = numberOfElements - 1;
};
virtual int current()

{
// return the value of working
    return(working);
};
// adding data to the collection
// add this pointer to the end
virtual int addItem(void *);
virtual int addItem(void *,int);
// add this pointer after the specified index
// deleting from the collection
virtual void deleteItem();
// delete working element from collection
// delete the indexed element
virtual void deleteItem(int);
```

Virtual Functions

One of the noticeable differences here is the rather heavy use of the keyword **virtual** that precedes many of the function prototypes and definitions. The virtual keyword supports the inheritance capabilities of C++ and is a cue to the compiler and the linker that this function may be redefined in classes that are derived from this class. I once again offer as an example the case of the IndexedCollection class that is derived from the Collection class. The IndexedCollection, like the Collection, must support many of the same functions, such as **addItem** and **deleteItem**. These functions behave quite differently in the case of the IndexedCollection, as they must also manage updates to the collection index and to the collection data itself. We must tell the compiler that we intend on using many different forms of the same function, depending on exactly with what class of object we are dealing.

What "virtual" means to the compiler and linker is that it should search upwards through the class hierarchy, starting with the object class we are using, to locate the first virtual function that seems to fit the bill. For example, if we were dealing with an IndexedCollection and we wanted to add an item to it, the call:

```
myIndexedCollection.addItem("ACollectionKey","A New Item");
```

would call the addItem() function defined within the IndexedCollection class, not the addItem() function in the Collection class. This is only the tip of the iceberg that we call **virtual functions**. In the next chapter you will see how you cannot only redefine the behavior of virtual functions within the class hierarchy, but also how you can incorporate the behavior of virtual functions at higher levels within these new functions. In other words, the virtual functions at lower levels can "inherit" the capabilities of virtual functions at higher levels, leaving them free to do only what is necessary to change their behavior. For example, in the IndexedCollection class, the addItem function now has to deal with updating the collection's index list, but it still deals with adding the raw data to the collection in the same way as we have done here in the collection class. Rather than having to re-implement this behavior at lower levels, there is a mechanism by which you can reach up through the hierarchy and use existing functions. The IndexedCollection addItem() function does its own thing with the collection's index list, and then gets Collection's addItem() function to do the update of the actual collection data list.

There is a complex relationship between virtual functions and overloaded functions; a function declared to be virtual may actually end up being an overloaded function in derivations from the class where it was originally declared virtual. In many cases, a hierarchy of classes will use the same function name, but each class, as it deals with a different data structure, will use different parameters for the function; resulting in an overloaded function. Technically, a virtual function definition is only needed when a derived class exactly duplicates the function name and the parameters of one of its base classes. The run-time penalty for declaring virtual functions is quite small, especially compared to the design and coding penalties that arise from not using them. Do yourself a favor and declare all functions that you expect base classes to reimplement, as virtual functions. Spending an afternoon carefully comparing function prototypes to find out why the wrong function is being called isn't any fun. At the highest level of the hierarchy where you declare a virtual function, you must implement the function. We can't define the virtual addItem() function and then refuse to produce any code describing how it operates. At levels underneath the highest declaration, you do not need to define the function again if its behavior is identical to that of the level above it in the hierarchy. If your last definition of the function's behavior was good enough for you, then you can simply depend on the system to locate this particular function. All you must do is declare the virtual prototype for the function—the compiler and linker will do the rest.

External Function Definitions

You may have noticed that only prototype definitions were given for some functions. This is because the "prototype only" functions are larger than the functions that were fully defined and are therefore defined in an external file, which will include the class definition file.

To be more specific, in Zortech C++ all class definitions are placed in files that end with the extension **.hpp** and all external member function definitions are placed in files with the extension **.cpp**. In the case of the Collection class, this would give us two files:

- Collctn.hpp—The class definition
- Collctn.cpp—Class member functions

Notice that the entire Collection object class is defined in two files, with the name of the collection (albeit somewhat condensed) forming the name, and the standard .hpp and .cpp extensions giving you the two related files. All you need to do to use the collection class in your next project (in source form) is move these two files to your project directory. This is why it was so important not to let Bancroft-specific details creep into the Collection specification.

As an example of a member function to be defined in the implementation file, consider the **changeItem(void *)** function required to change the currently selected item in the collection. If this were the only function we needed to place in the implementation file (it isn't), then the implementation file would contain:

```
#include "Collection.hpp"      // MUST include class definition file

void Collection::changeItem(char *newObject)
{
    if(numberOfElements == 0 || working = numberOfElements)
    return;                              // working isn't valid

    elements[working] = newObject;
}
```

Summary

In this chapter you have implemented the basic Collection class, which was derived from the GenericObject class. You have seen how constructors and destructors work together to allocate and release dynamic memory used by instances of the Collection class, and you have seen how to use the private/public element separation to keep users of Collection objects away from dangerous functions like the element array shifters. We have also seen how objects deal with dynamic changes to their sizes over their lifetimes—through the use of the grow function.

Further Enhancements

Extend the Collection's capabilities so that it can also release excess storage that isn't being used. You will need to find some breakpoint, such as the number of elements in the collection being less than 25 percent of the capacity of the collection. You will also need a mechanism for carefully controlling this storage release, since it could get over-enthusiastic and release all the memory of a newly allocated collection.

CHAPTER 10

DERIVED SYSTEM CLASSES

Chances are if your parents never had any children, neither will you.

Before we move on to the Bancroft application classes, we will deal with the final remaining generic system class, the **IndexedCollection** class. The IndexedCollection class is derived from the Collection class that we created in the last chapter, and is designed to handle collections where each object in the collection has been assigned a unique keyword.

One of the horses almost beat to death in the Strategy section was how you should try to avoid extra work at all costs. Most success stories in programming involve those that deliver on-time and on-budget, rather than those that deliver three years late and cost 10 times as much as initially estimated. In using OOP in a standard programming shop, you can raise the ante and deliver ahead of schedule and under budget, given that all of your original estimates were for how much time it would take to code the project in a non-OOP language. Or you can hide this great progress and take a lot of vacations.

In implementing the IndexedCollection class, we can see exactly what steps need to be taken to reach this goal. As you learned in the Strategy section, you must first ask yourself, what does my immediate base class, in this case the Collection class, already do? And then you need to determine exactly what has to be done to its existing behavior to get it to meet your new requirements.

In this case, the Collection class manages lists of objects, allowing you to retrieve specific objects either by directly indexing them or by searching sequentially through the collection. It makes one very strong assumption, namely that you know exactly what kinds of objects this collection contains and exactly how to determine in which objects you are interested.

The IndexedCollection class adds a single new twist to this concept, namely that every object in the collection is associated with a keyword. Instead of physically examining elements within the collection to determine which is of interest to you, you now can ask the collection for the object it contains that is associated with a specific keyword.

What this means is that we can use most of the existing capabilities of the Collection class to implement the IndexedCollection. We don't need to worry about maintaining the actual elements contained within the IndexedCollection, as the Collection class functions can already do this. All we really need to do in an IndexedCollection is to maintain the list of keywords associated with each element of the collection, and ensure that changes are made so that the list of keys we maintain in the Indexed-Collection always corresponds to the list of elements that the Collection maintains. Here is a general list of requirements for the Indexed-Collection class:

- Creating the Collection (Constructor functions).
- Destroying the Collection (Destructor functions).
- Accessing elements by keyword.
- Adding elements with keywords.
- Deleting elements by keyword.

Constructor Functions

From the work we just did in creating the Collection class, we know that the constructor function for a standard Collection will initialize the collection's control variables and allocate space for the element list of the collection. We also know that we are obligated to call it, if for no other reason than to ensure that within the context of a **GenericObject**, this new instance is correctly identified as an IndexedCollection. We also know that since this is an IndexedCollection, not only do we have to maintain a list of elements within the collection, but also we need to maintain a corresponding list of keywords that are associated with each of the elements in the IndexedCollection. We will therefore state that the class IndexedCollection contains a member element that contains the keywords assigned to each of the objects in the collection. We will define that element as:

```
void **keys;                    // keywords used for collection objects
```

We must remember from this point forward that we are assuming the relationship between a keyword in the keys list and an object in the elements list that we inherited from collection, is purely positional. This means that if we had a collection containing three keywords, the first object in the elements list is associated with the first keyword in the keys list, the second object with the second key, and the last object with the last key.

There are two very different opinions as to what you can use as keywords to an IndexedCollection. First, you can elect to construct a homogeneous list of strings or numeric pointers (or some other type of data) and use them as keywords. For the truly brave, you can use other objects as keywords and get a powerful indexed collection indeed. I say for the truly brave because you can easily create complex indexing systems where the index keys actually react to being looked at—by modifying the collection they are keying. This type of behavior is encountered in the latest hypertext systems, where almost any element of the systems be linked to almost any other element. While powerful, these systems can often defeat efforts to understand their internal operations.

In any case, we are going to need to implement three constructor functions because we want to provide the same set of constructors in the IndexedCollection's context as we do in the Collection's context. This isn't actually a requirement that C++ has placed upon us; however, uniformity of behavior within a class hierarchy makes it much easier to remember how to work with each level of the hierarchy. It would really be nice if IndexedCollections were assembled in roughly the same way as collections. This would mean we could easily apply our knowledge of how collections behave to the behavior of IndexedCollections. In doing so, we would implement these three constructor functions:

```
IndexedCollection(int)          // standard empty IndexedCollection

IndexedCollection(int,int)      // user sized empty IndexedCollection

IndexedCollection(void **,void **,int,int)
                                // initialize with fixed data
```

In the third constructor, we have deviated from the exact form used by the Collection constructors, since we require two lists of character pointers, instead of the single list used in the Collection's context. Because this is an IndexedCollection, we have to initialize the list of keywords as well as the list of elements in the collection, so the difference is easily remembered. When constructing a derived class, if you have a valid reason for the class' methods to behave differently, this really isn't a problem as the differences are based on the contextual differences between the base class and the derived class. It isn't bad to assume that the programmer will remember that they need to supply a list of index values along with the list of collection objects, after all, they did pick the IndexedCollection class over the Collection class in the first place. One technique that works well is to put the the new parameters in front of the parameters that are required already by the base class. If the Collection class requires:

```
Collection(<object list>,< size>)
```

then the IndexedCollection class would require:

```
IndexedCollection(<list>,<list>,<size>)
```

In the previous chapter you saw how the Collection class called the GenericObject constructor functions in order to ensure the object was correctly initialized at the GenericObject level. In this case you should be concerned with calling the Collection object's constructor function to ensure that the object is properly initialized at the Collection level. The cause the GenericObject constructor to be called. This allows the Indexed-Collection constructor functions to concentrate on initializing only the Index List and passing the rest of the parameters back to the Collection constructor, which will in turn invoke the GenericObject constructor function. This sequence of constructor activation illustrates how an object is built from its lowest base class up to the specific derived object being constructed. This is because the calls to the base constructor functions precede the body of code that actually initializes the class within any given context. What this means is that you can safely assume that when you are *inside* your local constructor code, all of the variables you inherited from your base classes have been correctly initialized already in terms of the parameters on which you are currently operating. One concern we must deal with is the constructor function at the IndexedCollection level. It creates an empty instance of an IndexedCollection with a default size that was established at compile time:

```
IndexedCollection()
```

This constructor does not necessarily know the value of the default collection size (**collect_dflt_size**) definition that was established in the Collection class definition. You could copy this parameter from the Collection class into the IndexedCollection class, but that puts extra work on your shoulders. More importantly, provides a portal for bugs to enter should you change this constant in one class, but not in the other. For this reason, a constructor that creates an object containing a certain default amount of dynamically allocated memory should never depend on its base class to share the same default. In an environment where you are concerned with memory usage, it is quite likely that the default size of an IndexedCollection could be smaller than the default size of a Collection. An IndexedCollection needs more physical memory to hold the same amount of information because of the fact that it has a list of keywords in addition to the Collection's list of elements. Therefore, both our default size IndexedCollection constructor and our programmed size IndexedC-ollection constructor use the programmed Collection constructor. Neither of them depends on the Collection constructor to know how big it should make the collection; they both tell it specifically how big it really should be. In short, the derived classes all use programmed functions of their base class when using default initialization values, they do not assume that they use the same default values as does their base class. Constants are always propagated upwards through constructor functions, as it is dangerous to assume that the base class default values are identical to those of their derived classes. This means you can modify either the IndexedCollection's or the Collection's default size without ending up with an IndexedCollection containing differing amounts of storage for its keyword list and its elements list.

Unlike the Collection class, we have not used an integer variable within the IndexedCollection class to tell us how many keywords we have. This is because the number of keywords will always be equal to the number of items in the collection itself. We can therefore use the *numberOfElements* variable within the context of a Collection to keep track of the number of keywords in the list. By not duplicating this counter at the Indexed-Collection level, we avoid the possibility that the Collection and Indexed-Collection can develop two different ideas as to the size of the dataset contained within the IndexedCollection.

Destructor Function

The IndexedCollection destructor function is responsible for destroying the local contents of the IndexedCollection, meaning that its only respon-sibility is to release the storage occupied by the keyword list. The compiler will ensure that destructor functions are called automatically whenever the object in question goes out of scope, or no longer exists. Once again, the compiler will first call the destructor for the derived class and then move up through the class hierarchy, calling each destructor in turn. In this case, when the compiler determines that an IndexedCollection should be destroyed, it would perform the following sequence of destructor calls:

- IndexedCollection Destructor
- Collection Destructor
- GenericObject Destructor

Accessing Items in the IndexedCollection

In constructing the functions to access the elements of an Indexed-Collection class, the idea is not to completely reduplicate the functional capabilities of the collection class, but rather, to do selective extensions and revisions to the existing functions in order to provide the needed functions that support operations on IndexedCollections.

We have inherited functions from the Collection class that retrieve items from the collection by either the current working position or by specification of a positional index within the collection. Since the actual elements list of the Collection is not publicly available, we must use these functions to access the elements list. The primary concern of the functions provided at the IndexedCollection level is to convert the keywords we are passed into positional indices that can be used to retrieve data from the collection.

For example, the Collection class implements the function **selection(int)** where int is an index within the collection. This function will return the data pointer stored in the collection at that position. The IndexedCollection class also implements the selection function, but in this case it implements it as **selection(void *)** where void * is a pointer to the keyword of the desired item. What this function must do is to look up this keyword in the keyword list, and use its index position as a parameter to the Collection level selection(int) function.

There is one special consideration we must address. As stated previously, we don't dictate exactly what kinds of pointers are used as keywords, because we want to allow the programmer a wide range of choices for keywording a collection. If we had limited the collection to character pointers, then we could simply check for keyword equivalence by performing a **strcmp()** between each item in the keyword list and the keyword we received as a parameter. Since we didn't establish that limitation, we really don't know how to determine if two keywords are equivalent. For this reason, the IndexedCollection contains a function pointer variable, defined as:

```
int (*keyTest)(void *,void *);
```

This statement tells the compiler that the variable *keyTest* is the address of a function that accepts two void pointers and returns an integer. We are expecting the function to implement some arbitrary logic to determine if the two arguments refer to the same keyword, returning zero if they do, and non-zero if they don't. A more common example of this type of relationship exists in the **qsort()** function found in most standard C libraries. Although the function knows all about sorting, it too requires that the programmer provide it with a function for comparing two elements against each other. We haven't made any consideration in the constructor functions for this value, so it would end up being a NULL pointer when the constructors finish their jobs. That isn't really acceptable, since using a NULL pointer as a function address won't result in anything resembling a stable system. We could go back and modify all of the constructor prototypes so they accept another parameter that supplies this function address, but there is a simpler solution. Given the fact that we can assume many keyword lists will be composed of character pointers that really do point to character strings, we will make the constructors put the address of strcmp() into this variable when they initialize the indexed collection. If another function was to be used in place of strcmp(), then an update method could be used to change the function pointer.

Now that the issue of determining keyword equality has been addressed, we can define the steps necessary to implement the selection function:

1. Use the collection level function numberOfElements() to find out how many keywords exist.

2. For each keyword that exists, use the keyTest function to determine if the keyword we are testing is equal to the keyword we got as a parameter to the selection() function.

3. If the keyword wasn't in our list, return a NULL pointer as the result of this function.

4. If the keyword was in our list, use the index of the matching keyword as the parameter to the Collection level selection function and return the result from executing that function.

In this algorithm there are two points where we need to call functions in our base class, the Collection class. They are public functions, so we know that it's legal to call them, but exactly how do we tell the compiler we want to do this? What we need to do is to explain to the compiler the context or scope in which we wish to call these functions. As it trundles along compiling something, the compiler's usual concept of the scope is the current function it is compiling and the class of which that function is a member, if the compiler happens to be compiling a class at the time. In these two cases we want to override the compiler's normal assumption by telling it to use a function that is in one of our base classes, specifically the Collection class. The function that implements selection() in C++ is:

```
char *IndexedCollection::selection(char *theKey)
{
    int nElems;              // number of elements in the collection

    short i;                             // loop index

    void *result;                       // returned value

    nElems = numberOfElements();
    for(i=0 ; i < nElems; i++)
        if(!(*keyTest)(theKey,keys[i])
            break;                      // break if the keys are equal

    if(i == nElems)                     // keyword wasn't found

        result = NULL;
    else                                // use as collection index

        result = ::selection(i);
    return(result);

}
```

The first thing to understand about member functions is that they all have an implied parameter which is a reference to the object that they are being applied to. C++ applies member functions to instantiations of that object; therefore, every member function has implied knowledge of the object on which it is operating. If necessary, such as for passing the object as a parameter to some external agent, the object itself is available through the keyword list. In any case, the object's local class variables are available for its immediate use, as you see where the **keyTest** function is being called.

In the two cases where we need to access the more general capabilities inherited from the Collection class, we must specifically inform the compiler that we are not referencing the current object as an instance of an IndexedCollection, but as an instance of a Collection. This is done through use of the **scope resolution operator (::)**. You can see that in the above line of code where we called the Collection class' **selection()** function.

This is declaring that the compiler should not use the immediate context when executing the function, but instead should use the same function in the closest higher context, in this case using the selection() function found in the Collection class instead of the one found in this class. This is how we gain access to the data and functions we inherit from our base classes. The compiler will not let us tell it to treat an orange as an apple, however it will let us call either one of them a fruit, via the scope resolution operator and deal with them in terms of being a fruit. Remember, at the level of a fruit, we can no longer tell whether they are apples or oranges. The specific base class to use can be placed in front of the scope resolution operator when you wish to bypass a function of the same name that lies between the function in the current derived class and the function in the desired base class. For example, if we had to find out what the subclass ID of a GenericObject was, and we were attempting to do this from inside an IndexedCollection member function, we'd couldn't just write the following:

```
genericObjectClass = subclass();
```

This is because we'd get the class ID of an IndexedCollection. We also couldn't write the this:

```
genericObjectClass = ::subclass();
```

The reason is because we'd get the class ID of a Collection, since the compiler would search for the first occurrence of the subclass function above the IndexedCollection. We therefore would have to specifically resolve the scope by writing the following code to give us the answer we desire:

```
genericObjectClass = GenericObject::subclass();
```

Adding Items to the IndexedCollection

We know from our work on Collections that there are already mechanisms available for adding items to a Collection. Since the IndexedCollection keeps its actual set of items at the Collection level, we must use these existing mechanisms to maintain the set. What we need to implement at this level are functions that add to the list of keywords. We must then ensure that the same alterations are performed at the collection level, positionally speaking.

To add an item to an IndexedCollection, we need to know both the actual data to be loaded into the collection, and the keyword to be associated with that data. This results in the **addItem()** function being implemented as:

```
int addItem(void *,void *);
```

Here the first parameter is a pointer to the keyword, the second parameter is a pointer to the data, and the result of the function is the physical index position of this item. The reason that this function returns a physical index, in spite of the fact that we are dealing with a keyword indexed collection, is that it must. *All C++ functions declared as virtual must have the same return data type.* Therefore, every addItem function in every collection must return an integer that we will attempt to ensure is always the position of the item in the collection. By doing this, the function loading data to an IndexedCollection can use these indices to the data it has loaded, thereby treating the IndexedCollection as a Collection and significantly improving its performance. However, when it returns or passes this instance of an IndexedCollection, the recipient can use keywords to access the members of the collection. The specific steps necessary to accomplish this are as follows:

1. Loop through existing keywords in the collection to see if the key is already there.

2. If it is, then this won't be an add operation, it's a change operation. At the collection level, you must first change the value of working to the index of the located keyword, and then you must use the **change()** function to load the new object to the indexed collection.

3. If it is an add location, add the keyword to the end of the keys list and then get the collection to add the data pointer to the end of the elements list.

4. Return the index position where the pointer was stored.

In an IndexedCollection we are using the addItem() function to do more than add items to the indexed collection. Since we do not allow duplicate keywords in an IndexedCollection, addItem() is obliged to search the list of known keywords before it adds a new item to the collection. If it finds the keyword, we change the current value associated with that keyword, rather than adding a duplicate copy to the end of the list. There are many different ways to share this responsibility between addItem() and **changeItem()**, in this case we have elected to have addItem() do all the work.

Deleting Items from IndexedCollections

In order to delete an item from an indexed keyword, we need to know the keyword associated with that item. We will delete this keyword from our local keys list, and we will delete the pointer with which it's associated from the collection. To accomplish this we must manipulate our list of keywords in exactly the same way as the collection does.

You will recall that the Collection class implements a private member function called **krush()**, which is used to shift a collection's elements down so that the collection does not contain NULL references in the middle of its data lists. You may have been disappointed by the fact that the actual code for krush() was not given when it was first mentioned. As it turns out, if the code has been written then, all we would be doing now is rewriting it, carefully changing the existing references to elements to references to keys.

While you are constructing the C++ class definitions, you should defer definitions of the larger functions until you have completed all of the class definitions. This is because you will find, as in this case, that you have member functions in two classes that perform the same operation on different data. In this case, we have the requirements for the Collection krush() routine:

- Loop to copy each item in elements from start +1 to finish down one unit.

The requirements for the IndexedCollection krush() routine are:

- Loop to copy each item in keys from start + 1 to finish down by one unit.

As you can see, the krush algorithm is identical for both, it's just that each of these classes supplies different parameters. What this means is that you need to write one standard C function that implements the krush() algorithm, accepting everything it needs as parameters to the function, such as:

```
void InternalKrush(void *baseAddress,      // base of list to krush

            short elemSize,

                        // size in bytes of each list element
            short start,                    // starting point

            short end);                        // ending point
```

It then becomes a simple matter to implement the krush() member functions in the Collection and IndexedCollection classes. Each of these member functions simply acquires the parameters that it needs and calls the **InternalKrush()** function. In the case of an IndexedCollection, the actual definition of the krush() function would be:

```
void IndexedCollection::krush(int startAt)
{
InternalKrush(keys,sizeof(char *),startAt +
1,Collection::numberOfElements);
}
```

Summary

In this chapter we have used inheritance and polymorphism heavily to construct a class implementing a new collection behavior, but using as many of the existing collection behaviors as possible. We have defined the IndexedCollection class where the only real work done by this class is the maintenance of the keyword list. All other operations are performed by existing routines at the collection level.

CHAPTER 11

SIMPLE APPLICATION CLASS

The problem-solving process will always break down at the point at which it is possible to determine who caused the problem.

In this chapter we will begin to deal with the implementation of the Bancroft application specific objects. These objects are considered to be more a part of the Bancroft system than of the core OOP class library. They are valuable outside of the Bancroft system because they deal with the kind of general information encountered in many business applications.

Review

An instance of the class Entity contains two elements, the name and address of the entity. The value used for the name is usually a pointer to a string, but it actually can be a pointer to anything. Any user of the value held here is supposed to know exactly to what they have a pointer. On the other hand, the address element has been declared to always be an instance of an Address object; therefore, we must enforce this when we load values into this element.

Unfortunately, this design system causes a bit of a problem because the design says it must be an Address object that we place in the address element, however, we know that an Address object is an **Abstract class**, meaning it serves as a common base class for DomesticAddress and ForeignAddress, but is never instantiated itself.

We have two possible solutions to this problem in C++. First, we can simply put logic into the Entity address element update function to allow the update to occur if the passed address' type is equal to a Domestic-Address or a ForeignAddress. The problem with this approach is that if we later derive the **ElectronicAddress** class from Address, the Entity won't accept it as a legal address until we modify the Entity class' address change function. This solution is a technical violation of the laws of OOP, because you have now introduced a dependency in the system where if one class is modified (Address) then a completely unrelated class must also be modified (Entity).

The second solution supports pure OO design, but it is considerably more expensive. It involves building a memory resident table of every single object id, and the id of that object's immediate base class. With this table you can generate the entire inheritance chain for any object, by constantly using the parent you just found as the new search term, until you get to the root object, which has no parent. The problem with this approach is that you must update the data in this table every time you modify the class hierarchy. This would allow us to use the Address class ID as the test parameter, and to search the hierarchy of classes associated with the address parameter to see if we could find the Address class ID in the hierarchy. The reason that there are two conflicting approaches arises from the differences between strong and weak typing.

In the first approach, the strong typing model is used, which means we must specifically recognize each possible derived class of Address that the Entity may ever see. In the second approach a weak typing model is used, but it requires that we have a complete map of the hierarchy available to separate it. In this book we have implemented much of what is necessary to use weakly typed designs in C++, however this particular area would entail too much work for too little gain, at least as far as this book is concerned. Therefore we will support strong typing for interobject links such as this, which means we will hardwire the Entity class specifically to recognize each possible derived class of Address it should accept. If, at a later time, we add the ElectronicAddress derived class, we will then alter the Entity class to reflect this change. Although this is not as graceful as the loosely typed solution, where class relationships can be determined at run-time, it's a lot more efficient. This particular problem isn't due to C++ as much as it is due to the subclass() virtual function we have implemented in our design. Pure C++ can easily circumvent this problem through the use of a **casting operation**. For example, in pure C++, we could simply cast any derived Address class such as ElectronicAddress to an Address class, and we wouldn't have any problem. Unfortunately, our subclass() function, which we must have in order to support our heterogeneous lists, does not understand typing. We therefore would have to add extra run-time logic to the system to allow the subclass function to map the relationships between classes.

Constructors

The default Entity constructor function doesn't really have anything to do. There's no dynamic storage to assign and there are no control variables to initialize. In cases such as this you usually don't need to declare a constructor, but it is a good idea to declare one anyway, even if all it does is fill pointers with NULL. In our case, we must provide constructors because we need to get the subclass ID back to our base class, the GenericObject. There are three cases where there might be some real work for Entity constructor functions. These are when the name, the address, or both are supplied to the Entity constructor function:

```
//build new entity
Entity();
// must type the parameter to determine element
Entity(GenericObject *,);
// set both parameters
Entity(Name *,Address *,int)
```

Notice that the second constructor receives a GenericObject parameter, which could be any object in the system. The third constructor receives a **Name** object and an **Address** object. Although we are primarily designing in a weakly typed model, there isn't anything wrong with using strong typing when you can clearly define the possible types of a parameter. In the second constructor, we had to use a GenericObject type because we don't know whether the function will receive a name or an address. The only object that is a common ancestor of these two classes is the GenericObject itself. In the third constructor we were able to define the types more accurately; therefore, we made this information available to the compiler. At the very least, the compiler can now warn you when you accidentally reverse the name and address in a static call on this constructor function. Making names specific objects instead of simple character strings helps us with this process, both for type identification and for proper operation of the second constructor.

The second constructor actually has to do the work of two constructors. It does not know beforehand whether it will receive a value representing an address or a value representing a name. Therefore, it must somehow determine this from the parameter we receive.

The solution is to perform an **aram-subClass()** call to determine what kind of object we are looking at. But this brings up another problem, specifically, what do we do if they use a character string for a name. Attempting to get a character string to tell its subclass will cause many problems.

This means we need yet another new object, as we must require that all parameters received by this constructor are objects, making this a First Class Object Oriented Function. We now can require that all name values for Entity be instances of a name object, and addresses must be instances of an Address object or one of its subclasses. The second constructor function can be implemented with:

```
Entity(GenericObject *value) :

{

    switch(value->subClass())

    {

        case NAME_CLASS :
```

```
            name = (Name *) value;
            break;
        Case DOMESTICADDRESS_CLASS:
            address = (Address *) value;
            break;
        case FOREIGNADDRESS_CLASS:
            address = (Address *) value;
            break;
        default:
            system_error("Entity doesn't accept this
            class!");
    }
    value->incReference();
}
```

As with previous examples, the first thing that happens in executing an Entity constructor is that its base class' constructor is executed. Before we actually initialize the object in the context of an instance of Entity, we initialize the object in the context of a GenericObject. This provides the GenericObject constructor with the specific subclass ID of the object that is being instantiated.

Following the initialization of the GenericObject level data we will then initialize the name or address field of the new Entity instance, but first we must determine the exact subclass of our parameter. More importantly, typing any instance of any class as a GenericObject will prevent typing warnings from the compiler, as all classes are derived from it. If we had declared the input class to be either a Name class or a derivative of the Address class, we would have been wrong about the class of the parameter half the time.

As you can see from the code, the way to deal with functions that accept many different types of objects is to say that all parameters the function receives are the base class and will cover all the possible classes the function might get. In this case, since the Name and Address classes are only related at the GenericObject level, we have declared the function parameter type as a GenericObject. In a function that worked only on ForeignAddress and DomesticAddress objects, we could define the parameter as being a reference to an Address object. For the above reasons, it is important to always cast the value being passed to the function to the same type the function thinks it is.

Converting a pointer from a GenericObject reference to a more specific reference is a simple cast, as shown in the body of the switch statement. You are not limited to casting between the GenericObject class and the terminal class of the object; you may cast to any class between the GenericObject and the terminal class.

The last statement in the definition is used to increment the reference count to the item that has just been loaded into Entity. This is the primary function performed by reference counting, and is indicated when a given object has been appropriated as a component of another object. If this element is referenced by two Entities, destruction of one of the Entities won't cause the element to be deleted.

Destructor

The only tasks required of the Entity destructor function is to indicate that it is no longer referencing the name and address objects and to delete the objects if there are no longer any references to them:

```
Entity::~Entity()
{
    if(name->decReference() == 0)              // no reference
    {
        name->release();
    }
    if(address->decReference() == 0)
    {
        address->release();
```

```
        }

    }
```

In defining this function we have made use of a **release** function instead of the **delete** keyword that C++ provides. This is because these are objects we are pointing to, and only they know if there is internal storage to be released. It is not Entity's responsibility to know if there is internal storage in the name or address object.

The release function is a virtual function which should be implemented within every class in the system that contains references to other objects or that dynamically activate memory. This function provides the same functionality as the class destructor function, but it is meant for use on dynamically allocated objects, for which the compiler never generates destructor calls. All release functions work their way back through all of an object's component classes, until they reach the GenericObject release function. The GenericObject function is responsible for physically deleting the object, as the lower levels have finished deleting all of its internal data.

In the call on **release()** we have used the virtual release method associated with the Name class. The call to this function is set up by the compiler and linker, by using the compiler's knowledge of the class hierarchy to determine exactly which virtual function to call. The major piece of information used to locate this virtual function is the declared class of the pointer.

One critical issue is the means by which the name and address instances were created originally. You must use the new keyword to allocate storage for any object you intend on allowing other objects to reference through their member variables. If you were to use a static variable in one of these objects, their destructor functions would attempt to delete the storage, usually producing complaints about trying to free memory the system never gave you in the first place. If you create an object on the stack, as an automatic variable within a function, you never want to give this object to another object for its internal reference. After the function finishes, the stack space that contains the object is released, but the other object still references where the object used to be on the stack.

Access Functions

Entity provides two functions that will return its name and address parameters to the caller. The functions are:

```
Name *name()
{
    return(name);
}
```

and:

```
Address *address()
{
    return(address);
}
```

The only interesting thing here is the fact that the name function return type is the exact class of the returned object (Name), but the return type from the address() function is the abstract base class of the class returned. This name is always an instance of Name, whereas address may be an instance of DomesticAddress or of ForeignAddress.

Update Functions

Once again we provide two functions, this time allowing the user to change either the name or address:

```
void name(Name *aName)
{
    name = aName;
}
```

and:

```
void address(Address *anAddress)
{
    address = anAddress;
}
```

Notice that we have been bound to the same real and abstract typing conventions that we had to follow when writing the access functions. This means that all well behaved callers of main say:

```
anEntity->address((Address *) aPtrToADomOrForeignAddress);
```

C++ does do implicit type conversions from derived to base classes when it feels it's called for, but there are times when using an explicit cast can help readers to understand the program. If explicit casts are used when parameters are being passed to a function that deals with them in more generalized terms, it tells the reader that the called function is ignorant of the details that distinguish foreign from domestic addresses.

Summary

We now have implemented the Entity class, which is the abstract base class for the classes Supplier, Customer, and Employee. In doing this we have begun to exercise the reference counting mechanism inherited from GenericObjects, and we have detailed how the deallocation of dynamic objects works.

Further Enhancements

Entity is the first object in which we have supported reference counting. Go back and modify the Collection class to support reference counting on the items in its collection. You could also implement switchable reference counting for the IndexedCollection keywords, if they happen to be objects. Remember, you need to implement the virtual **release()** function and the master **terminalRelease()** function. In the code so far, an entity can be constructed with a name, address, both, or neither.

We also provide functions to change the name and address. This isn't the way things should happen. Change the system to require at least a name for the constructor functions and then remove the function that allows name editing. This gives you an Entity that is always instantiated with a name and will never change over its lifetime.

CHAPTER 12

BUILDING CLASSES IN PARALLEL

I don't mind fighting fires. But they keep giving me gasoline, and telling me it's water!

In this chapter we will implement the Address class and its derived classes, DomesticAddress and ForeignAddress. As the class name implies, these objects represent addresses for Bancroft's customers, suppliers, and employees.

In a change from previous sections, we are not going to implement the three classes in a linear fashion, instead, we are going to code them all simultaneously. Although this may seem to be a foolhardy step, it actually represents a coding method that you can use when you are defining a group of related classes and you know that there really isn't much substance to the group. You usually will find this to be the case when you are implementing a simple abstract class and a few simple classes derived from the abstract class.

Review

In the Strategy section, we defined the Address class and two subclasses, DomesticAddress and ForeignAddress. The address class is an abstract class, meaning that we will never create and use instances of the address class itself, but instead will use its derived classes which represent foreign and domestic addresses. The address class only contains data that is common to both foreign and domestic addresses, which implies that it can only deal with local address information, such as the street, city, and local phone number of the address. Details such as area codes, states, or provinces have a definition that is dependent on whether the address is within the United States or is in a foreign country. In the simplest case, foreign address must state for which country it is an address, whereas the fact that an object is a domestic address already suggests that the country is the United States.

Variables

As was discussed in the Strategy section, the Address class contains that data which is common to both foreign and domestic addresses. The data that fits this criteria is the street address of the addressee, his or her local phone number, and the city or town in which the person lives. Regardless of whether the individual at this address was located in Des Moines or Djakarta, this information is always applicable.

Notice that we have said simply that there is a local address—instead of saying that there are lines one, two, and three for every address. The latter approach wastes time and space when there are fewer than three lines and infuriates the user when the address absolutely must have six lines. Therefore, we will say that the local address information is simply a pointer to a string which contains as much text as is required for the local address. The variables that will then be implemented for the address class will be:

```
char *localAddress;                    // whatever it takes

char *city;                            // the city or town they live in

char *phone;                           // their local phone number
```

All of these variables will be private, which means that no other objects will be allowed to directly access these variables. We will, however, use the friend keyword to allow the two classes derived from Address to access these values directly.

We must also define the variables used by the foreign and domestic subclasses. In the case of the DomesticAddress we have:

```
char *state;                    // *usually* a two letter abbreviation

char *zipCode;                  // five or nine digits long

char *areaCode;                 // three digits
// In the case of a ForeignAddress, we would implement the variables
char *province;                 // e.g., Quebec, Queensland

char *postalCode;               // comes in many flavors

char *country;                  // e.g., England, Japan

char *intlAccess;               // international direct dial prefix
```

There is much similarity between the values held in the foreign and domestic addresses because provinces in Canada are similar to the states in the U.S.A, at least as far as a mailing address is concerned. It would be very dangerous to say, however, that all addresses are the same based on the fact that the data used to represent them is similar. It is dangerous because this viewpoint has not addressed the procedural knowledge that is associated with addresses. This procedural knowledge is represented in C++ programs by the functions that have been defined as members of a class. Consider the feature found in many modern mailing list managers, where the city and state information is derived from the zip code. These systems do not require that the operator enter the city and state directly, instead it looks up these values in a table, using the zip code provided by the operator as a key. This procedural knowledge embedded in the system prevents the operator from entering any foreign address.

This is not to say that procedural knowledge is bad. On the contrary, it is a vital component of any system, OO or not. Procedural knowledge operates on a set of assumptions about the data which it manipulates. In the previous example, the assumption is that all addresses are in the

United States and the zip code will identify the correct city and state. This means we cannot define a single class to represent any address, foreign or domestic, and then expect to implement procedural knowledge that can deal with a class' instances which don't follow the rules. If we want to use procedural knowledge (given the fact that we are using objects, we do want to use it), then the objects must be defined under the same constraints that the procedural knowledge will assume to be true.

In previous examples, this hasn't been much of a concern for two reasons. First, the previous objects were implemented for very limited purposes, so there wasn't much difficulty in seeing the relationship between the data and the procedures that operated on it. There was only one way to do things. Now, we are starting to deal with hierarchies of objects, where they all represent the same essential information, but each derived class does it a little differently. For that reason, we must now sensitize ourselves to the inter-relationships between data and the functions that operate on the data.

Constructors

In order to easily implement constructor functions for a set of related objects as a single task, you should exploit the hierarchal relationships between the classes for which you are creating constructors. For example, we know that the Address constructor function will only be used by the DomesticAddress and ForeignAddress classes. No other object or external program is ever going to deal with an Address because it is an abstract class, used only to group the common characteristics of the foreign and domestic address classes. Since this is true, we can decide that there will be only one constructor function for the Address class. This means that the domestic and foreign addresses must match the parameter list of the Address constructor exactly, they cannot rely on the presence of overloaded constructor functions using "nicer" parameter lists. This means that we have only one single definition of the Address class constructor function:

```
Address(char *l,char *c,char *p) :
    {
```

```
localAddress = strsave(l);
city = strsave(c);     phone = strsave(p);
}
```

In this example we have used the **strsave()** function, which duplicates any string passed to it, making it handy to create more permanent copies of local variables. This allows the domestic and foreign address constructor functions to provide their local data as parameters to the Address constructor, with the advance knowledge that the constructor will duplicate this data and will use the duplicates internally.

Proceeding to the constructor for domestic addresses, we have three new data elements, specifically the values for the state, zip code, and area code of this new DomesticAddress. There are two possible ways of constructing this object. First, the user may provide only the zip code, hoping that the system can figure out the area code and state from this value. On the other hand, the user might assume that the program is a cretin, and therefore would provide all three values. As far as the user providing either the state and zip, or area code and zip, we shall exercise our "divine/design" authority and pronounce those conditions illegal, as both would produce exactly the same parameter list. This cannot be done because it is the differences in parameters that the compiler uses to determine which overloaded function should be invoked. This leads us back to the idea that you can't just initialize an address with a zip code and a state or area code. Keeping that in mind, we would write the following two constructors:

```
DomesticAddress(char *l,char *c,char *p,char *zip) :
(l,c,p)
{
    zip = strsave(zip);
    areaCode = strsave(fetchZipArea(zip));
    state = strsave(fetchZipState(zip)); }
DomesticAddress(char *l,
char *c,
```

```
char *p,
char *s,
char *z,
char *a,
: (l,c,p)
{
    zip = strsave(z);
    areaCode = strsave(a);
    state = strsave(s);
    saveZipState(zip,state);
    saveZipArea(zip,areaCode);
}
```

These two constructors have introduced a new set of functions, which we used to link the zip code with states and area codes. The following table provides a definition of each function:

FUNCTION	DESCRIPTION
fetchZipArea(z)	Given a zip code, return its telephone area code fetch.
ZipState(z)	Given a zip code, return the state its for.
saveZipArea(z,a)	Learn the zip code/area code link.
saveZipState(z,s)	Learn the zip code/state link.

This provides the best of all possible worlds. As the user gets smarter (or more tired of entering addresses), the system is compensating by learning the zip code associations itself. This is a desirable goal in many designs, but it can be attained easily in OOLs. Since objects are self-contained, we can implement private capabilities within them without worrying about what kind of havoc it will cause with the other software. With the additional fact that each object performs a very specific job, we don't have to look very far when deciding where capabilities should be implemented. In this case, a long term memory of zip code assignments is obviously a component of the DomesticAddress class. After all, it's the only class that cares about these relationships.

Moving on to the foreign address class, we find that the initialization of this class is straightforward. Once again we can elect to provide a single constructor function, although for different reasons. All we really know about foreign addresses is that they may contain all of this same data. On the other hand, they might not contain a lot of it. If we look at providing constructor functions to handle every foreseeable case, we end up with quite a batch of possible functions. Many of these functions couldn't be implemented because the compiler can't tell the difference between two overloaded function calls if they don't use a different parameter list. For example, it can't tell the difference between:

```
ForeignAddress("10 Downing St," "London," "England")
```

and:

```
ForeignAddress("10 Rue Montmartre," "France," "hZip")
```

because they both have the same name and identical parameter lists:

```
ForeignAddress(char *l,
char *c,
char *p,
char *prov,
char *pCode,
char *cntry,
char *intAcc,
int sClass): (sClass,l,c,p)
{
    province = strsave(prov);
    postalCode = strsave(pCode);
    country = strsave(cntry);
```

```
    intlAccess = strsave(intAcc);
}
```

Destructor

We must implement three destructor functions for destroying the Address class and its two subclasses. All of the destructor functions have the same basic task, to release the memory allocated to hold their private values. This illustrates the fact that the majority of destructor functions are very necessary, and very boring:

```
~Address()
{
    delete localAddress;
    delete city;
    delete phone;
}
~DomesticAddress
{
delete zip;
    delete areaCode;
    delete state;
}
~ForeignAddress()
{
    delete province;
    delete postalCode;
    delete country;
    delete intlAccess;
}
```

The only observation that can be made here is that these destructors do show how the class hierarchy is used to ensure that all necessary destructors are called. Although both of the derived address classes contain their own internal private copies of the Address class elements, they aren't responsible for actually deleting these elements. The compiler will ensure that whenever the destructor function for either derived class is called, the Address class destructor will be called immediately after the derived class destructor returns. This is a definite contributor to the rather dull nature of the average destructor, it just doesn't have a hard job. The compiler does most of its work for it.

Although a destructor's job is quite simple, it is extremely important. The destructor is responsible for ensuring that all of the information referenced by that object is deleted. Which means, any objects that use pointers must release these pointers within their destructor functions, if they still exist. If this isn't done, the system can completely lose pointers to allocated memory, which in turn will cause system demands for more memory to become major issues. Given the abandon with which OOPs create and destroy objects, a well behaved program might allocate and release several thousand objects over its lifetime. If these objects were all in memory simultaneously, as would be the case if the destructors weren't doing their job, megabytes of memory would be wasted.

Access Functions

In implementing the access functions for these classes, we must remember that the system treats them in a rather cavalier fashion. There is no element of the original design that cares whether it deals with a domestic or foreign address. We are faced; therefore, with a bit of a paradox—while the system does not distinguish in any way between two classes of objects, it has nevertheless provided them, because of their internal behavioral differences. Each class' internal behavior is different and each one responds to its external environment in an identical fashion, which implies that they all have the same access protocol, but this protocol is different in each object. Going back to the earlier discussion of polymorphism, it was said that polymorphism was a means by which different objects did the same thing, but each object achieved the goal by following a different path. The case of domestic and foreign addresses is a concrete example of polymorphism because we are making an apparently single function sensitive to the context of the object to which it is applied. If we define a set of functions that can be applied to either domestic or foreign addresses, we come up with:

- fullAddress(): A string representing the formatted address.

- phoneNumber(): The full phone number for this address.

- state(): The U.S. state or the foreign country.

The first function is used to generate the full address of the Entity as it would appear on a shipping label; the second function can produce the phone number; and the third is a bribe to the demographics freaks in the marketing department. It is this third function that makes the most interesting use of polymorphism. While the first two functions essentially produce the same data, albeit by different means, the third function actually returns one of two quite disparate elements. In the case of a domestic address, it returns the state. In the case of a foreign address, it completely ignores the province and selects the name of the country itself. The user of this function just treats foreign countries like states in the U.S. The coding for these functions is not too complicated, as you can see from this example:

```
char * DomesticAddress:fullAddress(char *name)
{
    char buffer[512];
    sprintf(buffer,"%s\n%s\n%s, %s\n\t%s",name,localAddress,
        city,state,zipCode);
    return(strsave(buffer));
}
```

We have used the friendly relationship between the DomesticAddress class and its Address base class to access directly the contents of two private variables in the base class, specifically the *localAddress* and the *city elements*. While one may be tempted to allow a lot of friendly relationships to exist in the system so that external functions can operate on the contents of another object without harassment, it violates the entire principle of OOP, except in a very few cases. By making someone the friend of an object, what you are doing is making that object sensitive to changes within the object of which it is a friend. This can lead to endless headaches. However, we also don't like making an element of an object public, because this implies roughly the same thing. All public really means is that everybody is this object's friend. If we were to stringently enforce each object's individual privacy, then the system would spend more time calling member functions to access data items in other objects than it did doing anything useful.

When you have a derived class of an abstract class, you can safely assume that all the abstract class is doing is grouping some common functions and data for this class and some of its immediate family, and that clear dependencies between this abstract class and its derived classes are reflected in the class hierarchy. Abstract classes may specify their immediately derived classes as friends. This allows the derived classes to operate on the private variables of the abstract base class, but it also ensures that they are the only ones who can. This alleviates the need for making member variables of the abstract class public and guarantees the following:

1. The classes derived from the abstract class can access the data in the abstract class by direct reference, instead of using an access function in the abstract class to provide this value.

2. No other classes can access the abstract classes member variables.

Update Functions

Updating these values is a complicated procedure for two reasons. First, as we have noted, the system doesn't actively distinguish between foreign and domestic addresses, making its opinions about the validity of this data questionable. How can it decide that the province in a foreign address is incorrect when it doesn't even bother to distinguish between foreign and domestic addresses? The ability to deal with objects in general terms is one of the greatest benefits of OOP. But this does not mean that work, in the form of coding, has simply evaporated. Whenever you create a specialized object, and then allow the system to deal with it on general terms, you allow the system to assume that the object is capable of running its own life. Therefore, you don't have to write any code in the general program to truly support this object. All you have really done is to shift that burden onto the object itself. Looking back at the domestic address, you can see that although the overall system didn't have to do anything special to handle addresses that were capable of learning their own zip codes, the DomesticAddress class itself did. OOLs don't make programming tasks evaporate, their primary contribution is to help guarantee that you only have to do these tasks once.

Consider a function called when the user has decided that a zip code is invalid. If the user is treating all addresses the same, as does most of the system, then the first thing we have to do is to figure out whether the user is talking about a foreign or a domestic address. This isn't too hard, as the complaint about a specific zip code is always expressed in terms of the object that carries the offending zip code. Remember that the definition of the bad zip code function starts off something like:

```
DomesticAddress::badZipCode(...
```

This is a statement that implies that the domestic address object carrying the bad zip code is available within the bad zip code function itself. After all, if we examine a hypothetical call of this function, we see that the real element we are dealing with is the address object itself, not its internal Zip code element:

.

.

.

```
// we know we are working with a domestic address
theZip = theAddress.zipCode();
```

.

.

```
// user doesn't like this zip code
theAddress.badZipCode(newZipCode);
```

As you can see, the offending instance of a DomesticAddress is always right at hand. If another **badZipCode()** function was declared in the ForeignAddress class, our problem would be unchanged, because the function can assume that, if it's called, it's in the right class. This illustrates how OOPs can function at multiple levels. There are sections of the code that operate on a variable as an abstract concept, in this case an Address object. These sections simply assume that any instance can respond to some simple message such as **load,** by verifying and loading the data. The system can then deal with the Address class as an abstract quantity, and can use a limited set of polymorphic functions to drive the behavior of any object derived from the Address class. In short, there are cases where the system in general never knows exactly to what kind of object it is talking. It doesn't have to, it can depend on the fact that receiving functions always knows exactly what kind of object is involved, a binding that occurred when the program was compiled.

In any case, the badZipCode member function is an example of an update function, although it has a few more twists than most. It not only needs to load the new zip code into the address, it first must delete the existing links between the bad zip code and the state and area code. The code to accomplish this would resemble:

```
DomesticAddress::badZipCode(char *lng)

{

    clearZipState(zip,state);

    clearZipArea(zip,areaCode);

    delete zip;

    zip = strsave(lng);

    saveZipState(zip,state);

    saveZipArea(zip,areaCode);

}
```

As you can see from the example above, there are three main tasks that must be accomplished by the badZipCode function. It must undo the internal links it has built to the bad zip code, release its storage, and reallocate and relink the new zip code.

In general terms, when you are implementing update functions, you must always ask yourself, *"Is there something that the last update or initialization did that will no longer be true after I perform the update?"* The answer is often yes, and often for the simplest of reasons. Whenever any object uses dynamic storage to hold its values, at the very least you must delete the old storage before loading the new value. In cases where other objects are referenced, you must determine if the object itself should be destroyed, based on the number of other references to it. If you are the only one referring to this object, you must destroy it. In more complex cases you must also correct any internal data that is invalidated by the new data.

In general, the average complexity of update functions within any class is determined by how far down the class hierarchy the class is. As we have seen previously, generalized classes near the top of the hierarchy, such as Collections and Entities, have very simple update functions. As they deal with the most general cases, they aren't overflowing with specialized code for rare conditions. On the other hand, classes further down the hierarchy, such as DomesticAddresses, are more specialized and tend to perform longer sequences of specific actions. Essentially, the more general classes embody knowledge about the system itself, whereas more specialized classes are specialists, designed for operating on a very small subset of the applications data. Update functions for general purpose classes tend to be simpler than update functions for more specialized classes.

Summary

1. We used a parallel implementation technique to produce an abstract class and two related subclasses. By performing this operation in parallel, we were able to save ourselves some coding work, as we could quickly establish a limited set of relations (via member function calls) between the implemented classes. At the same time we were able to guarantee that this limited set of relations would satisfy all of the current requirements, and not interfere with any new requirements that might arise.

2. The relationship between the procedural knowledge and the data that an object contains was shown. The primary reason for the separation between the domestic and foreign address subclasses is not based on differences in data, since they could both be represented by a common structure. It is the procedural knowledge, about such things as the correct format of a zip code or phone number that makes them distinct. Objects are not defined in the terms of the data on which they operate. They are defined by this data and the functions that the object provides to operate on the data.

3. Polymorphism allows an apparently single set of functions operate on both classes. Both classes provide the **fullAddress()** member function, but the actions of this function differ between the classes.

4. OOP is not a panacea. It does not make programming tasks evaporate. It can help you to make sure you only do each of them once.

Further Enhancements: Implementation Decisions

In this chapter we are dealing with coding three distinct classes as a single task. In all of the previous classes, we can divide the implementation into three major sections. There are the initialization functions or constructors, the functions that implement the special behavior for the class, and the function that deletes the object or destructor. The constructors represent a great deal of work on our part, primarily to save us time in the future by providing a wide range of ways in which we can initialize the object, depending on exactly what data we have. In some cases this isn't necessary, because the object will be accessed from a limited set of functions, where each function provides an identical set of parameters.

This is often the case when dealing with an abstract class such as Address and its real subclasses such as DomesticAddress and Foreign-Address. Both of these derived classes will probably operate from the same basic set of data, therefore it isn't too difficult to ensure that each of these derived classes provides the same set of parameters to the Address class constructor, which in turn means we only need to implement a single address class constructor. We aren't going to be overly inconvenienced by giving up overloaded constructor functions in the Address class, and this in turn means we are going to be greatly convenienced because we no longer have to write the overloaded functions themselves. Notice the use of words such as "usually" or "probably." This represents a form of thought used by many successful object programmers. You never want to be in the position of saying something is true forever for all classes, because if you do this, you lose the ability to say, "Add a new subclass? No problem."

In the last chapter we said that we might someday implement an electronic address subclass of the Address class. Now, if we had built some piece of code that forced all classes to act a certain way and the new electronic address class had problems with this, adding the electronic address subclass becomes quite expensive. On the other hand, if we had left flexibility for unknown future developments, then these developments don't have to incorporate modifying everything we've already done into the cost of implementing them. Since domestic and foreign addresses already cover most of the spectrum of address flavors and the electronic address is the only conceivable subclass that might pop up one day, it's safe to assume that using the single existing constructor function isn't going to be a big problem to new subclasses. If it is a big problem, we can add a new initiator and don't have to do anything else to the foreign or domestic address classes—or to the Address class itself. The future cost of adding the electronic address class is likely to be quite small. While this may seem to be a trivial observation, real world observations tell otherwise.

In many systems, programmers tend to implement what they believe are private data structures and algorithms to accomplish a specific job. Then their program goes into the field, and the users start requesting extensions to the system's capabilities. Most user requests are expressed in terms of a difference between the real system and their model of a perfect system. For example, with an inventory package they might say, "Well, you've got the size. How about taking the color too?" In conventional systems, this kind of request is often more expensive to satisfy than it appears on the surface. This is because the modules within the system are so tightly locked to a single viewpoint, that they must all be modified to account for what appear to be surface changes in the characteristics of the program. By using the class hierarchy, objects are constructed where changes made at any level in the hierarchy are guaranteed to apply to all levels that are affected by these changes. There are times where it is convenient to simply assume that all lower levels of the hierarchy will do some task in the same way. Because we are doing all of our work in this class hierarchy, we aren't eternally damned with this decision. We can always add new features to a class at a later point, if one of its subclasses insists that it must have this feature. When implementing any new object, the constructor functions are often the first defined. This allows you to divide the various processing responsibilities between the object itself and the objects that use it.

CHAPTER 13

RELATIONS AND LIFECYCLE

The leg bone is connected to the hip bone, the hip bone is ...

In this chapter we will build most of the classes we need to implement the Inventory database. This includes the Inventory class itself and the associated Supplier class. This chapter discusses some implementation level considerations as they relate to future program maintenance, and illustrates how object oriented programs are constructed on a much more general level than are their straight C counterparts.

Review

In the design section we determined that the Inventory database was actually an IndexedCollection of instances of InventoryItems—where each InventoryItem represents one item in Bancroft's inventory. From the design of the InventoryItem class arose the requirement for Supplier objects that represent Entities from which Bancroft buys products. In designing the Supplier class, we determined that we also needed a **SupplierInventory** class to map supplier inventory codes and prices onto the InventoryItems with which they are associated.

Variables

The variables provided by the inventory class are:

```
char *partNumber;                // part number code for this item

int onHand;                      // number of items on hand

float price;                     // the price per item

OrderedCollection *suppliers;    // place to order from

IndexedCollection *salesHistory; // the sales history for this item

char *description;               // a text description of the item
```

As you can see, some variables refer directly to a data item, such as the integer *onHand*, while some refer to other objects, such as the *Ordered-Collection* referred to by suppliers. The variables that refer directly to individual data items are **terminal** variables, while the ones that refer to other objects are **non-terminal** variables. The word terminal in regards to variables has effectively the same meaning as it does with trains. The end of the line, no further travel possible. First specifying the variables we are implementing for a class allows us to estimate reliably the complexity of the code for the class we are going to implement. The presence of terminal variables implies that the object containing them is likely to be the one operating on them, and it also implies that none of these operations should be too complex, as the terminal variables themselves aren't that complex. This fact can be easily verified in a traditional C program, as functions that tend to operate on structures (objects) tend to be more complex than those that operate on individual data items. Conversely, the presence of object references indicates that the immediate class does not have to implement logic to manipulate this data, it only needs to make the proper member function calls to accomplish its objectives.

The general sequence of implementation is to start with the most general classes and work through the hierarchy, moving to more and more detailed classes which are derived from base classes that have been implemented already. When non-terminal variables are encountered, we simply assume that the object implements a reasonable suite of member functions, and we make calls to these member functions as needed. In short, we constantly focus on solving small implementation details (terminal references) with which we can easily deal, and continue deferring larger details (non-terminal references). The end result is that we implement the entire system by doing this because all of the objects we are creating end in terminal references (after all of the non-terminal references have been passed through). We will have constructed all of the complex system operations as a set of cooperating simpler operations. It could be said that we never even had to understand how these complex operations worked, we only had to know how all of the pieces work. There are two distinct cases for deciding to use non-terminal references. First, the non-terminal may be used to provide the object with some internal capacities it might otherwise have to provide itself. For example, if Bancroft were to ask that we track the amount of merchandise on hand in several warehouses, then we would most likely use a Collection of some type to hold each of the warehouse's on hand values. We would do so by replacing the terminal on hand reference to an integer with a non-terminal reference to this new collection. In this case, we are using Collection to provide the InventoryItem object with certain skills to manage a specific group of data even though InventoryItem is still responsible for managing the data within the collection.

In the other case, we might actually create a separate object to support some specialized component of the inventory. For example, if Bancroft decides to enhance the description field, we might convert it to an object that has internal elements which define such things as color and size. The InventoryItem would not need any new code to manipulate this new object. It would simply inform the object of its general desires via the use of member functions and wait for the object to perform the requested actions.

In the InventoryItem as it has been defined, we've actually conducted a marriage of convenience between these two cases. In managing the information about suppliers and sales for each inventory item, we have used Collections of specialized objects. We've ordered both items on the menu.

This event is fairly common in the case of Collections of various types, as you will find Collection and its subclasses to be among the most ubiquitous objects in the system. After all, the response of any OOL programmer, when hearing the words "one or more of..." is to substitute instantly the words "collection of ..." OOL programmers in weakly typed OOLs also manifest a supreme indifference to the exact contents of the collection, instead they simply assume that all collections are full of "stuff." In any case, the InventoryItem is responsible for managing access to the collection, and the actual objects contained within the collection are expected to do what the InventoryItem expects of them.

Therefore, when you lay out the variables for implementation, look at what you've got. If some of them are specialized objects then you know that you won't have to deal directly with them, but you do need to know how to communicate with them, by using member functions. If some of them are standardized system classes, such as Collections, then you know that while you don't have to understand exacxtly how a collection works, you do need to know how to call a Collection's member functions to make the right things happen. You will have to deal with the terminal objects by writing code to perform the desired operations on them. Through this analysis, you will form a much clearer idea of what it is that you must implement for this object.

Constructors

In constructing a new instance of an InventoryItem, we will assume that we can always count on getting the part number, the price, and the description. We have the choice of implementing a single constructor function to handle these three values, or to implement a series of constructors to handle parameter lists that provide one or more of the optional values. The decision to implement more constructor functions at this time is based on the convenience it will provide future programmers, as the underlying functionality will also be given by some of the update functions.

They don't really need a lot of different constructor functions for the inventory item. If we provide facilities to update each of the optional values they might provide, then the constructor can simply set all these values to NULL and the update functions can be used afterwards to load the various optional data that wasn't required. For example, if someone also wanted to supply the value for onHand, they could call a standard constructor function, which would set onHand to zero, and they could then call the **onHand()** update function to set the onHand value after the constructor finished. The decision to implement or not to implement a constructor function, is more critical when constructors that carry a single parameter are implemented. This is because constructors with a single parameter are used by the compiler as mechanisms for performing type conversions, or casts. For example, an Entity's constructor which accepts a single string as a parameter, forms an implicit type conversion, showing how to convert a string to an Entity. Although this is not bad, you must keep track of a relationship such as this, because it is used whenever an attempt is made to convert a string variable to an Entity variable. When there are many of these implicit type conversions, determining which overloaded function just committed electronic suicide could be tough.

As it so happens, we will have enough problems with the InventoryItem constructor. Remember that one of the primary elements in the Bancroft system, from the user's point of view, is the **InventoryDatabase**. This is nothing more than an IndexedCollection, containing a reference to every InventoryItem in the system and keyed by the InventoryItem's part number. As the InventoryDatabase is supposed to contain an accurate list of InventoryItems, the best time to ensure that this list is correctly maintained is when we create and destroy InventoryItems. Since we can trust each InventoryItem object to police its own behavior, all we need to do is to control the gateway.

Therefore, the constructor function is going to have to ensure that this database is correctly maintained. This means that is must ensure that the following conditions are satisfied:

1. Every InventoryItem created by this constructor and still in existence can be located in the InventoryDatabase by using the part number that was given to the constructor when it was called.

2. No two items in the InventoryDatabase have the same part number.

Given these two conditions and the normal requirements for constructor functions, we would end up with the following InventoryItem constructor function:

```
InventoryItem(int sClass,char *p,float c,char *d):(sClass)
// see if this is really a new part number
{if(InventoryDatabase.selection(p) != NULL)
    error("Part number is already used");
// initialize the new InventoryItem
partNumber = strsave(p);              /* link duplicate of the part # */

onHand = 0;                            /* CLEAR ON-HAND */

price = c;                            /* set the unit price */

suppliers = OrderedCollection new;
salesHistory = IndexedCollection new;
description = d;                       // update the database

InventoryDatabase.add(p,*this);

}
```

As you can see, the constructor first checks to make sure the key isn't used in the database. If it isn't, it proceeds to initialize the new instance of the InventoryItem and then to add this item to the database.

Destructor

The InventoryItem object does not accomplish its assigned duties by itself; it needs the help of Collections of Supplier objects. In turn, the Suppliers need the SupplierInventory object to support the translation between Bancroft's part numbers and the supplier's part numbers. The Supplier object is not the exclusive property of a single InventoryItem, it may be shared by a large number of InventoryItems. We are confronted by a tricky situation here. We can't just go about arbitrarily deleting suppliers because we are deleting an inventory item, for the supplier might be linked to other InventoryItems. On the other hand, deleting an inventory item means that we must adjust the supplier's internal data because in deleting this item we have to delete the supplier's reference to the item. This is an example of one of the few areas where object oriented design is more complex than procedural design. Very subtle relationships can exist between objects, where any operation on one object means another related object must also be modified. There really isn't any such thing as a simple deletion of an element in Bancroft's inventory. Instead, we are dealing with a set of deletions, one in Bancroft's inventory and a corresponding deletion in the inventory of each supplier that provides this item. On top of this, we have the same basic problem we had with the constructor function—ensuring the reference to the inventory item we are destroying is also removed from the database. To implement the destructor function, we need to perform the following actions:

1. Delete the reference to this item from the InventoryDatabase.

2. For each Supplier in the supplier's collection, delete the supplier inventory item corresponding to this item. If the supplier inventory collection is now empty, delete the supplier itself.

```
~InventoryItem()
{
    Collection dumpList;
    SupplierInventoryItem *sId;
    int running;                    // see if we might have a *big* problem

    if(InventoryDatabase-selection(p) == NULL)
        fatalError("PART NOT FOUND IN DATABASE!!!");
                                    // loop through the supplier list
    firstSupplier = suppliers-first();
    running = 1;
    while(running)
    {
        theSupplier = suppliers-selection();
        theInventory = theSupplier.inventory();
```

```
        if(theInventory-selection(partNumber) != NULL)
        {
            theInventory-delete(partNumber);
            if(theInventory-isEmpty())
                    deleteSupplier = true;
            else
                    deleteSupplier = false;
        }
        else
            fatalError("Inventory references bad supplier");
        if(deleteSupplier)
            dumpList.add(suppliers.currentIndex());
            running = (suppliers-next() !=
            firstSupplier) ? TRUE : FALSE
    } while(suppliers-next() !=firstSupplier);
    // clear out the deceased suppliers
    if(!dumpList.isEmpty())
    {
        firstSupplier = dumpList.first();
        do {
            suppliers-rDelete(dumpList.selection());
        } while ((dumpList.next() != firstSupplier);
    // now delete the part from the inventory database
    }
    InventoryDatabase-delete(
}
```

Access Functions

Since the InventoryItem object is one of the system's real workhorses, we will save ourselves future problems by implementing an access function for each element contained within this object. Although this is not technically necessary, given our design, it's a good idea. The reason is simple. If you implement an object that you expect to use a great deal, it is fairly safe to assume that you are going to use it in all sorts of ways you never originally thought of. This is not to say that the design of the object itself is wrong, or that you will be using it improperly. It is simply a realization that before you are done, you will probably come up with a reason to access each and every element of this object.

We can also assume that the InventoryItem class is likely to have a horde of specialized functions, and that it is likely that this horde will multiply during the life of the program. This is because the InventoryItem represents a central component of the system, and its behavior has strong effects on the behavior of the system in general. It is likely to have to do many special things for a large number of client objects, a community in which the users are also found.

Earlier, with the Collection class and its derived classes, we limited the rampant growth of member functions with a two pronged attack. We first divided the concept of "Collections" into a class hierarchy, so that we could implement only the unique aspects of a particular collection in each class, rather than being forced to go through the whole development process again. Secondly, we acknowledged the fact that the Collection classes represented general system capabilities, and for that reason we provided a single general purpose interface, where each of the derived classes modifies or extends the behavior of the collection. Such a general purpose interface is itself polymorphic, as it can perform many distinct tasks, depending on exactly what derived class it's operating. In this case, we aren't making a general purpose system module, we are implementing one of the key objects in the application. While system objects are meant to provide general solutions to a wide range of similar problems, application objects are used to provide specific solutions to specific problems, which tends to limit their ability to interact through a polymorphic interface. Not all application objects act this way. Many objects, such as we have seen up to now, perform supporting roles. But in the case of the InventoryItem, this is definitely not the case. The InventoryItem is something of direct interest to the user, and they are likely to have many questions they wish to ask it.

In the cases of objects such as the InventoryItem, there are certain constants on which you can depend, although not all of them are pleasant. Items such as these go through a standard kind of evolution, which starts at the point we are at now. Other than keeping a collection of all the ones we know about, we really haven't said what it is that InventoryItems do, or more importantly, how we introduce them to the user, who is still suspicious of their very existence. We've built the system with the goal of implementing these things, and now that we are there, we don't know what to do with them.

Common sense tells us that we will probably hook these items up to screen programs and some kind of user query support function, so that we can display this data for the user, and they can ask questions about it. We already know one question they are going to ask—and that is why can't it be faster and easier? This is one constant on which we can depend however, this doesn't mean that new capabilities are added directly to this object. As a matter of fact, these new capabilities, represented by new member functions and variables, tend to spring up like mushrooms in other parts of the system. Maintenance is what harvests this crop of capabilities and transports all of them to the InventoryItem.

We can also look at the various member functions that we've decided an InventoryItem must have. As we are responsible for maintaining the values contained within the InventoryItem, we have already presupposed that there are member functions available to access and change each of the variables. We usually just assume we can implement an access and a store function for each element of the InventoryItem. We can then safely forget about them, as we should never have to alter them again, unless of course we decide to redesign the system from the ground up to eliminate a bug (**scorched earth policy**).

The general process starts off with an application object like Inventory-Item being implemented and other objects accessing and manipulating it by the simple access and update functions, as we see in this case. These functions are quite straightforward, as their only purpose in life is to allow other objects to manipulate the elements of an InventoryItem. As the system matures, we may notice that a sequence of access operations is duplicated by many users of an object. For example, let's say that Bancroft uses two inventory coding schemes in parallel and often needs to know which coding scheme was actually used for a part. We would find a lot of code fragments in the user interface functions that go somewhat like this:

```
.

.

. pNum = invItem-partNumber();
if(strncmp(pNum,"PN",2))
    pCode = OLDCODE;
else if(strncmp(pNum,"II"))
    pCode = NEWCODE; .

.

.
```

Some readers may be pointing out that if we already knew that, why didn't we remember to put it in the design in the first place? More importantly, why don't we put it into the InventoryItembecause that's where this test belongs? Well, that's a good point. We try to put anything we do know about in the design and we try to put functions in the right places, where they are of most use. But software doesn't get released once and then live forever in that single form. Instead it gets released, released again, and so on, until the version number has to be given in exponential form. It is a necessary process because this is how software is fine-tuned to the demands of its user community.

And then it's version 5.7, and you find a horde of the above mentioned fragments living in your program. When you started this process, you didn't know that this was such a common question because the users never told you. This leads us back to the subject of OOP maintenance. Identifying common fragments such as these and upgrading them to the status of object member functions is the most important aspect of OOP maintenance. By promoting these fragments to member functions, you are simplifying the overall structure of the program, as well as significantly decreasing its overall size. You are also saving yourself from future coronary problems when users mention the third type of part number coding that they forgot to tell you about when you did the first two types. Instead of having to hunt through a program and identify each of the fragments that needs a third conditional, as in:

```
        .

        .

        .

pNum = invItem.partNumber();
if(strncmp(pNum,"PN",2))
     pCode = OLDCODE;
else if(strncmp(pNum,"II"))
     pCode = NEWCODE;
else if(strncmp(pNum,"ZZ"))
     pCode = OTHERNEWCODE;

        .

        .

        .
```

you can make this change in one place, to one function, giving you the InventoryItem member function:

```
InventoryItem::partCode()
{
     int returnValue;
     if(strncmp(partNumber,"PN",2))
          returnValue = OLDCODE;
     else if(strncmp(partNumber,"II"))
          returnValue= NEWCODE;
     else if(strncmp(partNumber,"ZZ"))
```

```
        returnValue= OTHERNEWCODE;
    return(returnValue);

}
```

Connecting this to the subject of access functions, recall our earlier decision to simply provide basic access to each of the inventory fields, leaving it up to the callers of these functions to do something intelligent with the data. This approach will eventually lead to the situation described above, where you are performing the same operation on data from the InventoryItem, in many different places in your program. One problem initially confronted by new OOP programmers is the decision of what to, and what not to, implement. What happens is that they successfully make their way through the design process, feeling that they are now in possession of a complete definition of the program's requirements. Then they begin implementing the design and become horrified as they realize their beautiful design doesn't clearly delimit the responsibilities of each object. Not only that, the design of the system itself appears to be an agent for change! This is an understandable position for a programmer who has previously worked from rigid procedural designs, many times represented by hundreds of flowcharts, dataflow diagrams, and the like. This information is necessary for constructing programs in C. C is a structured language, but the structure only details how elements of the program are defined. Other than to say that programs are collections of functions which all have a certain surface similarity and that main() is the first one called, C imposes absolutely no constraints on the running characteristics of a program. This is the root of the difference between C and C++. C++ is a programming environment, where all programs and data (objects) are structured in a certain way, as opposed to straight C, a programming language where all program elements are structured the same way.

Therefore, growth is a phenomenon that is institutionalized in C++ programs, that is to say that the system recognizes this phenomenon, and that its design took this into account. Unfortunately, while C++ does allow for growth, it still takes human intervention to ensure that this growth is orderly. And this occurs in the implementation maintenance cycle:

1. Add known function requirements to an object definition.

2. Wait for some time to pass, and some changes to be made.

3. Examine all of the users of the original functions, and see which are performing duplicated actions.

4. Move these duplicated actions to the object on which these functions were operating, and replace the actions in the original functions with a call on the new object member function.

5. Go back to step two.

Here is the first set of access functions that will be implemented by the InventoryItem. These functions will serve as building blocks for new functions that operate on InventoryItems, and will in turn be captured and added to this set:

```
char *
partNumber()
{
    return(partNumber);
}
int
onHand()
{
    return(onHand);
}
float
price()
{
    return(price);
}
OrderedCollection *
```

```
suppliers()
{
    return(suppliers);
}
IndexedCollection *
salesHistory()
{
    return(salesHistory);
}
char *
description()
{
    return(description);
}
```

Update Functions

In implementing the update functions, we must pay attention to both the design specification of the program and to any requirements placed on us by the implementation as it currently exists. For example, the design says it is very irregular to have someone arbitrarily change the onHand quantity, as they usually wish to add or subtract something from it. In another case, the implementation places restrictions on how we change the part number because it's used as an index in the inventory database.

Given all of these unpleasant little details, how shall we begin? The first step isn't too surprising, we'll define all of the functions that don't have any external relationships and see where that leaves us. To begin with, we will define the functions necessary to adjust the quantity on hand, the price, and the description:

```
InventoryItem::addOnHand(int quantity)
{
```

```
    if(quantity > 0)
        onHand += quantity;
    else
        < report attempted fraud>
}
InventoryItem::removeOnHand(int quantity)
{
    if(quantity  0)
        onHand -= quantity;
    else
        < problems,problems>
}
InventoryItem::price(float thePrice)
{
    price = thePrice;
}
InventoryItem::description(char *theDescription)
{
    if(description != NULL)
        description release;
    description = strsave(theDescription);
}
```

Now we can proceed to the more complex functions. Starting right off with a real beast, we will examine the part number **update** function. If the system needs to change the part number of a defined inventory item, it must delete and reload itself into the inventory database, to ensure that the database has a correctly updated reference. It must also disallow changes in the part number where the new part number is not unique. If this wasn't enough, it has to change all the supplier inventories that refer to it.

For these reasons, we are not going to attempt to actually change the part number on the fly. It's just too complicated, especially since there is a much simpler solution. We can create a new inventory item, copying all of the old information to it, with the appropriate substitutions along the way. After we have finished this entire process, we will destroy the original inventory item.

This is a preferred solution when you are modifying data that objects use to establish links between themselves. In this case, many of the items that an InventoryItem refers to will refer back to it, using its part number to do so. This means that you will have to loop through collections of objects, such as SupplierInventoryItems, and modify the collection underneath yourself as you perform this search. The process can become too complicated. If you copy the pieces of the old object to the new object, substituting values where necessary, you have a much simpler problem. The destructor is the only function that must know how to undo all of the connections between the object being destroyed and other objects:

```
InventoryItem::partNumber(char *thePartNumber)

{

    // is there an entry for the new part number
    if(InventoryDatabase.selection(thePartNumber) != NULL)
    {                           // oops, there's already an entry for that code

        return(NULL);
    }                                              // the change should be OK

    < BUMP THE REFERENCE COUNT>
    InventoryDatabase.delete(partNumber);

    partNumber release;

    partNumber = strsave(partNumber);

    InventoryDatabase.add(partNumber,(void *) this);
```

```
< UNBUMP THE REFERENCE COUNT>
}
```

In this function, we had to increase the reference count by one before we called the InventoryDatabase **delete** function. This reflected the fact that we needed to make sure the system knew we had an internal reference to this object. Recall that the collection delete utilities will automatically call the **decReference()** function, which will in turn destroy the object if this count goes to zero. While in previous cases we have not had to worry too much about the reference count, at this point we must. The InventoryDatabase is the only object that normally refers to InventoryItems; therefore, if we don't note our own reference to the object, the system will cheerfully delete the InventoryItem before we have a chance to reload it into the database. When we decrement the reference count at the end, it will go to zero and the system will then delete this object.

Summary

Implementing classes is primarily a process of implementing the logic that operates on their terminal references. Where non-terminal references to other objects are encountered, the object holding the references contains logic to communicate with the objects on the other end of these references. The end result of this implementation path is that the entire system will be implemented as a set of operations on simple data types. The more complex operations involving objects are created from these simple operations—sequenced together with member function calls. This results in that more complex operations are a by-product of the implementation of the simple operations.

There are two main types of non-terminal reference usage. First, there is the use of other objects to provide special skills to the object referencing them. Collections are the common example of this, where objects use Collections to give them the ability to manage lists of data. The second type of non-terminal reference is where specialized objects are used to provide specialized subcomponents of the object referencing them. Many application specific objects fall into this class, where they provide special capabilities to a larger or more generalized object. Care must be exercised when implementing single parameter constructors. These constructors represent implicit type conversions between the type of the constructor parameter and the type of the object to which the constructor is bound. Careful attention must be paid to non-terminal references. These references to other objects form a path for dependencies, created through circular references between objects.

Circular references often require specialized logic to ensure that changes affect all of the objects linked together. Objects that represent major conceptual parts of the application, such as InventoryItem, are likely to have a great many specialized functions to support the user interface. In addition, they are likely to grow steadily because they are in the foreground, as far as the end user is concerned. Standard system classes tend to have simple, polymorphic interfaces. Application classes that are directly tied to the user interface tend to have many specialized service functions, resulting in fairly complex interfaces.

Further Enhancements

Implement a description object, as mentioned above. Alter the behavior of InventoryItem so that the color and size fields are automatically incorporated in the keying.

You can populate a collection of InventoryItems using the old (char *) definition of the description element. Change this to the newly defined InventoryDescription class, automatically propagating the information from the old class to the new class.

CHAPTER 14

META-OBJECTS

The first rule of intelligent tinkering is to save all the parts.

In this class we will implement the Customer subclass of the Entity class. This class is used to maintain information on each customer and all instances of this class are collected together into the customer database. In implementing this class we will examine the use of class data, where all objects of a particular class share a common variable.

Review

The Customer class is a high level object within the Bancroft application, that is structurally equivalent to the InventoryItem class. The Customer class is responsible for dealing with the same structural requirements as InventoryItem's. Because Customer represents a more complex entity than does InventoryItem, the problems are compounded. The Customer object must manage this information that is associated with the customer:

- Name and Address
- Transactions
- Advertising

Variables

The Customer object needs four private variables to support the information associated with customers. It does not need to implement name and address information, as this is already done by its base class. These variables must be implemented as private variables of the Customer class:

```
char *customerID;

IndexedCollection *orderHistory;

IndexedCollection *dropShips;

Collection *mailHistory;
```

As you see from the definitions, with the exception of the customer ID, we will be dealing with various flavors of Collections to support the Customer class data.

Constructors

In order to decide on what constructor(s) should be provided, we should consider the likely way in which new customers are identified. As a customer needs to make an order to become a customer, we are probably going to have to create new Customer objects during the order entry cycle. If this is true, it then follows that the name and address is available for this customer, as well as a single SaleTransaction object representing the current purchase.

What we don't have is a customer ID. To create a customer ID, we keep track of the number of customers we have, so that we assign a unique number to each customer we get. Then, to aid the users of the system, we add the first five letters of the last name, which would produce a customer ID that looks like:

- Smith00001

In order to accomplish this, we need a single variable that is shared between every instance of the customer class and that is used to count the number of customer objects which have been created. This variable must; therefore, be a static variable. Remember that all member variables for a class are duplicated for every instance of the class, so we must inform the compiler that all of these refer to the same piece of memory.

We could simply define the customer counter as a static member variable within the class. This also makes the variable available to every member function of the class, at a minimum, which is not that desirable. However, by examining exactly how this variable is used, we can do this in a more elegant fashion.

The only function that really needs to know the value of this variable is the constructor function itself, in order to create the new customer ID. We can define the variable *customerCounter* to be a static variable within the constructor function itself, instead of making it globally available within the class, as the earlier approach proposed. By doing this, we have hidden the variable within the Customer class constructor function. The limitation on using a static variable is that you may only have a single constructor, but this can be circumvented by using static functions in place of the variables.

Returning to the definition of the constructor function, we can now write:

```
{
Customer(Name *name,    Address *address,
    SaleTransaction *currentOrder) : (name,address)
{
    static int customerCounter = 1;    // our global class variable
    char cID[11];                      // a buffer for the customer ID
                                       // make and save the customer ID
    sprintf(cID,"%5s%05d",name.name(),customerCounter++);
    customerID = strsave(cID);  // initialize the collection variables
    orderHistory = IndexedCollection new;
    dropShips = IndexedCollection new.
    mailHistory = Collection new;
```

/ / put the current order into the order history

```
orderHistory.add(currentOrder.transactionID(),currentOrder);
}
```

Destructor

Implementing a customer destructor function has far reaching ramifications because of the relationship that exists between Customer and InventoryItem objects. You will recall that an InventoryItem object contains a salesHistory element, which is an IndexedCollection of Sale-Transactions. The Customer object also contains an IndexedCollection of SaleTransactions. More importantly, each instance of a SaleTransaction is referenced by both a Customer object and by an InventoryItem object. For any reference to a SaleTransaction in a Customer, we will find corresponding relations between this SaleTransaction and various InventoryItems (based on what the customer ordered). This isn't surprising, since a SaleTransaction object represents a customer order and is tied to the customer that ordered it and each of the items the customer ordered.

What this all means as far as the destructor is concerned is that because the Customer and InventoryItem objects share objects and these shared objects reference both this Customer object and an arbitrary set of InventoryItem objects, our destructor function cannot obliterate the Customer object without taking these relations into account. If we arbitrarily delete the Customer object without doing this, we would end up with a set of SaleTransactions that no longer refer to a valid Customer object. Worse yet, we wouldn't be able to ascertain this fact until after we tried to use the old, invalid reference to the customer and the system crashed.

To solve this problem, a Customer object must ensure that all InventoryItem objects that share references to a SaleTransaction with the customer be updated to remove these references. The Customer object must then destroy each of the SaleTransactions before it can finally self destruct. You must always be sensitive to the kinds of relationships between objects where data structures are distributed over other objects. If you find this to be the case in any destructor function, then that function must take steps to ensure that this distributed data map is updated to account for the deletion. This is the same problem with non-terminal references that we encountered in the previous chapter, although more complex. In this case we are operating on a meta-object described by all of the physical objects connected in a network of non-terminal variables.

While the InventoryItem class also dealt with distributed data, we did not discuss it then, because we had other things to talk about. Many of the decisions we made were still based on the fact that we were dealing with distributed data.

As we saw in the InventoryItem and Customer constructor and destructor functions, the complexity of these functions is dependent on how closely the object we are working with is tied to other objects in the system. We also saw that the constructor's job is usually simpler than the destructor's, as the constructor must integrate the new object with the existing objects, whereas the destructor must make it seem like the destroyed object was never there in the first place!

In many OO programs, you will find that there are two distinct kinds of data. The first, and simplest, are those objects which implement concrete concepts. In fact, this is true of all objects that we have implemented in the Bancroft system. They all represent some specific self-contained portion of the overall application. They all have a specific job to do and they carry all of the internal data and knowledge (member functions) necessary to accomplish that job.

The second kind of data are the **meta-objects**, which represent objects that don't exist and control the behavior of the system. Meta-objects implement complex abstractions based on cooperating physical objects– abstractions based on a very high level view of the system's behavior. You cannot point to any single object and immediately know that it is a meta-object. However, this does not make them any less real. It is these meta-objects that are causing us so much trouble with our constructors and destructors. It isn't hard to see that concrete concepts, manifested as objects, represent concrete things. What you must also see is that abstract concepts, implemented by several cooperating objects, also represent concrete things. A meta-object is formed from two or more distinct objects, which may themselves be meta-objects.

These relationships were discovered during the design phase and have affected all the objects of which the meta-object is composed. In this specific case, the relationship between a single Customer and multiple SaleTransactions (and in turn between each SaleTransaction and multiple InventoryItems), is a meta-object implementing a meta-object that represents customer purchase orders. The purchase orders aren't physically implemented by any individual object within the system. It is the responsibility of each object involved to support its end of the relationship, so that between all of the objects involved, the relationship is correctly maintained. If we had actually implemented a **PurchaseOrder** object, we would then be confronted by a rather strange object indeed. It would be both a concrete object and a meta-object. It would be a concrete object because of the fact that it was physically represented in the system. It would also be an meta-object because its definition still involved the relationships established between Customer, SaleTransaction, and InventoryItem objects. In this case, we have a complex relationship established between a single Customer object, a group of SaleTransactions, and a group of InventoryItems. The Customer has a reference to a Collection of SaleTransactions, and each of those SaleTransactions has a reference to a Collection of InventoryItems. In addition, we know from the previous design of the InventoryItem class that each InventoryItem refers back to each of these SaleTransactions.

To properly implement relationships such as these, you must be sensitive to the self-imposed dynamic organization of your system, which originates from the meta-objects. In coding most functions, you can depend on the C++ compiler to help you be a good OOP programmer, because the compiler guarantees that the structures you are defining will produce either a well behaved OOP, or a list of errors. However, in a dynamic object relationship that embodies a meta-object, you are actually implementing the structure at run-time, so the compiler isn't going to be of much help. Instead of depending on the compiler to guarantee you are a well behaved object oriented programmer, you must make this guarantee yourself.

Consider implementing a function that would tell you the most expensive item on a customer's order. If we examine the situation, we could say that the function would do the following:

- Get the current selection from the orderHistory collection; Consider that to be the current order.

- Convert the currentOrder from a saleTransaction to a Collection of inventory items.

- Search the inventory items in the orderedItems list for the one with the highest price.

As you can see, although the function to drive this process might reside within the Customer class, the operation requires cooperation between multiple classes. To accomplish this, you depend on the dynamic relationships between the objects involved. These relationships are critical to the function of the program, but because they are created, used, and destroyed at run-time, the compiler can give little help in guaranteeing that they will operate correctly. It will bless each piece, but it is ignorant of the whole they form at run-time. It is up to the programmer to ensure that the rules which each piece follows are always consistent and always obeyed.

In conclusion, when you begin to implement any object, you must first determine whether the object is a component of any meta-objects. If it is, you must ensure that all operations which the new objects perform, adhere to the rules that the meta-object assumes to be true. By doing this in every individual object involved, you will end up with an implementation of the abstract object, even though you cannot point to a single section of code that actually does the job.

In implementing the customer destructor, we now know we have to not only delete the customer, but also we must ensure that the abstract purchase orders which the customer is involved with, are deleted to reflect the deletion of this customer. This means we need to physically delete the SaleTransactions of this Customer, and all references to these SaleTransactions made by InventoryItems. The code to accomplish this goes something like this:

```
{
~Customer()
{                                      // start at the beginning of the collection

    firstTrans = orderHistory-first();
```

```
        do
{
                                                // get the current item
        theTrans = orderHistory-selection();
                        // get the list of items for this transaction
        transItems = theTrans-orderList();
                                // now update the inventory database
        firstPart = transItems-first();
        do
{
                                        // get the line item object
            theLineItem = transItems-selection();
                                // get the part number of this item
            thePartNum = theLineItem-partNumber();
                                // get the inventory-item record
            invItem = InventoryDatabase-selection(thePartNum)
            // get the inventory sales-history
            invSales = invItem-salesHistory();
                                    // delete this transaction from it
            invSales.delete(theTrans-transactionID());
        }while(firstPart != transItems-advance());
    // delete the transaction storage itself
        delete theTrans;
}
while(firstTrans != orderHistory-advance());
{
                                // now delete all of the transactions
                                // start at the beginning of the list
    firstTrans = orderHistory-first();
                                    // and delete every transaction
        do
```

```
{
            orderHistory-delete();              // delete current selection

    } while(!orderHistory-isEmpty());
                                        // delete the orderHistory collection
    delete orderHistory;
    // delete all of the mailing history records
    firstMail = mailHistory-first();
    while(!mailHistory-isEmpty())
      {                                    // get each mailing record object
            mailItem = mailHistory-selection();
                                              // delete the physical object
        delete mailItem;

      }
      // delete the mailHistory collection
    delete mailHistory;
}                           // DROP SHIPMENTS HAVE BEEN IGNORED
```

As you can see, in order to successfully delete the SaleTransaction records associated with a customer we had to:

1. Delete the reference to a SaleTransaction from the salesHistory collection in each InventoryItem (to which the SaleTransaction referred).

2. Release the physical storage occupied by each saleTransaction.

3. Release the physical storage occupied by the Collection of saleTransactions.

The actual code for freeing drop shipments is not shown because it would make the function much larger. Its general requirements, however, are as follows. Recall that our design stated that records contained in a customer's mailing history could be either plain Entities, or Customers when the goods were shipped to this or another customer. In other words, if we have a Customer object representing the name and address we sent the goods to, we put a reference to that customer in the collection of drop shipments. If we have never seen this name and address before, we then create a new instance of Entity, filling in the name and address references.

Notice that we are using the Entity class directly in this operation. Prior to this we have always assumed that Entity is the base class of some derived class in which we were interested, such as Customer. Given that Entity has been used primarily as an abstract class, what are we doing using it, instead of one of its subclasses? In cases where you may not have enough information to define some specific class completely, the information that you do have may be enough to populate the class' base class. Abstract classes can be of great service in cases such as these, but some care must be taken. Because it is likely the abstract was written with the idea that it is only used to flesh out its base classes, it may require some extensions to support direct use.

Access Functions

The area of customer access functions is one where we can expect continued, heavy growth. This is because the Customer object is a central component of Bancroft's database, and will likely be subjected to a great many queries, in a myriad of forms. When we consider the fact that connections extend from the Customer objects to many other objects in the system, such as InventoryItems, and that these items are in turn linked to even more items, such as Suppliers, we start to see the spectrum of queries that the Customer object may have to support.

When implementing any system, OO or not, you must identify the primary interface between the user of the system and the system itself. Much of the guts of any large software system has very little direct contact with the user, as it is being used to support the lower level operations of the system. Users come into contact with top levels of the system, which then fans out their requests across a much larger number of lower levels.

Identifying these points in a traditionally designed program is quite straightforward. The user interacts with the highest level functions in the program. After all, that's what they are there for. In OO systems, this is not the case. If you look at the program as being represented by the class hierarchy, you notice that the user definitely does not interact with the Object class. This is because the class hierarchy contains some truly sweeping generalizations at the top, defining what is common to every program ever written, not just this specific application. The application code itself is scattered over parts of the hierarchy at lower levels. Which makes it seem harder to locate those parts of the program that interface with the user.

Actually, it's really not hard to find these points. Because this is an OO program, and the objects it contains are modeled on their real world counterparts, the user will themselves name the points of contact, using words like "Customer." We can safely assume these are the points that will be the primary focus of communication with the user. We stated long ago in the design phase that one of the primary benefits of Object Oriented Program System(OOPS) was that it was effectively a model of the application, and there was a high degree of correspondence between the way that the problem was defined and the resulting design of the OOP. We are now exploiting this relationship, one where the program and the user share a great deal of common terminology. To locate the most important parts of an OOP, from a user's perspective, simply requires that you figure out which elements the user interacts with the most. As the system is essentially a model of the real world, the way that users do things on the system is going to be directly related to the way that they do things in the real world.

With that in mind, we shall totally ignore the traditional element access functions, concentrating instead on some of the more specialized access functions that we might expect to see the customer develop over time. One such function might be the **repeatOrders()** function, used to identify all of those items in inventory that the customer has ordered more than once.

This function would have to search through each of the Sale-Transactions contained in this Customer's orderHistory, and in turn it would have to search though every InventoryItem listed in each Sale-Transaction. In all, as you can see below, it's a well behaved OO function, if a trifle large because of the search it has to do:

```
{

Customer::repeatOrders()
```

```
{

    IndexedCollection *compositeOrders, *orderItems;
    Collection *resultList;
    SaleTransaction *aTrans;
    InventoryItem *anItem;
    char *partKey;
    int firstTrans, firstOrder, firstItem, nextItem, count;
                        /* create a scratch collection where we can count the
                           number of times each inventory item was ordered*/
    compositeOrders = new
            IndexedCollection(INDEXEDCOLLECTION_CLASS);
                          // return empty collection if there are no orders
    if(orderHistory.isEmpty())                      // no orders

        return(compositeOrders);
                              // starting at the first transaction filed
    firstTrans = orderHistory.first();      // first transaction
    do
                                        // get the current transaction
    {

        aTrans = orderHistory-selection();
                          // get the items ordered from the transaction
        orderItems = aTrans-orderList();
                                        // from the first item ordered
        firstOrder = orderItems-first();
        do
                                  // get the current inventory item
    {

            anItem = orderItems.selection();
                                  // get the partnumber of the item
```

```
        partKey = anItem-partNumber();
                // use the key to find out how many times we've seen it
                        // if never seen, we'll end up with 0
        count = (int) compositeOrders.selection(partKey);
                        // reload the (count + 1) into the collection
        compositeOrders.add(partKey, (char *) ++count);
    }
while(orderItems-next() != firstOrder);
                        // end when we get back to the first item

    }
while(orderHistory.next() != firstTrans);
                // end when we get back to the first transaction
                // now we remove all items which were only ordered once
    firstItem = compositeOrders.first();
    nextItem = firstItem;
                // from the first item in the total list of ordered items

    do
{                       // how many times was this item ordered?

        count = (int) compositeOrders.selection();
                                        // if only once

        if(count == 1)
        {                       // delete it from the collection
                // collection class behavior automatically moves
                        // us to the next element.

            compositeOrders.delete();
        }
        else
        {                       // OK. advance to the next item

            nextItem = compositeOrders.next();
```

```
        }
    } while( nextItem != firstItem);
                        // quit when we get back to the start of the collection
                        // quit if nothing was ordered more than once
    if(compositeOrders.isEmpty())
        return(compositeOrders);
                            // build a collection of InventoryItems for
                            //all those elements left
    resultList = new Collection(COLLECTION_CLASS);
    firstItem = compositeOrders.first();
    do {                        // the key for the indexed collection is the
                                // inventory part number
        partNum = compositeOrders.key();
                        // get the inventory object itself from the database
        anItem = InventoryDatabase.selection(partNum);
                                // and add it to the new collection
        resultList.add(anItem);
    }
    while(compositeOrders.next() != firstItem);
    return(resultList);
}
```

As you can see from this example, much of the work accomplished within an OOPS is done through the cooperation of many objects. In order to find the items that were ordered more than once, this function used the member functions of the Collection, InventoryItem, and SaleTransaction classes.

If you examine this code closely, you notice that the function limits itself to defining how lists of multiply ordered items are built. Nowhere does it dictate how the objects it uses to accomplish this job are supposed to function.

Update Functions

As in the case of the access functions, we will ignore the various standard elemental update functions we might implement for this class, concentrating instead on a more complex example. Specifically, we shall address the issue of updating the Customer object when a new order is received.

To update the Customer object correctly, we must first remember that the information we are using is not the sole property of the Customer object, as it is also used to relate Customers, SaleTransactions, and InventoryItems together through the meta-object purchase order. If we analyze how this event is most likely to start, we see that the brunt of the work falls onto the Customer object.

When a customer order is received by Bancroft, it is entered into some user interface package, preferably an OO one, and thereby transferred into the core Bancroft system. Now, as user interfaces are not mechanisms for maintaining databases, we don't want to force the user interface to support the relations between the Customer and other classes. The logic simply doesn't belong there. If we examine what the user interface is likely to have as data for the core system, we can see which object is truly responsible for integrating this new information.

Specifically, the user interface is likely to have three distinct pieces of data for us. First, it will have a reference to a Customer object, which defines the previously known Customer placing the order. Even if this is their first order, we can assume that the user interface acquired all of the necessary data on the customer prior to collecting information on the order itself. We can further assume that the user interface would have also given this new customer information to the core system before proceeding with the order entry, and the core system in turn would have created a new instance of Customer containing this new data and returned a reference to that instance to the user interface.

The second piece of data that the user interface will have is information regarding where this order is being shipped to. In the case that the customer has had the order shipped to themselves, the user interface will supply the customer reference twice, first as the actual customer, and then as the shipping information. On the other hand, if the shipping address is different, the user interface is going to use a (as of yet undefined) Customer access function to convert the name and address it gets as a shipment address to a Customer object reference. We must note that if there isn't any such customer, then this function will return an Entity object with the name and address fields filled out.

The final piece of data that the user interface will provide is an IndexedCollection which tells us what specific items have been ordered by the customer this time. The keys to this collection would be Inventory-Item part numbers, and the values associated with each key would be the quantity ordered.

We must implement a Customer member function to handle adding new customer orders received from the user interface. We know that the user interface will give us:

- A reference to the customer making the order.

- A reference to some kind of Entity giving the shipping information.

- An IndexedCollection, keyed by inventory part numbers and giving the quantity ordered for each item.

Considering the way that Customer itself works, and then considering the way our abstract concept of purchase orders is represented, we can say that the function to add new customer orders must take the following steps:

1. Create a new SaleTransaction object that is linked to this customer.

2. Add the shipment information data into the dropShipments collection, using the new SaleTransaction as a key.

3. Loop through each inventory item.

4. Add it to the SaleTransaction

5. Add a link to the new SaleTransaction from the InventoryItem.

Converting this to C++ code, we would get:

```
{

Customer::purchased(Customer *thisCustomer,
```

```
            Entity *shipInfo,
            IndexedCollection *theOrder)
                                    // create the new SaleTransaction
{
    saleTrans = new SaleTransaction(thisCustomer);
                                    // add the shipment information
    dropShips = thisCustomer-dropMailings();
    dropShips-add(saleTrans,shipInfo);
    firstItem = theOrder.first();
    do {
        thisItem = theOrder-keyword();
        numOrdered = (int) theOrder-selection();
        saleTrans.addItem(thisItem,(Object *) numOrdered);
        invItem = InventoryDatabase-selection(thisItem);
        sales = invItem-salesHistory();
        sales.add(saleTrans);
    } while(theOrder-next() != firstItem);
}
```

Summary

Class variables are those variables that are shared by all objects in a class, as opposed to instance variables, which are duplicated in every existing object. Class variables are often control values used at a single point in the system, and in these cases may be hidden within the object itself by declaring them as static local variables within the member function that uses them.

A meta-object represents an abstract object, which is physically implemented by several cooperating objects. Although meta-objects are not physical entities, they are nonetheless extremely important. The complexity of a meta-object cannot be described in mere code, because it is a product of the dynamics of the physical objects that form its parts.

Abstract classes can make good holders for data when you don't have enough data to initialize one of the classes derived from the abstract class.

The application code in an OOP is scattered through the class hierarchy tree; usually some distance removed from the Object class. Where the top level in a conventional program makes sweeping generalizations about the behavior of one program, the top level of an OOP program makes even more sweeping generalizations about all programs.

OOPs are models of real world systems. The way in which a user views an OOP should closely match the concepts manifested by the objects in the system. The user and the system share the same viewpoint.

Further Enhancements

If we were to implement new constructor functions, we would have a problem with the fact that we've put a static variable in the existing constructor. This can be fixed by creating a small static defined function that manages this variable, and calling this function from the constructors. It is not quite as neat, but still neater than putting it directly into the class.

We could also implement a customer function that generates reports based on the purchase order meta-object.

CHAPTER 15

COMPOSITE OBJECTS

If you have something to do, and you put it off long enough, chances are someone else will do it for you.

In this chapter we will implement the Employee class and some parts of the required supporting classes. We will also focus primarily on the complex interrelations that can be established between the Employee classes and its supporting classes, by building upon the discussion of dynamic objects presented in the previous chapters. Instead of using dynamic behavior to implement meta-objects in this chapter, we shall use it to construct **composite objects**, which are more limited in scope than meta-objects. We have constructed composite objects already, most notably the Entity class itself, but we have not yet closely examined the concept.

Review

The Employee object is used to maintain data on employees. The Employee object by itself is relatively useless, as it depends on several specialized objects to accomplish its tasks. For example, the employee uses a kind of EmployeeSalary object to maintain information on the employee's salary, so this implies that the average Employee object can't even directly tell you an employee's salary, but instead it must use a member function of the EmployeeSalary class to accomplish this task. As the Employee class is derived from the Entity class, it does start life with the capability to manage the employee's name and address. However, for almost everything else, it relies on more specialized objects, to which it holds references in its member variables.

The fact that the objects of the Employee class depend so heavily on classes specifically constructed to help them do their job, is a strong indicator that they are composite objects. This is because a composite object is one that is dealt with in terms of the object itself and all specialized helper classes that the object directly references through a member variable. Unlike a meta-object, which is a synergistic product of classes cooperating together, *a composite object is where one object totally controls the lives of the objects it references*. It is customarily dealt with as though it directly possessed all of the capabilities that are implemented by the classes it controls. The difference between meta-objects is admittedly separated by a somewhat fuzzy boundary, but nevertheless, this distinction is important because there are uniformly different behaviors that can be attributed to meta-objects and to composite objects.

Variables

All of the variables in this class hold references to other classes. In the case of the salary and tax information, a reference to a single object is used. In the job classification, benefits, and employment history, we use collections of objects:

- OrderedCollection *jobClass;
- EmployeeSalary *salary;
- OrderedCollection *benefits;
- EmployeeTaxInfo *taxes;
- IndexedCollection *history;

As each new instance of an Employee object is created, an instance of each of these object types must also be created, and the references to the newly created objects must be placed in the appropriate member variable, a responsibility of the Employee constructor functions. This style of construction involves the integration of multiple objects, as do constructors that operate on components of meta-objects. The difference is that the constructors for meta-objects must integrate the newly created object with the existing components of the meta-object, whereas the composite object constructors trigger the creation of all of the helper objects when the primary object in the constructor is created.

Constructors

An Employee constructor must create five new objects and install references to these objects in the new Employee object. This means that the most important job of the Employee constructor function is to route each of its parameters to the appropriate object constructor.

What do the subclasses need? If we were to write it out we would get:

- jobClass   Department and Job Title
- salary   Depends on whether this is a fixed or hourly worker
- benefits   Sick Leave, Vacation Leave, Benefits information
- taxes   Deductions
- history   EMPTY

As you can see, that's a fair amount of data required to initialize the employee. In addition, the salary field can be defined in two radically different ways:

```
HourlyEmployeeSalary(salary,standardHours,overtimeRate)
```

or:

```
FixedEmployeeSalary(salary)
```

If we use this information to determine the parameters to our constructor functions, we find we will need two constructors, defined as:

```
Employee(department,title,salary,standardHours,overtimeRate,
```

```
        sickLeave,vacation,benefitsInfo,deductions)
```

and:

```
Employee(department,title,salary,sickLeave,vacation,
        benefitsInfo,deductions)
```

Notice that we have not specified whether a fixed or hourly salary object needs to be constructed. We have only provided the arguments that would be necessary to accomplish one of the initializations. If you examine this event at a deeper level, you can see this implies that overloaded functions are sensitive to the context in which they are used. In implementing a group of several overloaded functions, you are creating a single function that operates in several distinct contexts, these contexts being differentiated by the parameters to the function. This example, using standardHours and overtimeRate implies that we are dealing with the employee in the context of being an hourly worker, then if we omit both of these terms we are dealing with the employee in the context of being a salaried worker.

One can make the observation that this really doesn't save us much, as we still have to implement a new function for every context in which we refer to this object. So what's the big deal about making each function do its job a slightly different way? All we appear to have gained is the ability to use the same function name with a couple different sets of parameters, and an implicit type conversion in the case of single parameter constructors. This is no small gain, as it greatly enhances the overall structure of the program, but we are still writing all the initialization functions that we would in straight C, and duplicating a fair amount of code in each function.

How much of the function are we truly required to define each time? If we have to reduplicate a great deal of standard code within the body of each constructor function, we are asking for trouble. If we were to do this, then modifications to the logic in one constructor function would have to be duplicated by modifications to all of the other constructor functions, which is in direct opposition to the goals of OO design.

If we consider carrying our design into the world of straight C, we can see both the existing relationship between OO and traditional modular programming, and we can see how to exploit this relationship to solve our problem. We can build all of the necessary constructors in a modular fashion, where we separate the code needed to support the specific peculiarities of each constructor from the more general code that physically initializes each new Employee object.

In implementing the constructors for the Employee class, we can see that both do many of the same operations. The only distinction between them is the type of EmployeeSalary they create. We can assume that the system itself will make this distinction for us, so that we know that each constructor is selected based on what kind of EmployeeSalary object it will create. It will create either a FixedEmployeeSalary or an Hourly-EmployeeSalary object, depending on whether we called the constructor function using a salary alone, or a salary in conjunction with values for the number of standard hours in a pay period and the overtime rate. After this, the steps to initialize the new Employee object are identical. In summary, the steps taken by any constructor are:

1. Create whichever type of EmployeeSalary object is required.

2. Copy the passed parameters and the new EmployeeSalary reference into this class.

If we were to implement the second step as the private member function **initializeMyself(arams)** then we might call it from the constructors in the following fashion:

```
                    // Create a new employee with an hourly salary
Employee(name,address,department,title,salary,
        standardHours,overtimeRate,
        sickLeave,vacation,benefitsInfo,deductions):
    (name,address)
  HourlyEmployeeSalary *sal;


  sal = new
  HourlyEmployeeSalary
```

```
                (salary,standardHours,overtimeRate);


    initializeMyself(department,title,sal,
                        sickLeave,vacation,benefitsInfo,
                        deductions);
    }
```

// Create a new employee with a fixed salary

```
    Employee(name,address,department,title,salary,sickLeave,
            vacation,
            benefitsInfo,deductions): (name,address)
    {
        FixedEmployeeSalary *sal;
        sal = new FixedEmployeeSalary(salary);
        initializeMyself(department,title,sal,
                            sickLeave,vacation,benefitsInfo,
                            deductions);
    }
```

From these examples, we can see how the addition of any new kind of EmployeeSalary object means that we only need to write a new constructor function the first calls the appropriate salary constructor function and then calls the standard constructor function to actually initialize these variables. This is much easier than duplicating the entire logic of the initialization step.

In general terms, you can identify the necessary supporting functions, such as initializeMyself() in this case, by writing out some rough pseudo-code of each of the constructors you expect to implement. If you find that you are duplicating "chunks" of this pseudo-code, you may wish to examine the possibility of making these chunks into private member functions for the use of the constructor functions. In fact, you can do this with any group of member functions you plan on implementing. If you feel that any group of member functions are duplicating the same action, it is your duty to locate these common operations and make legitimate member functions out of them.

We still must define how the support function initializeMyself() operates. We know it will be a private member function of the Employee class, because it is only meant to be used by the constructor functions. We would therefore like the compiler to inform us if any other object is rude enough to try and use this function. We also know that its primary job is to initialize of the member variables of the Employee class, and that to accomplish this initialization, it is going to have to create some new objects. Given all of this, we will first lay out the problem in pseudo-code, before we try and write the C++ version:

1. Create a new ordered collection and put a reference to it into the job-Class element.

2. Create a new EmployeeJobClass object using the department and title parameters as arguments to the constructor function.

3. Add the new EmployeeJobClass object to the empty collection referred to by the department element.

4. Create a new ordered collection and put a reference to it into the benefits element.

5. Create a new EmployeeBenefits object using the sickLeave, vacation, and benefitsInfo parameters as arguments to the constructor function.

6. Add the new EmployeeBenefits object to the empty collection referred to by the benefits element.

7. Create a new EmployeeTaxInfo object, using the parameter deductions as a parameter to the constructor function. Put the reference to this new object into the taxes element.

8. Create a new indexed collection and put the reference to it into the history element.

Recall that we said that because of relationships between the Customer, SaleTransaction, and InventoryItem classes, we had implemented an meta-object. In this class we are creating a composite object, which is another dynamic construction, but has different operating characteristics.

A meta-object has certain traits in common with composite objects, one being it contains references to external objects within its member variables. Composite objects have one internal object that serves as the primary object. In these examples the Employee object is the primary object within the composite Employee object. Only the Employee holds references to the other objects that form the composite Employee object. There are no reciprocal paths back from the rest of the objects within the composite object. Defined as a network topology, it's a star with the primary object at the center and one helper object at the end of each arm.

Meta-objects, on the other hand, can be completely accessed through many of the objects that form them because many of these objects tend to contain references to each other. In my experience, the majority of meta-objects go so far as to use a large number of circular references between all the objects that form it. This essentially means that, as a network topology, a meta-object can be anything.

Consider the following case. Some arbitrary function in the user interface gets the salesHistory collection from some arbitrary inventory ite and selects an element from it. Following this, another function in the user interface selects some Customer object and selects an item from the orderHistory element of this customer. What happens if both of these SaleTransaction references refer to the same SaleTransaction? This is often going to be the case because that's why the relationship was built in the first place.

The key issue is that we have accessed the same object via paths from two different objects and that all three objects in turn are components of a meta-object. In order for an object to be truly defined as a meta-object, there must be more than one way to form the abstract object; otherwise, it's a composite object. As you can see in the example, we can form the abstract object by going either from the InventoryItem to a SaleTransaction, or from a Customer to a SaleTransaction.

Returning to the Employee class, if you examine the objects mapped by instances of this class, you can see that they have no meaning outside the context of the Employee object with which they are used. Unlike InventoryItems and Customers, each of which can stand on their own, the objects mapped by an Employee object, such as the EmployeeBenefits object, have no lives of their own. An InventoryItem does not need a Customer object to be complete, but an EmployeeBenefits object only has meaning in terms of the composite object with which it is associated.

Given all of this, the code necessary to implement the initializeMyself() function would be:

```
void
Employee::initializeMyself(char *name,
                   char *address,
                   char *department,
                   char *title,
                   EmployeeSalary *salary,
                   char *sickLeave,
                   char *vacation,
                   char *benefitsInfo,
                   char *deductions): (name,address)
{
    OrderedCollection *oc;
    EmployeeJobClass *jClass;
    EmployeeBenefits *bInfo;         // copy the salary object pointer

    salary = theSalary;        // create and initialize jobClass collection

    oC = new OrderedCollection(ORDERED_COLLECTION);
    jClass = new EmployeeJobClass(department,title);
    oC-add(jClass);
    jobClass = oC;          // create and initialize the benefits collection

    oC = new OrderedCollection(ORDERED_COLLECTION);
    bInfo = new EmployeeBenefits (sickLeave, vacation,
                              benefitsInfo);
```

```
oC->add(bInfo);

benefits = oc;            // create and initialize the tax information

taxes = new EmployeeTaxInfo(deductions);

                         // file the new employee in the database
EmployeeDatabase-add(this);

}
```

The first thing to notice is that this function, which is primarily responsible for initializing new instances of the Employee class, does not interact with previously existing instances of any other class, proving that it is indeed a composite object. The function also shows how the classes, such as EmployeeBenefits, are truly support classes for the Employee class. The only entity that creates instances of these classes is the Employee class itself. No other objects need to be aware that these classes exist, as they will be managed automatically based on the interactions between other objects and instances of the Employee class.

This illustrates a kind of relationship that isn't recognized by the class hierarchy. In this case, we have a direct relationship between the Employee class and a support class such as EmployeeBenefits, but the only relationship they have in the class hierarchy is the fact that they are both objects. The relationship between the Employee class and the EmployeeBenefits class is dynamic, which means that it is assembled and managed by the run-time system, unlike the static relationships between classes in the class hierarchy, which is managed by the compiler.

Destructor

The Employee destructor function's primary job is to undo everything that the Employee constructors did. While we do not have quite the same level of complexity in this task as we would if Employee was an abstract object, we must still ensure that we release all of the objects serving Employee. If we don't, then they will remain in memory for the duration of the program, and we will have no way to remove them since we no longer have references to them. When we destroyed a component of a meta-object, we had to ensure that the meta-object was correctly updated to reflect this, or we faced immediate catastrophe. In destroying a composite object , we must ensure that we destroy all of the referenced supporting objects. If we do not, the end will not come as quickly as it does with a mangled meta-object, but come it will.

In general, if you find yourself confronted by a program exhibiting steady, insatiable memory growth when it should not, one of the first things you should suspect are support objects for the various composite objects that you are creating and destroying. Just because you destroy the primary object does not mean you automatically destroy the servants, a condition that is often missed on the first few cuts of a program.

Summarizing the actions we expect the Employee destructor to perform, we have:

1. Destroy the EmployeeSalary object.

2. Destroy the EmployeeJobClass object.

3. Destroy the EmployeeBenefits object.

4. Destroy the EmployeeHistory object.

5. Destroy the EmployeeTaxInfo object.

6. Remove the Employee object from the database.

If we examine these operations more closely, we can see that steps 1-4 require that we first destroy all of the objects within the referenced collection, and then destroy the collection itself. In the first three destruction operations, this isn't a big deal, as the collections only contain one type of object. However, in destroying the EmployeeHistory, we must do more work. This is because while the first three only contain one kind of object, the fourth collection can contain any combination of EmployeeSalary, EmployeeJobClass, EmployeeBenefits, and EmployeeTaxInfo objects. In fact, the implementation of the EmployeeHistory destructor is so complex, we will split it into several parts. The most critical part, which destroys arbitrary Employee support objects, is the first one we will deal with.

The **destroyArbitraryESO()** is used to destroy arbitrary Employee Support Objects. It takes a reference to the object to be destroyed as a parameter, and then destroys it. While this might not seem too complicated, it is.

The first problem is that we must declare the parameter type to be the common denominator of all the possible types of class we might pass as an argument. For example, when we deal with foreign and domestic addresses within the system, we often don't really care whether they are foreign or domestic, instead we only care that they are some kind of Address object. In this case, the Address class is the common denominator between the DomesticAddress and the ForeignAddress classes. Returning to the destruction of Employee servant objects, the first observation we can make is that they do not fall within some distinct subset of the class hierarchy, unlike the previous example. Instead, the only common denominator between them is that they are all objects. This implies that their common denominator is the Object class itself.

However, we must referee a difference of opinion within the system, one that arises from the interactions between the strong typing of the compiler and the weak typing of our design model. If you recall that the means by which destructors are invoked is the delete keyword, a rather pressing question appears. How does the compiler know which destructor function it should use? The answer is that it uses the type definition of the variable to determine what kind of object it's looking at, and calls the destructor for that type. Unfortunately for us, all we've told the compiler so far is that the parameter is an object. Asking it to delete this reference in this case would only release a portion of the actual object, as only the generic object information would be deleted by the Object destructor, which is what the compiler would use to accomplish this for us.

So, once again, the compiler and our run-time system are slugging it out. The compiler insists on setting up the destructor calls when we compile the program, but it's the run-time system that knows which object is actually supposed to be destroyed. A solution to this problem is shown in the following function:

```
{

Employee::destroyArbitraryESO(Object *eso)

{

    EmployeeJobClass *ejc;
```

```
EmployeeFixedSalary *efc;

EmployeeHourlySalary *ehc;

EmployeeBenefits *ebc;

EmployeeTaxInfo *etc;

switch(eso-subClass())

{
    case EMPLOYEEJOBCLASS_CLASS:
        ejc = (EmployeeJobClass *) eso;
        delete ejc;
        break;
    case EMPLOYEEFIXEDSALARY_CLASS:
        efc = (EmployeeFixedSalary *) eso;
        delete efc;
        break;
    case EMPLOYEEHOURLYSALARY_CLASS:
        ehc = (EmployeeHourlySalary *) eso;
        delete ehc;
        break;
    case EMPLOYEEBENEFITS_CLASS:
        ebc = (EmployeeBenefits *) eso;
        delete ebc;
        break;
    case EMPLOYEETAXINFO_CLASS:
        etc = (EmployeeTaxInfo *) eso;
        delete etc;
        break;
    default:
        fatalError("Illegal element in
```

```
EmployeeHistory class");
    }
}
```

We have coupled the compiler's knowledge of which destructor functions go with which objects, using the run-time system's ability to specialize object references. The compiler can successfully link each of the needed destructors to each delete statement, as each delete is tied to the specific type of object we wish to delete. We pass a generic Object reference to the function, and it uses the derived class ID this object can produce to determine exactly what kind of object it is. We then cast the object pointer into the appropriate form and perform the deletion.

You must exercise caution when using techniques like this. These techniques are meant to provide some of the capabilities of a loosely typed OOL, which can sometimes conflict with the strong typing enforced by C++. One situation that would be fatal to your running system is putting a char * pointer into the EmployeeHistory collection because this pointer would be handed to the destroyArbitraryESO() function which; in turn, would attempt to execute its member function subclass(). As string pointers don't know a thing about derived classes, you would be jumping to a random location in your program.

You will be far safer if you use objects throughout your system, using the standard C types only within individual objects and functions and then only when you can clearly identify all users of this value. The ability to assume that everything is an object and; therefore, that everything in the system knows how to perform basic object operations, is the key issue in a loosely typed OOL. While you do incur some extra overhead when making objects out of strings and ints, you can save yourself a great deal of future pain. Once you have the system debugged and running to your satisfaction, you can always switch back without much trouble.

Concluding this example, here is the code for the Employee destructor function:

```
Employee::Employee()
{
    EmployeeJobClass *ejc;
```

```
EmployeeFixedSalary *efc;

EmployeeHourlySalary *ehc;

EmployeeBenefits *ebc;

EmployeeTaxInfo *etc;

if(!jobClass-isEmpty)

{
     first = jobClass-first();
     do {
         ejc = (EmployeeJobClass *) jobClass-selection();
         delete ejc;
     } while(jobClass-next() != first);
}

if(!benefits-isEmpty)

{
     first = benefits-first();
     do {
         ebc = (EmployeeBenefits *) benefits-selection();
         delete ebc;
     } while(benefits-next() != first);
}

delete salary;

delete taxes;

EmployeeDatabase.delete(this);
}
```

Access Functions

The most important access functions in the primary element of a composite object are the ones that provide references to each of the supporting objects. The only object that can deliver these references is the primary object. As a result, the primary object is responsible for implementing member functions that will return the support object references.

For this reason, the access functions required in a composite object can always be divided into two sets, the first being those that return references to the support objects and the second being everything that's left. The composition of the second set will vary widely, but the composition of the first set is more consistent. At a minimum, it will contain functions to return a reference to each support object.

We will disregard the application specific Bancroft messages and concentrate on what might be done with the first set of messages. We could simply implement a set of functions, as in:

VARIABLE	MEMBER FUNCTION
jobClass	Employee.jobClass();
salary	Employee.salary();
benefits	Employee.benefits();
taxes	Employee.taxes();
history	Employee.history();

It is important to note that no such functions have to be provided by a composite object. A composite object may only provide application messages, where no other object is allowed to communicate directly with any of the support objects. The fundamental issue in this case is the scope of communications between a composite object, its supporting components, and any arbitrary external object. On one hand, we can make this scope very broad, by implementing functions to return the references to each of the support objects. On the other hand, we can make this scope very narrow, by not allowing any direct communication with the support objects. This reduces the scope of the communications from the capabilities of all objects within the composite to the scope of the capabilities of the primary object alone. In real projects, the mixture of capabilities lies between these two endpoints with security issues limiting the communications and flexibility issues extending them.

Update Functions

Update functions for composite objects can be structured in much the same way as the access functions. By doing this; however, you are reducing the amount of code within the Employee class by distributing it across all of the classes that use it. In short, the cost of flexibility is that more objects need to know how to directly communicate with other objects.

This cost is one item that composite objects are very good at controlling. By providing update and access functions that operate in terms of the complex object, the workload is naturally distributed across the system. For example, consider updating an employee's salary information.

To do this, the current EmployeeSalary object must be added to the history collection. A new EmployeeSalary object must then be created with the new values, and referenced by the salary variable. It is unreasonable to expect external objects to go through this process, as it is the responsibility of any object to maintain its own internal data. Therefore, we can't expect outside objects to transfer the old salary value to the history collection, it is a job that the Employee object must do. If we were to force external objects to do this for us, we would have violated two basic OO design elements. First, we have made all the users of Employee objects understand and support the internal workings of an Employee object. Secondly, we have taken this illegal code and liberally duplicated it through the system wherever Employee objects are used.

To see this, consider the following two sequences to change an employee's salary. The one on the left represents code that has to be implemented once, as a member function in the Employee class. The sequence on the right represents code that would have to be duplicated in every object that needs to make this change:

EMPLOYEE SCOPE	SALARY, HISTORY SCOPE
Accept salary params	Accept salary params
Add salary to history	Get employee history
Create new salary	Get salary
Done	Put salary into history
	Create new salary
	Update employee salary
	Done

For this reason, the orientation of update functions is skewed in the opposite direction from that of the access functions. Update functions tend to consolidate operations at the primary object level, whereas access functions tend to distribute them over them over each of the support objects.

Summary

Composite objects are related to meta-objects, but they have distinct characteristics. Composite objects are often used when a concept is simply too complex to represent as a single object, but none of the pieces of the concept are of much interest to any other object. The physical objects that form composite objects are always related in a star topology, whereas the relations between physical objects in a meta-object are a unique network structure for every meta-object.

Constructor functions can be evaluated in terms of what they all do the same way, and what they each do differently. For common operations, the code can be moved to a private member function and called from each of the constructors. After this has been done with the constructors, it can be applied to many other groups of functions. Stamp out code reduplication!

The primary difference between meta-objects and composite objects is that meta-objects have many points of contact with the system, any one of which may be used to access the entire meta-object. Support objects within a composite object may only be referenced from the primary object.

Conflicts between the strong typing of C++ and the weak typing of our design model can crop up when virtual functions are not used, as in the case of the destructor functions, as they are currently implemented. The subclass() function is used to synchronize the compiler's type definition with the run-time system's type definition.

Composite object access functions are biased towards allowing client objects to directly communicate with the support objects in the interest of flexibility. Composite object update functions are biased the other way; directly implementing all support object communications in the interest of program structure and stability.

Further Enhancements

Bancroft has defined a new Employee class, the **Contractor**. These employees are all hourly workers with an overtime rate equal to the standard rate, and no benefits or tax information. Implement changes to support this by extending the constructor mechanism. Perform this extension along the same lines that the constructor already uses to differentiate between salaried and hourly workers.

The destructor mechanism shown in the example is not the optimal solution. Change the entire Bancroft application so that every destructor calls the virtual function **selfDestruct()**. Implement this virtual function throughout the class hierarchy. Watch most of the destructor problems evaporate.

CHAPTER 16

IMPLEMENTATION SUMMARY

Any object, regardless of its composotion or configuration, may be expected to perform at any time in a totally unexpected manner for reasons that are either totally obscure or completely mysterious.

Although the Bancroft system is not completely implemented, the portions of the system that have been implemented were carefully selected to illustrate the various OOL /OOP design and implementation techniques. With the techniques you read about in design and implementation of object oriented programs, you should be able to finish the Bancroft system, or any parts of it that particularly interest you. As you confront each new problem, see if you can find a comparable problem in this book.

Review

In Chapters 8-15, we designed various system and application components of the Bancroft system. The following list shows which objects were discussed in each chapter:

- 8 The Object Class
- 9 The Collection Class

Chapters 8-10 described system classes that will be used by many future programs. Chapters 11-15 describe application classes, which we expect to be used by a limited set of programs.

The Object Class

The requirement for the Object class was introduced and then its operating features were defined. Although our design never specifically stated a requirement for this class, it does require that this class be present because it assumed that we could use weak typing in dealing with object interactions brought about by parameter passing.

In a weakly typed design we implement functions that accept many different types of objects as parameters. This is where an argument is declared as any member of a set of possible argument types. This is accomplished by declaring it in terms of the common subclass of all objects it may receive. Collections are an excellent example of this, where the flexibility of the collection class arises from its ability to treat all objects in an identical fashion. On the other hand, C++ requires that we be more explicit about the specific type(s) of parameters the function receives. C++ can relax its typing somewhat, as it allows the passing of a reference to a derived class where a base class parameter is declared. For example, C++ would allow us to declare a function:

```
foo(Entity *anEntity);
```

We could then pass a derived class of Entity, such as Customer, as a parameter. It should be noted that the more specialized information associated with Customer would not be available, because **foo** would be operating on the object passed as an instance of Entity.

Weakly typed systems often require far more definition versatility than C++ is willing to provide, because the only assumption some weakly typed functions can make about their parameters is that they are some type of object. If you examine the Collection classes, you will see that they depend heavily on this assumption. To do anything else would be to severely restrict their abilities because they can only manage objects that are instances of the declared class or derived from it.

For this reason, all loosely typed designs should be initially implemented in a class hierarchy with an Object class at the root, and all classes in the design should be derived from the Object class. This makes the development system very flexible, for when you do not know what kind of object the system will be dealing with, you can always declare that the function accepts Objects. By doing this, you have allowed the function to accept any object the system can generate.

When the development cycle is finished and the software is to be released, you can analyze the system to determine which instances of each class are used. You will often find that after the system begins to stabilize, especially when the user interface and error control have been completed, it tends to use a restricted set of classes. The internal logic leans more towards a strongly typed model than did the development prototype. This is primarily due to the fact that the best enforcer of strong typing is testing, as it keeps failing the program for accepting illegal input, and doing other disgraceful things. Where traditional programmers often have to fight with the compilers to override the machines imposed strong typing, OO programmers move along a path from no typing to strong typing as required by the user interface.

At this point in the development cycle, you can elect to remove some of the more general classes such as Object, thus breaking the class hierarchy into a number of separate groups. This does have an adverse impact on the maintainability of the software and should only be necessary because of extreme run-time speed requirements of a real time application.

You must always be aware of the potential for conflict between the strong typing of C++ and the weak typing of our design. During compilation, both strong and weak typing can be used together to construct extremely powerful and accurate typing that reflects the benefits passed on by both of the typing mechanisms. While running the system, only the program's weak typing information is available, as it is reflected in the overall architecture of the system and in the subclass() virtual function.

This means you must always be sure your compiler type assumptions are in sync with those of your run-time system. The fact that subclass is a virtual function is quite useful in guaranteeing this behavior, as we know that it will always return the specific class of an object, regardless of how generalized the type declaration is. In short, if we have an instance of Employee we are pretending is an Object, we will still get the Employee class identifier if we use the subclass function on it. Beyond using this function, you should pay special attention to all of your conversions between standard C types and object types.

The Collection Class

The Collection class was implemented to allow one or more objects to be grouped together within a single object. As the Collection is not a concept unique to the Bancroft application, it was implemented as a system class instead of an application class. Because it was expected to be very flexible, its contents were declared as Objects; the loosest possible type we can specify.

The collection class itself isn't that interesting. It manages lists of data in a simple-minded fashion. But the concepts a collection represents are of great importance:

- A System Class
- Loose typing of paramaters

System classes are those that are generalized enough to be used without change by any other current or future object. Application classes are those that are of interest to only a few programs. Together they form the class hierarchy of the complete program. If you were to view this as the roots of a plant, then the large central roots represent the system classes and the smaller roots extending from them represent the application classes. There is a steady pattern exhibited over the life-cycle of an OOP development environment, where each new application contributes some new capabilities to the system environment, much as a plant's roots grow thicker over time. System classes develop over time and represent a great deal of development power as each new project is built on the shoulders of the previous project.

One other element that the Collection class illustrates is the flexibility which loose typing provides. By declaring that a Collection manages lists of Objects, this means that a Collection can manage any kind of object that is derived from the Object class. By doing this we have guaranteed that a Collection object can hold anything. If it can be disrobed as some kind of object, the Collection class can definitely hold it.

Certain mechanical details involved in the construction of a C++ program, such as the mandatory constructor and destructor functions implemented for each class, were illustrated during the implementation of the Collection class. We saw the sequencing of the base object constructor and destructor calls, which relates to the discussion in Chapter Seven about the true nature of an object. As the instantiation of an object is a de facto instantiation of all of its base classes, the invocation of a constructor function is also a de facto invocation of every base class' constructor function.

The IndexedCollection Class

The algorithms behind the implementation of the IndexedCollection class are as trivial as those of the Collection class. However, the implementation process illuminates two key points.

The first, and most important, is the creation of a new class by refining the behavior of an existing class. When we implemented the Indexed-Collection, we used the existing capabilities of the Collection class to manage the actual data contained within the collection, which meant that we only needed to manage a list of indices. What we have essentially done is to refine the behavior of the Collection class by adding mechanisms for keyword access to its existing capabilities.

This is the primary method by which all classes are constructed in a loosely typed system. The entire system is represented by a single class hierarchy, and all of the classes within it refine, or specialize, the behavior of the classes above them in the hierarchy. Individual classes such as Collection can evolve into large trees over time, as new kinds of collections such as matrices and sorted collections are created by deriving them from the closest existing Collection class, by refining the behavior of the existing class.

The other element we used in the implementation of the Indexed-Collection was the concept of plug-in operations. In the IndexedCollection class, we are going to spend our time primarily searching for specific indices, which implies that we need a means for comparing two values, to see if they are similar. Unfortunately, our design allows these values to be just about anything, so there isn't really a single satisfactory comparison function. A test to see if the pointers to the two parameters are equal isn't necessarily applicable to all cases. Therefore, it's quite difficult for us to implement a comparison method directly within the function, because this function is sensitive to the data the object contains, whereas the object itself ignores this information. To embed this logic within the class itself would mean that we would have to create a new derivative of the IndexedCollection class for every type of comparison we perform between elements of the collection.

As C++ and C are closely related, we can use many of our C techniques in C++. In doing this, some of these techniques take on a new life, as their powers are increased by their shift to an OO paradigm.

In C, we can deal with the address of a function as a discrete value, which means we can make a function programmable by passing it the address of a function it should call to perform some internal task. The most common example of this is the **qsort()** function found in most C libraries, where the address of the element comparison function is passed into qsort() as a parameter.

We have done almost exactly the same thing in the IndexedCollection class for exactly the same reasons. Through the *keyTest* variable in the IndexedCollection, we can provide whatever specialized comparison function is required, without altering the general behavior of the class. In short, the selection of the appropriate comparison routine is driven by what data is being compared.

Plug-in classes can often be used to cap the growth of a particular subset of system classes, without adversely affecting their flexibility. This capability is of great use in the system's classes, to help meld the system class' goal of generality with the application's classes goal of precision. By providing a set of plug-in functions, the system can allow an application to refine the behavior of a general system class without requiring that a new class be derived to accomplish this. Plug-ins help system classes from being covered in derived application classes, preventing them from growing barnacles on their hulls.

The Entity Class

The Entity class is the first Bancroft application class we implemented. It is an abstract class, meaning that we never intend to use it directly. Instead, Entity is used to group together certain basic characteristics of a set of derived classes that we will use. In our system, the Entity class provides the ability to manage names and addresses to the derived classes Supplier, Customer, and Employee.

The Entity class represents a composite object because it depends on the support class' Name and Address to operate. Interestingly enough, each of Entity's subclasses is also a composite object in its own right. Instances of Entity, or more correctly, of its derivatives, are the primary objects in each of the composite objects that will be formed.

The Entity class is an illustration of where an instance of an abstract class can be used, specifically when we used Entity objects to hold drop shipment addresses to non-customers. Abstract objects are used when not enough information is available to differentiate between the derived classes, but more information is expected. An instance of an abstract class provides a ghostly image of an object that is expected to resolve itself into something more concrete in the future. In the meantime, there is a limited set of operations that are available to both ghosts and real instances alike, in this case accessing and editing the name and address elements.

In designing the Entity class, we elected to implement a single parameter constructor function that could handle the initialization of an Entity with either a name or an address. At this point we can observe that this is a bit convoluted, as we could have implemented two constructor functions, one for Names and the other for Address.

Whether you choose to experiment or not, the act of making the Entity constructors also showed us that new classes are often created to satisfy implementation criteria, but these classes never conflict with the existing design, they just add more detail to it. In this case, the design said we had some arbitrary piece of data that represented someone's name. When we began to implement the class, we discovered that the system would have to be able to determine the difference between a name and an address at run-time. To do this, they must both be capable of responding to a subclass() call, because the run-time system uses this virtual function to uniquely identify each object. This means that Names will also have to be implemented as a class.

A loosely typed OOL exhibits an inexorable growth towards a completely object-based system, where everything within the system is represented by objects. This allows the system to make some truly sweeping assumptions, such as the fact that anything it will ever see is an object, and all objects behave in a certain way, which includes being able to do such things as identify and destroy themselves. Because of the flexibility of such a system, you will notice a steady promotion of what appeared to be strings and custom data structures into full fledged classes. Much of the power of a loosely typed OOL lies in the fact that elements within the system are all objects, and therefore all elements respond to a basic set of member function calls. But this depends on the fact that the reference which the system encounters is indeed a reference to an object. A constant process of promoting non-objects to object status therefore becomes a part of the implementation process. This amounts to adding underbrush into the forest of classes defined in the design.

The Address and Derived Classes

The Address, DomesticAddress, and ForeignAddress classes illustrated the benefits of implementing a small set of related classes in parallel. By doing this, we managed to merge the requirements of each so that we could equally distribute the workload over all of the objects involved. The end result was that we implemented a single Address constructor, and constructed a single interface using a few high level polymorphic functions. And we did it with a minimum of wasted code between the sections involved.

We also examined the difference between procedural knowledge and data, and saw how they participate equally in the definition of an object. It would not have been much trouble to discard the domestic and foreign address classes completely, representing either kind of data at the Address level would not be terribly inefficient. However, there are strong behavioral differences between foreign and domestic addresses and these differences are represented within the member functions of a class.

When several classes are derived from a common base primarily for reasons of these behavioral differences, they tend to implement a common polymorphic interface between themselves and the base class. In other words, they all talk the same way, but they each do different things. When we have a series of specialized classes that all respond to a generic set of functions, we can afford to ignore the difficulties of dealing with each of the specialized derived classes, leaving that information encapsulated within the derived classes. Instead, we deal with all of the classes in terms of their base class and that class' generic virtual functions.

As an example of this, consider the chart options found in many popular spreadsheet programs. These options allow you to generate many different kinds of charts such as pie charts, line charts, and bar charts. If we were to implement the class hierarchy:

Chart

    LineChart

    PieChart

    BarChart

we could define a generic interface that would be structurally identical across all of the derived classes, and yet would produce different results in each case. Such a case, where a common set of member functions produces a much larger set of results across a set of classes, implies the existence of a polymorphic function or two.

The interface is simple. You merely create a new object from whichever class that does your desired drawing, send it the new data with one member function, and tell it to draw itself with another. Your selection of the class implies all other necessary data.

In implementing these classes we also saw how increasing specialization of classes tends to lead to increasing size of the class member functions. Although this is not an ironclad law of OOP, it is a statistical truth. The reason for this isn't hard to fathom—as the more general classes make assumptions about the regular behavior of all the objects they map, the specific application classes contain more logic defining their rather individualistic behavior. In short, if a member function is performing some unique operation for some class, it's likely to be larger and more convoluted than one performing a general function for a set of related classes.

The InventoryItem Class

In implementing the InventoryItem class, we focused on the difference between terminal and non-terminal references, a distinction which plays a central part in the definition of meta-objects and complex objects. We saw that objects within the run-time system can have complex links established to other objects through non-terminal references. Any kind of network can be constructed between running objects, but whatever kind of network is used—it can be decomposed into two distinct subnetworks. The first are the circular paths through the network, which form the nervous system of the meta-object. The second are those paths that lead directly to terminal objects. This allows us to view any path between any two classes as a pair of sub-paths. The first path moves along a circular path to the head of the second path, which leads directly to the class we want. An analogy to this is the phone system. You can consider the area code to be a path on a giant closed network, and the remaining part of the number as the path that leads out of the network to the terminal phone, or object.

Through the construction of networks of objects, meta-objects and composite objects are created. The basic set of capabilities of these objects is drawn from the set of all objects located on each path to every terminal reference. The primary difference is that this entire setof functions is available from any element of a meta-object, whereas it is only available from the primary element of a complex object. This arises from the fact that individual components of a meta-object can be used to link to any other individual component of the network, while the only links in a composite object are from the primary object to each of the helper objects.

We also dealt with the issue of a parameter constructor's functions, which can sometimes be bothersome. When a constructor for an object is defined with a single parameter, it serves as an implicit type conversion from the type of the parameter to the type of the object with which the constructor is associated. This is related to something we have not addressed up to now, the use of **overloaded operators**.

In the case of single parameter constructors we have to deal with implicit type conversion, which we can often use to our benefit. Consider three classes that represent the temperature scales: Fahrenheit, Celsius, and Kelvin. If we were to state that all internal temperature information was maintained in Kelvin, then the constructor of every class would have to convert arguments from the temperature scale of the class to degrees Kelvin. This has certain implications concerning the conversion of integers to one of these three classes. In essence, our constructor functions for these three classes represent three mechanisms for converting an integer to a kind of temperature object.

This is when C++ begins to permeate the fabric of C, in this case affecting what kinds of things the compiler does when it decides some type conversion is in order. To fully exploit and control this, you may wish to consider using overloaded operators, where you can redefine the behavior of various C++ operators, such as + and =, as they apply to classes. By doing this, you can make the behavior of a particular C operator depend on the class of its parameters.

By using overloaded operators, which are defined in much the same way as are standard member functions (except the function name is replaced with operator) you can create an even more powerful environment. In this environment you can implement such things as **fuzzy equality testers** (overlaid ==) and **optimized object copy** functions (overlaid =).

I strongly recommend you move to overloaded operators after you are comfortable with the basic premises of OO design. In creating situations where the compiler may perform a great deal of typecasting, such as in a program with many overloaded operators and one parameter constructors, you allow the system many avenues to do type conversions, conversions of which you may not be aware. Worse yet, many of these conversions may be incorrect. They will conflict with your assumptions about type represented in the run-time system's typechecking capabilities.

This isn't an insurmountable problem, just be aware that as you broaden C++'s horizon of type conversions, you raise the risk that C++ will perform a conversion you weren't expecting. You must therefore, scrutinize your programs carefully for conditions where these conversions might appear. Once again, the richer your Object class hierarchy, the more your program will be able to control this by giving satisfactory definitions of each data element by its place in the class hierarchy. The real risk comes as non-objects such as ints and floats meet Object classes.

The Customer Class

This class was our first encounter where the same variables are shared between every instance of the class, as opposed to variables which were duplicated in every instance of the class. As we saw in the implementation, class variables keep track of information that is shared between all objects in a class, such as the total number of objects that have been created.

In the case of the *customerCounter class* variable, we actually went so far as to determine that only one function actually needed this variable, so we hid the variable in this function. This is the goal in OOP, to encapsulate information in packages called objects, where the messy details are hidden within the object or objects that are actually responsible for them. This allows us to deal with the system in abstract terms, ignoring the horde of little details packed away within the objects themselves.

We built upon the basic network concept in the previous class to construct a meta-object in the process of creating a customer. Due to the interactions between the Customer objects and other objects within the system, meta-objects are created, which are defined by a networked grouping of distinct objects that have data or functional dependencies between each other. In this case, the relations established between Customers, SaleTransactions, and InventoryItems form a meta-object representing customer purchase orders.

We discovered, when implementing the destructor functions, that an object's membership in an existing meta-object means that the destructor function cannot simply destroy the object, as it would corrupt the meta-object, deleting some of its data. Instead, it must disengage itself from the system, performing the necessary updates and alterations to remove any references to itself from the system, and finally destroy itself.

This is the simplest and least efficient solution to the problem of deleting meta-objects. Far more elegant solutions modelled on semaphores exist, but such an algorithm is beyond the range of this book. When dealing with meta-objects, never overlook the fact that you can deal with the network of the meta-object itself as an entity. By installing objects that function as smart nodes within the network path or switches, you can implement universal solutions to problems involved in creating and destroying meta-objects. In this case, we have elected to make each destructor responsible for correctly adjusting the meta-object.

The Employee Class

The Employee class served to illustrate a composite object, showing how it differs from a meta-object. Like a meta-object, a composite object uses a network to establish relations between several objects, but a composite object is used to solve a much different problem. A meta-object represents a complex run-time entity where no single component dominates any of the others. The majority of objects contained within a meta-object are equal partners in the construction of a new meta-object that does not necessarily bear any surface resemblance to the objects that constitute it.

Composite objects are constructed for a much different reason. They represent single classes where the functionality required of the class would be too complex for implementation in a single class, but the rest of the system does not want to be bothered with these petty details.

When we designed the Employee class, we knew then that there was a need for some specialized helper classes to support specific subcomponents of the Employee class. We also know the rest of the system makes no such distinction, assuming that the Employee class directly maps all of this information.

To solve this problem, we implement Employee and its associated helper classes as a composite object. We make Employee the primary object within the composite object, which means that the rest of the system will use this object to perform all Employee operations. This is what the design already mandates.

Construction and destruction of composite objects is a fairly simple task. The system will call the Employee constructor or destructor, and this function is in turn responsible for calling the appropriate constructor or destructor for each helper object.

We saw how the specification of parameters for overloaded functions could be used to perceive context sensitive conditions. The two constructor functions are differentiated in terms of what salary parameters they accept, which in turn determines which derived class of EmployeeSalary object will be bound to the composite object.

Situations like this are fairly common, as this is an extremely useful capability of an OOL. They should be examined closely because they offer the opportunity to further modularize the code. If you examine the body of each constructor function, you may find that they perform many of the same operations, the differences being directly attributable to the sensitivity of their particular argument pattern or to the context sensitive part of their logic. In such functions, you can take the invariant part out of each function, place it in a single function, and make each of the now totally context sensitive functions call it. You will have greatly improved the system's structure by separating the constructors into their two natural halves, the **context free** part and the **context sensitive** parts.

Summary

In concluding the Tactics section, I hope you have seen how a range of OO techniques may be used in implementing OO designs and what the various goals are at each level of implementation. My intent has not been to provide you with cookbook recipes for solving problems. The raw code I've given is meant only to illustrate design principles, not to be used directly. By understanding the process of transforming a design into a program, what your goals are at each step, and what tools are available to you, you should be able to solve any OO project without difficulties. Compared to traditional environments, you might even have an easier job of it.

CHAPTER 17

FOUNDATION AND FUTURE

And then a miracle occurs here...

Object programming is primarily a process of model building, where we start with crude models of the system to be implemented, and progressively refine these models until we have finally constructed the system that we desire. The construction of an OO program is a continuous process, without any clear boundaries labeled with terms such as TEST or RELEASE-1. A later version of an OO program is simply a combination of all of the capabilities of its previous versions and the most recent changes. On the other hand, individual versions of non-object oriented programs can often be described as a series of "totally unique and unpredictable events" occurring over time, with very little similarity from one version to the next. Some commercial applications must obviously be developed in an OOPless environment!

The raw power of OOP is manifested in the subtlety of this concept of knowledge definition. Instead of focusing on how to do one thing, and communicating with the computer in terms of this single thing, we now begin to deal with programs as compositions of cooperating objects, and describing them in these terms. To truly understand this concept, means that you can move between almost any OOP system in existence, regardless of the language it uses. The act of learning the language is trivial in OOPS with large class hierarchies, because the programs are written at such a high level. Legend has it that there is an experimental OOP that implements the class "Brain," with one message, "think."

In stating that programs are **evolutionary** (defined as *a series of changes to a common set of information over time*), we are implying that the language these programs is written in is capable of describing them this way. To be capable of this, the language must go further than declare how products are constructed. It must also say how products are related to each other and it must always provide an environment where these products, or programs are available. In doing this, the goal of the language itself shifts from a jerky design-implement-test-release program to a continuous process of enhancing the class hierarchy, where individual programs are represented as a subset of this hierarchy.

This concept has already been used in the OS realm, and has proven to be extremely powerful, with UNIX being one of the best examples. The concept provides for programs to be run in controlled sequences and ensures that the output of any one program may be fed as input to another. By providing a large collection of basic "service" programs, many more complex tasks may easily be implemented.

Consider removing all of the duplicate lines in a block of unsorted input. The first step would be to sort the input, and then to remove adjacent duplicate lines. In UNIX, this can be accomplished with:

```
sort | uniq
```

This will send the initial input to sort, and then send the output of sort (sorted input) to **uniq**, which will strip out the duplicated lines. If we were to attempt to define these two programs in OO form, we could say that we have two classes, Sort and Unique, and each of these classes implements a single method **doIt** which causes them to perform their complete operating cycle. We trigger Sort with a doIt call with the input data, Sort does a doIt call with its sorted output to Unique, and we get the results from Unique.

The behavior of the UNIX system at the program level exhibits many of the strengths of an OO system, especially in the overall uniformity of programs within the system. Additionally, complete packages and revisions can be dropped into the UNIX environment at the program level with no marked effect on the system or existing programs. So how does a simple concept have such a dramatic effect at the system (UNIX) and language (OOLs) levels?

The reason for such a tremendous gain in capability from such a simple change in concept is due to *where* this change in concept is taking place. Pre-OO, programs were created from a void by the designers and programmers, then acted on by the compiler, and finally executed by the user. There was no mechanism to relate programs to each other in terms of their construction, outside of their use of a few function libraries. Naturally, this leads to an army of individually designed wheels, especially since many large programming tasks start off by trying to reinvent computer science. This isn't really hard to understand, as computer science has never quite managed to mesh successfully with the large human endeavor of creating the latest mega-program, primarily because it is not represented by the very tools it created. When we see a lathe, we see mechanical engineering. When we see a language compiler or interpreter, computer science is often irrelevant. What is missing is a **foundation**; something secure to seat these programs into, as well as a structure on which to hang all the pieces. Only when we have this will we have a common vocabulary for discussing the construction of all programs, as opposed to the vocabulary we now have, which is unique to each program.

OO systems, by their very nature, define both a foundation and a structure necessary to construct and manipulate modules within programs. The structure is the concept of objects themselves, and the structure is provided by the defined hierarchal relationships between the classes. Through this, we can build and maintain programs as collections of independently operable logic machines called objects. These machines can range in complexity from incrementing a value to drawing a 3-D solid, but they all retain a surface symmetry.

This means that we have a way of discussing any element of a program, representing some finite task and all of the data needed to perform it, in general terms that apply to any task, no matter how bizarre. Because we can take these descriptions of the tasks, now represented by objects, and plug them into a hierarchy of related objects, it means we have defined a mechanism that relates all objects to each other and defines a mechanism by which any object can communicate with any other object.

We are now looking at the fundamental substance of any OO system, regardless of how it actually makes this all happen. An OO system provides:

- The foundation necessary to discuss any finite task as a self contained entity in completely general terms. This is the system's definition of an object and the basic properties it possesses.

- The structure necessary to relate any given object to any other object in terms of their data and functional dependencies. This will be the system's definition of the class hierarchy. In C++ and Smalltalk it is base classes, derived classes, inheritance, and superclasses, subclasses and inheritance, respectively.

- A protocol by which any object may communicate with another object. In C++ this is implemented with member function calls.

Natural Patterns

As it turns out, many OOP practitioners discuss OO systems in terms of biological organisms. The reason for this is straightforward. OO systems do grow, or evolve over time, and the growth of an OO system is similar to the growth of a real organism. Additionally, the class hierarchy structure can be discussed in terms of genetic information for constructing and operating the objects.

The fact that there is this parallel we can draw between OO systems and biological systems raises some provocative issues. If there is some similarity between these two mechanisms, then is it possible for us to apply what we know of biology to OO design? Can the class hierarchy organization of an OOL be supercharged with our knowledge of the basic mechanism of DNA? In short, how far can these similarities be drawn out?

There are no answers to these questions, although there are those who are looking. For now, we can simply exploit this fact when it arises, using our experience in the world at large to help us with a computer model of a subset of this world.

Mechanical patterns also can be used to model or understand an OO system. In many cases, you will find that OO systems tend to assume the same structural configurations as the real world systems they are modelling. If we build a computer model of a car, it is likely to contain such objects as an engine, wheels, and a body. If we build a game with a Robot class in it, a Robot object is likely to use such objects as RobotArms and RobotLegs.

This close relationship of OO systems at their deepest levels and the real world systems they model, combined with the fact that the OO system itself can be defined as a biological model, has interesting implications for the future. The fact that OO systems possess this capability to a much greater extent than do normal systems, seems to imply the OO model is closer to the truth. In our terms, the truth is when the program we write to model something on the computer is a perfect description of that thing in the real world. With such a description, we have a common definition between the computer's universe and our own.

Future Directions

In this book, I ignored something called **multiple inheritance**. This is a condition where an object has been declared to be derived from more than one base class and therefore, it inherits from all of the base classes it has been derived from.

Part of my decision is based on my opinion that the entire issue has not been clearly defined as of yet. However, multiple inheritance is one of two areas I feel will be receiving much attention in the future. The other area that should receive a lot of attention are the communications between objects. The foundation of the system will still rest on the object, but the changes in these two areas could be quite significant.

As of this time, a very simple model of relationships is maintained within OO systems, the absolute minimum required to support such a system. In practice, many OO bugs are a result of this inadequacy. The root of the problem is that the class hierarchy defines only the functional dependencies between objects, it does not address their operational dependencies.

Multiple inheritance is a possible extension of the class hierarchy model currently implemented in many systems to augment the scope of functional dependencies represented by the class hierarchy. It is meant to solve a specific problem that arises under single inheritance hierarchies. The basic problem is encountered where a single object needs to perform the same set of functions as performed by another object, and building a composite object to accomplish this is in conflict with the design.

The best example of this comes from Bertrand Meyer, who showed how a Window class à la Macintosh could be implemented by having the Window class inherit from a Tree class and a Rectangle class. The Rectangle object provides the basic capabilities to support regions within each area of the window, and the Tree class serves to organize rectangles into windows.

In using multiple inheritance, the Window class simply needs to manage the interactions of the two sets of methods it has inherited. The low level logic stays within the Tree and Rectangle classes. If we were to use single inheritance, then we would have to derive the Window class from either the Tree or the Rectangle, and then copy all of the other classes member functions into the Window class. This could involve rampant duplication of code as all inherited functions would also have to be copied, until the common base object class was reached.

An area that has not yet been addressed involves the legitimization of composite objects. The main reason that composite objects must be created at run-time is that OO systems do not address anything but hierarchal relationships between objects. Consider defining a Car class, which could be defined as a composite object containing a body, an engine, and wheels. All of the burden of managing this composite object falls on the run-time system at this point, which means it falls on each of the objects that form this composite object.

This illustrates one place where the structural assumptions of OO systems can stand closer scrutiny. We could greatly reduce the size and complexity of many composite objects if we could support two more links in addition to the derived class and base class links we now associate with each class. We would use the two new links to indicate which object contains an object, and which objects are contained in the object. By implementing these links and functions to traverse them, we could greatly shrink the size and expand the power of composite objects.

The second major area of change in OO will be in the means by which functions communicate. One question that has continued to surface over the last several years deals with **distributed objects**. Distributed objects are effectively meta-objects where not every object is present on the same machine. In short, the message flow between the objects becomes much more physical, because it must travel over a communications channel between the two or more machines where the objects reside.

Consider if Bancroft were to link their warehouses all over the country together into a network to support this. This would mean that a corporate warehouse database meta-object would be created, composed of all the physical corporate databases available on the network. This meta-object would not truly contain any of this data, it would simply communicate over the network with the respective component. The end result is an object whose contents are transparently scattered all over the country. As far as any user of the meta-object is concerned, all of the data appears to be within this system.

Basically, a great deal of intelligence could be married to the message sending architecture, which would produce far more powerful systems. As an extreme view, merging message sends with the X.25 protocol specification could be a bit inefficient in some places. However, it could also be used to create very complex objects with components scattered all around a worldwide network, all functioning within a single integrated program.

In essence, the concept of an object is quite stable, and has proven to be satisfactory in all cases. The candidates for extension or modification in OO systems involve communication between objects. This communication occurs between running objects through message sending, and between static class definitions through the class hierarchy. Future activity in OOP systems will involve enhancing the current communications capabilities of OO systems.

Conclusion

Developing OO systems requires that one operate via a certain paradigm, or world view, as do BASIC, FORTRAN, and COBOL. The key difference is that whereas BASIC, FORTRAN, and COBOL all share a common concept of what a program is and does, any OO system works with a completely different concept.

The required paradigm shift means that you must stop viewing programs as large blocks of instructions that drive the computer around. Instead, you are dealing with a world where packets of data drive pieces of the program around. No longer do programs control things, now we deal with objects who do things. Control has been distributed to each of the objects that send out messages to have things done.

This shift is essentially a Eureka experience, as you break free of concepts that are bound to simple procedural languages. Until you do, you cannot truly exercise the power of an OO system, because you don't yet understand what it does. Once you do understand, you'll wonder how you ever got along without one. I sincerely hope this book has helped you reach that point sooner.

INDEX